The
Reagan Legacy

The
Reagan Legacy

John T. Stinson

iUniverse, Inc.
New York Bloomington

The Reagan Legacy

iUniverse books may be ordered through booksellers or by contacting:

iUniverse

1663 Liberty Drive

Bloomington, IN 47403

www.iuniverse.com

1-800-Authors (1-800-288-4677)

ISBN: 978-1-4401-5030-2 (pbk)

ISBN: 978-1-4401-5031-9 (ebk)

Printed in the United States of America

iUniverse rev. date: 6/19/2009

Contents

1

Establishing a Foundation in Foreign Policy

CONSIDERING THAT AT THE TIME of the American Revolution democracy was considered an extremist form of government, the founders were a remarkably even handed group. Their creation was politically conservative and so it remained. In reaction to a history of monarchy and dictatorship, postwar Europe adopted socialism in various degrees without dire consequences. If conservatives say Europe suffers as a result, painting today's American liberal as socialist is political name calling. Three of four Democratic presidents of the last fifty years, Kennedy, Carter, and Clinton, were only moderately liberal. Lyndon Johnson was an exception, though personally he was a typically opportunistic American. His Great Society was directed at bringing minorities, particularly African-Americans, into the mainstream. Hillary Clinton is portrayed as an extreme liberal because she led an attempt to establish a national health care system, hardly far out considering that most modern democracies have such a program.

Even Franklin Roosevelt was not an exception. My parents and grandparents, conservative to the core, could get apoplectic about the New Deal, but Roosevelt's socialism amounted to a series of temporary expedients directed at breaking out of the depression. Although arch conservatives still paint the New Deal as a flirtation with communism, this is nonsense. In Roosevelt's second term the more socialistic aspects of the New Deal were shut down. The failure of free market capitalism, expressed in the depression, led to a state organized form of capitalism that had prevailed through much of U.S. history. It worked before running into problems in the 1970s.

While conservatives griped about socialism and make work projects, a lasting aspect of the New Deal created particular passion - high income and inheritance taxes on the rich. When conservatives regained power under Reagan, their firepower was concentrated here. The results have not been favorable to the economy. Conservatives had long asserted that the economy could not grow with high taxes on the investor class, but the postwar years were the most prosperous in American history.

Conservatism in America had traditionally been close to that of President Eisenhower: cautious about government, supportive of business, and nonetheless socially progressive. The former general also followed the American model of caution about the exercise of military power. The present Republican Party is not that of Eisenhower or Prescott Bush, George W. Bush's grandfather, a senator for ten years. Prescott Bush was the polar opposite of his grandson: patrician and proud of it, progressive in domestic policy, internationalist in foreign policy, a stickler for decorum, and an avid supporter of planned parenthood. He would not have believed his grandson's presidency.

In modern times, conservatives moved in a new direction. One of their most distinguishing characteristics had been isolationism. That changed after Harry Truman's upset win in the 1948 presidential election, probably the greatest shock ever suffered by the Republican Party. Conservatives cast off moderation and launched an all out attack against Truman's conduct of the Cold War. Giving up whining about the New Deal, they took up lambasting Democrats as communist leaning traitors. Loss of China to communism was the central issue.

The American view of China was sentimental and unrealistic It had been built around anti-colonialism and missionary stories of a beautiful people eager to be converted to Christianity. China was seen as a troubled child the U.S. had an obligation to take care of. Feeding on this sentiment, conservatives manufactured the line that Chinese Nationalists had been sold out by subversive communist sympathizers in the State Department. In fact, considerable help had been provided to the Nationalists in the civil war with Mao's communists. At the end of the war, the U.S. sent troops into eastern China to relieve the defeated Japanese. All territory and arms were turned over to the Nationalist leader, Chiang Kai-shek, giving him a substantial advantage in the civil war. He lost anyway, overcome by corruption, military incompetence, and unwillingness to accept advice.

With Chiang losing ground, in January, 1947, Truman sent George Marshall in an effort to save Chiang through compromise with Mao. Not only was Marshall one of the most respected figures of the time, he was experienced in China, having served three years as American military attache. Marshall's attempts, including military advice, were dismissed. He concluded that the status was hopeless and the Pentagon Chiefs of Staff agreed, though for political reasons Truman continued to pour in money. The problem was Chiang Kai-shek, one of the most corrupt and incompetent men in all of history. Chiang, however, was quite a politician. Playing on American sympathy, the China lobby was influential in Washington, particularly among conservatives looking in election bitterness for an excuse to hammer the President.

The final verdict on China became apparent about the time of Truman's re-election. Shocked Republicans used the defeat as evidence of the Truman administration's subversion to communist influence. Some of the loudest voices had been isolationists, who would not have provided assistance, but this was politics rather than foreign policy. When the Korean War arrived a year and a half after the election, it was seen by the more reactionary conservatives as an opportunity to defeat communist China and reinstall Chiang, a lunatic idea supported by their hero, General Douglas MacArthur. Extreme partisanship ruled, as can be seen in the following quote from Republican Senator William Jenner of Indiana - "I charge that this country today is in the hands of a secret inner coterie which is directed by agents of the Soviet Union."

The subversion charge plagued Truman's second term. It was fed by the infamous Alger Hiss trial (Hiss, a former New Deal official on trial for treason, was convicted of perjury) and came to a head in the sensational claim by Senator Joseph McCarthy that the State Department had 205 communists, including all of the China experts. Not only was Truman treated as incompetent, his Secretary of State, Dean Acheson, was viciously assaulted. Truman and Acheson are credited with shaping America's Cold War strategy that prevailed for the next forty years, but the treatment they received at the time was disgusting. Marshall shared the brutality. Efforts were made to undermine the Marshall Plan to fight communism by supporting the economic revival of Europe. The outrageous campaign influenced future events in Korea, Vietnam, and our entire approach to the Cold War.

Truman faced a confounding problem, how to deal with the Soviet Union at the outset of the Cold War. George Kennan, a talented American diplomat with years of experience in Moscow, understood that Stalin was far more Russian than communist and his actions were likely to be determined by that heritage. Although communism might be out to convert the world to its philosophy, Russians were first of all defensively minded. In the 1920s Stalin had lived through expeditions sent by Western powers to overthrow the new communist government, leaving him instinctively suspicious of our intentions. He had defeated the invading Germans in history's titanic struggle and viewed American efforts to rebuild Germany as threatening. Stalin saw capitalistic encirclement, including the U.S. presence in Japan, another old enemy of the Russians. His overriding goal was safeguarding the homeland rather than spreading communism. While asserting Soviet influence over lands overrun during the war, he avoided confrontation with the United States.

Unlike most Americans, Kennan understood the Russian viewpoint. It meant that the threat was not as great as imagined. The Soviets could be relatively easily contained militarily, at the same time as their impractical economic system would eventually be self-defeating. Searching for answers, Truman adopted the Kennan approach. Containment was problematic for two reasons: 1) it required patience, something Americans are not good at, and 2) the irreconcilability of capitalism and communism inevitably led to a troubled relationship. To us, they were an oppressive totalitarian power out to conquer the world. They saw us in almost exactly the same terms: trying to impose an economic system that led to oppression of the working class and threatening them militarily. The ideological conflict was bad enough. When military confrontation was added, it led to always thinking the worst of one another.

The state of mutual incomprehension meant that incidents added to the tension. Churchill gave his famous Iron Curtain speech only ten months after the end of hostilities, despite having participated in the talks during and after the war assigning the territory in which the U.S.S.R. established satellites as a Soviet sphere of influence. The Iron Curtain was no surprise to him, he helped create it. Roosevelt had also agreed. Both leaders understood the terrible burden of the Russians in defeating Hitler and that the Soviet Union had been left destitute. They cut Stalin some slack.

Soon the American tendency to oppose any form territorial aggrandizement asserted itself. The satellites were not annexed to the Soviet Union, rather their people were forced into totalitarian communism. The Iron Curtain was seen as a fortress for persecuting whole nations. For its part, the Kremlin saw the Iron Curtain as a protective shield, a buffer against an unfriendly west. Concerned with defending themselves and struggling to make their economy work, spreading international communism was a secondary task. Little military support was provided to communist forces in China and elsewhere (Vietnam gained significant support in reaction to the U.S. presence). Russia recovered only slowly after the war, but the intensely hostile attitude precluded our recognizing that they had all they could handle at home. For their part, devotion to communism was sufficiently intense that they could not accept that it was not working.

Who started the Cold War? Between the Iron Curtain, the Berlin blockade, and allowing North to invade South Korea, the Soviets deserve that honor. On the other hand, as the conflict persisted the U.S. was the more aggressive party. Despite a number of overtures by the Russians directed at easing military confrontation, perpetuating the Cold War became U.S. policy based on the assumption they would attack if our guard let down. After outbreak of the Korean War in 1950, it became official policy to regard the Kremlin as utterly evil and intent on crushing the United States. Any interchanges were seen in terms of dealing with a hopeless liar. With such an extreme view as standard policy, there was no chance of ending the Cold War.

Vigorous opposition to the Soviet Union also became basic political strategy for both the Democratic and Republican Parties. Politicians found that an aggressive posture was necessary to getting elected. These extreme positions were sometimes costly. For example, the conservative attack on Truman over China precluded recognition of Mao's China and the ongoing charade of recognizing Chiang's exiled government in Taiwan as the legitimate China. Having won fair and square, Mao was enraged, all the more so when we defended Chiang's retreat. Mao's anger led to determination not to allow the U.S. above the former 38th parallel border during the Korean War. As the U.S. routed the North Korean army in the south, Stalin proposed a cease fire and an election, which the more populous south should have won, but anticipating complete victory, the U.S. pressured the UN into rejecting the overture. MacArthur's orders were conflicting - take North Korea and at the same time not engage the Chinese or Russians. As Chinese troops moved in, the U.S. was warned by routs of a Korean force and an advanced American probe. Failing to heed the warning, MacArthur split his forces, with the Chinese gathering strength in the gap. They fell on the Americans in late November, 1950, resulting in the worst ever U.S. battle defeat. Eventually, superior fire power turned back the Chinese to approximately the old line. The Russians were given no credit for failing to provide promised air support, the first step in the rupture between China and the Soviet Union.

While the Russians were not innocent bystanders, the U.S. was falling into the habit of blaming its international troubles on the Kremlin. We had invited the Russians into North Korea (as well as Manchuria) to disarm the Japanese and our own State Department established the arbitrary 38th parallel border, when a shorter and more natural division lay one hundred miles to the north. Stalin installed Kim Il Sung, a noted resistance fighter against the Japanese, as the leader in the north and trained and equipped his army. Kim wanted to unify Korea, but Stalin held him back. When the U.S. left South Korea, indicating it lay outside our western Pacific protective shield, Stalin allowed Kim to proceed. Had the U.S. indicated it would defend and train a South Korean army, the Korean War probably would never have happened. Although Stalin had no desire for a military confrontation with the U.S., we assumed he was behind the invasion. A similar instance occurred in 1990, when concentration on Russia led to neglecting Saddam's threat to Kuwait, leading to war in the Middle East. In turn that war led to the terrorist attack of 9/11.

Korea was the crowning blow in a series of events that escalated the Cold War. First came the Berlin blockade, starting in June of 1948. The blockade was a reaction to uniting Germany. Having just fought the most horrible war in history against them, Stalin imagined a new German military preparing another attack, this time backed by Western powers. Germans were seen as inherently militaristic and unusually skillful at the art. To the U.S., on the other hand, the blockade was a grab for Berlin, which like the country as a whole had been divided between the west and the Soviets. Loss of China to communism followed and in 1949 the Soviets successfully tested an atomic bomb.

These ominous developments resulted in a more belligerent attitude toward the Kremlin. Truman had originally felt he could work with Stalin, now he took to tough talk, encouraged by Marshall's hawkish successor as Secretary of State, Dean Acheson. Truman's tough stance on the blockade probably saved the 1948 election, a lesson not lost on Republicans.

Growing tension and political pressure took shape in NSC-68, a policy of extreme toughness toward the Soviets that had been lurking in the background. Adopted as official policy in 1950, it called for a military build up to oppose a Soviet Union that wished to "impose its absolute authority over the rest of the World". This extreme premise served as a backdrop to American policy for the next forty years. The difference with containment was emphasis on the military. Informed sources knew the Russians were struggling economically and were not involved in Korea, but NSC-68 set forth that the Soviet Union was an immediate military threat. It lumped China, Vietnam, and any other communist nation as a single entity controlled from Moscow. Hereafter the U.S. would be the Cold War aggressor. Thirty years later, despite the intervening peace and a gradually improving relationship, this same attitude of intense hostility was crucial to bringing Ronald Reagan to power. It was Reagan who finally brought about one of NSC-68's primary goals, an unrestrained military build up. Truman, Eisenhower, and later presidents had resisted this temptation as unnecessary and economically unsound. Reagan exercised no such judgment.

1950 reverberated in other ways. Ongoing support for Chiang in Formosa, soon to be known as Taiwan, and disdain of China as a mere Soviet satellite heightened Mao's thirst for revenge in Indochina, where the U.S. first supported the French, then a succession of weak rulers of South

Vietnam, and eventually joined the civil war. The aggressive approach led to the Vietnam War and later to the Reagan military build up, both destructive of the financial underpinning of the U.S. economy.

The lesson of Korea, do not fight on the Asian mainland, was lost in the urgency to thwart the Soviets in Vietnam. Eisenhower had provided financial support, Kennedy sent 16,000 military advisors. As the first president to recognize that instead of fighting a single Cold War against Moscow, a separate war was involved, Kennedy probably would not have gone on in Vietnam. He recognized that China was likely to prevent a U.S. win, as it had in Korea. Fighting to win in Vietnam could mean starting a big war, but fearing a repeat of Truman's political troubles over China, Kennedy deferred until after the 1964 election, only to die and leave the suspended mess to an overly prideful successor with less vision. Johnson got into a war he seems to have recognized was hopeless because, as a political animal, he feared a repeat of Truman's awkward position over China. Haunted by Truman's experience, he grasped the domino theory as an excuse for sending in troops. NSC-68 was on its way to running up a terrible bill for the nation. On the other hand, the policy was not entirely negative. It led to the preservation of South Korea and Taiwan, both of which evolved into successful industrial nations. Their success while remaining authoritarian provided a model for China, whose communist based efforts at industrialization under Mao had proven disastrous.

Luckily, serious consequences were avoided when North Vietnam turned us back in the south without China becoming directly involved, though both China and the Soviet Union provided substantial aid. The fallout from Vietnam tempered U.S. conduct of the Cold war, with positive results. Nixon's desperate search for peace with honor led to recognition of China. He also understood that Vietnam and dealing with the Kremlin were separate issues and that the nuclear arms race had gotten out of hand.

The U.S. attitude toward the Cold War was in part determined by a political struggle between Democrats and Republicans over who was the true defender of the nation. These were dark days for conservatives and they chose to stage a comeback by villainizing Democrats as soft on Communism. Truman's place in history is built less on adoption of containment than confronting Stalin. Although he routinely exaggerated the Soviet threat, conservatives always claimed he was not doing enough. The raw meanness of their attack, its personal aspect, the twisting of facts, set a new standard for the future. A number of precedents, or modes of operation, were established on which the conservative comeback was built. The mantra of attack employed issues less for their importance than their emotional appeal and adaptability to being twisted to reflect badly on Democrats.

Conservatives found media support for their comeback effort. The most influential publication then was TIME magazine. It had popular yearly quizzes on current events and all the answers could be found only in TIME. Publisher Henry Luce's romantic view of China came out of his father's China missionary experience. Any reference to China and Chiang Kai-shek was cast in a highly favorable light, leaving the sudden fall of the Nationalists in 1948 a complete surprise to readers. TIME continued to back Chiang and foster the fantasy of re-conquest with American aid. The right wing comeback was based on this kind of emotional media treatment to sell a twisted version of economics and foreign affairs.

Truman was followed by a sensible Republican president, Dwight Eisenhower, whose personal stature left him no need to bait communists for political advantage. Eisenhower brought common sense to the struggle over foreign policy. Truman was not a planner, he reacted to events. For him NSC-68 had the attraction of political popularity and gut feel. Eisenhower, a staff rather than a field general, had developed the habit of proceeding in accordance with a well thought out master plan. One of his first acts was to put together a group to study Cold War options. His carefully considered choice was a combination of containment, reliance on atomic weapons for defense, and making sure the economy was strong. Diverting from NSC-68, military spending was reduced. Eisenhower was a traditionalist, concerned about the influence of a wartime mentality on America's economy and habits. Given the horror of nuclear weapons, he recognized that open warfare was unlikely. When intercontinental ballistic missiles added to the danger, the strategy was already set and there was no panic or rush into larger military expenditures.

Except for the Vietnam build up, Eisenhower's controlled stance on military spending remained in effect, but NSC-68 continued to lurk in the background. A Soviet Union out for world conquest remained the conviction of most Americans. The NSC-68 approach was bound to produce a situation where aggression prevailed over reason and it happened in Vietnam. As Democrats realized the mistake and sought to get out, conservatives were able to identify with war protests and defeat with liberal Democrats. Although Nixon made the mistake of perpetuating the war, he still won the 1972 election in a landslide. The loss remained Johnson's. Conservatives seized the opportunity to become the party of determined communist fighters, while liberals were painted as soft in defense of the nation. Exaggerating the Soviet threat became fundamental to the conservative political rebirth. As the right wing marshaled its forces, NSC-68 was adopted as one of the foundations. Eventually an unwise presidential candidate was going to use anti-Russian sentiment to get elected and end Eisenhower's economically sensible policy. That candidate was Ronald Reagan.

History unfolded as Kennan foresaw, with no thanks to violently anti-Truman Republicans and their successors. Containment was affirmed under Eisenhower, but the right fought containment throughout the Cold War, claiming it was not working and that the Soviets must be dealt with aggressively. Reagan's rise was importantly based on abandoning containment on the trumped up theory it was causing us to lose the Cold War.

2

A Comeback For Free Market Economics

ALTHOUGH CONSERVATIVES INITIATED THEIR RETURN in the foreign field, domestic policy was their primary concern. Eisenhower supported business as good for the economy, but he was more moderate progressive than conservative. In his time businessmen accepted liberal progress and were pleased with the growing economy.

This left the conservative base a small group of old wealth, plus a few cranks in Congress still fighting the New Deal and sounding off about China. In 1955 conservatives found a fresh voice in the establishment of Bill Buckley's National Review. Buckley was an individualist who did not believe in government managed democracy. Unlike many deep conservatives, he was neither a cave man nor a monarchist. At a time conservatives seemed frozen in the past, Buckley could argue a liberal to exhaustion. He brought other attributes. He was ardently anti-communist, not so much in the military sense as maximizing resistance to the doctrine's dehumanizing effect. He was the first to introduce the values theme. A devout Catholic, Buckley believed in the importance of a moral life. In addition to a rallying point, he provided a well reasoned intellectual foundation.

Conservatism's theoretical basis came from Edmund Burke, an eighteen century British political thinker:

1) suspicion of the power of the state and skepticism about government supported progressivism,

2) preference for individual liberty over equality.

Burke's case amounted to being careful about change, but the new conservatives were not merely interested in holding the line, they wanted to turn back the clock. Suspicion of the state was converted into identifying government with all economic troubles. Devotion to the individual was directed at supporting freedom to acquire unlimited wealth without regard to social responsibility.

Although conservatism had enjoyed periods of popularity in the past, in general the United States had been progressive. Liberalism is by definition American to the core: favorable to progress or reform, favorable to or in accord with concepts of maximum individual freedom, free from prejudice or bigotry, open-minded, tolerant, and characterized by generosity. Except for maximum individual freedom, these were the values the right set out to oppose. They believed that individual freedom was more important than equality. Liberals saw government's role as fostering equality, conservatives saw these efforts as inhibiting individualism and national progress.

As Buckley gave conservatism a degree of respectability, things unfolded with surprising speed. In 1964 a far right conservative, Barry Goldwater, succeeded in becoming the Republican presidential candidate. The first think tank, American Enterprise Institute, was a primary force behind the Goldwater campaign. Later AEI was to become identified with the strong anti-Soviet position and after the Cold War with unilateralism, but originally it championed free market economics. Goldwater ran a dual campaign, a strong stance against the Kremlin and anti-government free market economics. These views were captivating to many wealthy conservatives, who became the financial angels of the new right wing.

Goldwater's campaign was so far ahead of the times that he drew the lowest percentage vote for a major party candidate in U.S. history when no significant third party detracted from the loser's total. He seemed deranged in a loose attitude toward use of atomic bombs to fight the Cold War at a time such weapons were recognized as the primary reason war had not broken out. Although inducing me and many other Republicans to vote for Lyndon Johnson, Goldwater carried six states, including most of the normally Democratic south. More importantly, conservatives found inspiration in his platform and his methods.

Four new elements in American politics came out of the Goldwater campaign:

1) The south, after voting Democratic since the Civil War, but conservative and out of tune with that party, was moving toward a more natural link with Republicans. After flirting with racist third party candidates, southern states joined the Republican Party and became the core territory of the right.

2) Beginning of a more broadly expressed disgust with liberal government programs. Johnson Great Society legislation was the high water mark for liberalism. Thereafter a decline set in that has lasted until the election of

Barack Obama. Taking advantage of negative reaction to Johnson's program, the right built its following around beating up on liberals. Although liberalism in the U.S. has been greatly tamed since 1964, the onslaught continues, for exaggerating the ills of liberalism remains a vital political tactic for the right. Needing to distract attention from their own wealth centered goals, they continued to attack even as liberalism faded away.

3) Resistance to civil rights. Goldwater voted against the Civil Rights Act and his opposition struck a chord among middle and lower class whites. New Deal programs that survived were broadly applicable and had become part of the landscape, but the Great Society, passed into law in 1964 and 1965, was different. Not broadly directed, it was aimed at bringing poor segments of society into the main stream. Primarily, that meant African-Americans.

Although the Civil Rights Act was accepted in principle, efforts by liberal Democrats and the courts at forcible implementation by busing, quotas, and affirmative action generated a backlash among lower and middle class whites. They bore the brunt of civil rights enforcement, as it was their jobs being threatened and their schools being integrated. Busing and affirmative action seemed all the more outrageous with the simultaneous outbreak of race riots, the black power movement, and the rapid rise of crime and people on welfare. Many working class whites, formerly stalwarts of the Democratic Party, reacted by turning away. If the normal consequence of a crushing defeat like Goldwater's was to write off the views he expressed, reaction against what was seen as special privileges for blacks was just getting under way. It brought dramatic change in the political climate in a mere four years.

4) Winning a major party candidacy for a far right figure like Goldwater awakened conservative Republicans to future possibilities. Here was a base that could be built on. Wealthy backers began to fund a comprehensive political effort built around Goldwater views. Conservative foundations and wealthy individuals funded think tanks. Before long, right wing think tanks were popping up all over the place.

Goldwater's principle themes, less government and larger armed forces, were not new, but his my-way-or-no-way approach was inspiring. If roughhouse tactics did not gain the presidency, for an outside the main stream candidate to gain the nomination of a major party was quite a feat. Although the wealthy backers of the new effort were hopelessly outnumbered, Goldwater demonstrated broad possibilities behind the themes and methods. Although a reactionary group of the wealthy would always be small in number, hardball tactics might enlarge the following. Winning the presidency was less a concern for Goldwater than serving as ground breaker for turning the Republican Party to the right.

At the beginning, the new conservative political effort was disorganized.

It consisted of a loose group of wealthy Californians rallying around Ronald Reagan following his highly regarded national television speech on behalf of Goldwater just prior to the 1964 election. They succeeded in moving Reagan into the California governorship in 1966, giving him a national platform as spokesman for conservatism. The strategy followed Buckley's call for individualism and against the shackles of big government. Individuals should be allowed to hold onto what they had. Sharing gave a free ride to the least accomplished members of society, leading to an ever increasing spiral of laziness.

The conservative line of attack was to go after government as a wasteful instrument for a variety of socialist giveaways that prevented capitalism from reaching its full potential. According to them, the New Deal had degenerated into interest group liberalism, an interesting argument in view of the complete capitulation of conservatives to special interest groups after they came into power. Not just welfare, but subsidies, government impositions on the marketplace, rescuing bankrupt companies and nations, had become so pervasive that economic progress was inhibited. Paying for the governmental apparatus led to confiscatory taxes on the most accomplished citizens, inhibiting entrepreneurial activity, innovation, and invention. Although there was no evidence to support these views, who was to say the nation might not have been more prosperous at lower levels of government and taxation. Besides, proof was not a concern, their beliefs were ruled by passionate self-interest.

With Buckley providing the inspiration, right wing strategy was based on dressing up free market ideology and controlling the terms of debate. Although free market economics had fallen into disgrace after bringing on the depression, they rewrote the history to capitalize on the fact that more than thirty years had passed since the depression and memories are short. They blamed the depression on government mismanagement as part of an assault on the evil influence of government on the economy. They benefited not only from short memories, but free market ideology has a utopian grandeur. Despite a miserable history, it sounds great. Buckley and others took on the task of dressing it up.

With its poor record, the free market did not have a wide following among economists. At the University of Chicago, however, free market economics was re-born after the war. Chicago spawned Milton Friedman, who became the foremost economist of the 1960s and 1970s. He gave the theory respectability, in part from offering a magic formula for implementation that, he claimed, would eliminate the business cycle by controlling money supply. Friedman had a talent for historical revisionism and developed the story that rather than the depression being caused by the free market system, it was the result of mistakes by the Federal Reserve Bank and the Hoover administration. He rewrote the record to fit his theory, a lesson the right was to apply to its own future failings.

As Friedman became well known, inflation was on the rise and he sold the idea that it could be controlled by keeping money growth within a narrow range. Slow growth in money supply would permit steady non-inflationary growth, allowing the economy to reach full potential. Friedman became a one man think tank serving right wing economic theory. Friedman was the most famous and highly regarded economist in the world, winning the Nobel Prize in 1976. Today he has faded into history, but at that time no one understood that his theories did not work, though early experiments were a warning. Nixon tried tightly controlled money supply and the economy immediately weakened. Chile was next, again with depressing results. Great Britain followed, with the same results, though Margaret Thatcher got deserved credit for ending the the socialist period and privatizing British industry. Attempted in the United States between 1979 and 1982, it eventually broke an inflationary spiral, again after a long recession.

The right had help from another economist. Money supply and free market economics were not inspiring, no matter how much right wing think tanks and business publications might build them up, but a new theory came along to popularize the free market - supply-side economics. According to the theory, tax cuts would so stimulate the economy that growth would make up for the lost tax revenue if a free market prevailed that provided full scope for capitalism to work its magic. Supply-side theory was the work of Arthur Laffer, whose low regard among economists was more than overcome by enthusiastic support from right wing think tanks and The Wall Street Journal. A Journal reporter developed the Laffer Curve, an entrancing explanation of why tax cuts and free market economics would create a paradise of prosperity. Ronald Reagan was attracted to rosy myths and made supply side the basis of his economic policy.

Underlying supply side was the theory that taxes were a key determinant of the economy. A low tax rate created higher incentive and a stronger economy, a high tax rate acted as a disincentive to hard work and entrepreneurship, slowing the economy. Overlooked was that at the 70% top bracket rate prevailing prior to Reagan, much lower capital gains rates left ample incentive, while the high rate on ordinary income was a disincentive to less productive pursuits, such as securities trading and high corporate salaries that encouraged management decisions based on short term factors. The theory was disproven when Clinton raised the top bracket from Reagan's 28% to 39.6% and the U.S. enjoyed a burst of entrepreneurial activity. The low top bracket rate under Reagan and George W. Bush set off a frenzy of corporate misbehavior and Wall Street activities that almost brought the country to a new depression. The capital retained by high earners because of a low tax rate did not necessarily flow to productive investments. Often it went into speculation and fast reward ventures like mergers that destroyed jobs.

Supply side might not work, or to the extent it did, only slowly, but above all the wealthy founders of the new right wing wanted tax cuts and the theory fit that goal perfectly. The question for those claiming to be fiscal conservatives seeking a balanced budget was how to pay for the tax cuts. Supply side said they would pay for themselves. If tax reductions paid for themselves, then cuts could be larger. Later, when the theory failed and deficits did not sink the economy, they decided deficits did not matter, so they could keep on lowering taxes. If some supply side backers recognized that economic growth would not cover the lost revenue, they planned to make up the difference by cutting government services, of itself a major right wing goal. Supply side's attraction was not that it worked, which many suspected it would not, but that it perfectly fit conservative goals.

To a degree supply side did work. Clinton balanced the budget on the massive earnings of a greatly enlarged group of rich paying taxes at almost half the rate that prevailed prior to Reagan. If the immediate effect was deficits, the economy absorbed the shortfall more easily than supply siders had thought. At least, that was true until 2007, when the piper finally had to be paid.

During the years prior to Reagan, government participation capitalism began to run into trouble from deficits caused by the Vietnam War and social spending. About 1965, inflation picked up. Capital shortages developed out of the limitations of the Bretton Woods monetary agreement tying worldwide currencies to a gold backed dollar. Bretton Woods depended on the United States having sound fiscal policy and inflation strained the system. Nixon found the gold standard too difficult to maintain, abandoning it in 1971.

The result was a period of what was termed stagflation, or slow growth accompanied by inflation. If economic growth in the 1970s was in line with subsequent decades, at the time it seemed slow because of dropping from 1950s and 1960s rates. The stock market suffered a long slump from 1966 into 1982. Imports began to threaten some of our established industries. Moderates and businessmen who might not have lined up with a reactionary effort were converted by the pressures of inflation and decline in their stocks and bonds. Government participation capitalism took the blame, giving new life to free market theory. The groundwork was laid for a new experiment in free market economics under a right wing president.

Although winning the presidency in a progressive democracy might seem improbable for a tiny group of wealth, Goldwater had won the candidacy and their man was governor of the largest state. Think tanks were conceptualizing a basis for persuading a wider following. The campaign was built around making right wing doctrine an appeal to idealism, religious values, and fear of foreign threats, liberals, and unruly racial minorities. In the early days they had ample material to work with. There was plenty of room for complaint that liberalism had become excessive. Although remarkably free of corruption, the system was full of excesses. The federal budget was a growing monster of endless programs on top of new projects. Temporary expedients became self-perpetuating.

The new right spoke out for ending this folly through minimal government, arguing that capitalism would then be unleashed to the greater good of all. The few people who might be hurt were lazy. The great majority would be better off if this massive government structure was unwound. Reagan was effective at picturing government as the cause of our problems rather than the solution. Incentive destroying policies that erected barriers to economic activity should be replaced by a free market that opened up capitalism's natural capacity to expand and generate new wealth to the benefit of all. Thousands of inefficiencies in government programs provided a rich field for cultivating an anti-government attitude among voters.

Other factors were working away in these years to boost the right. During the long period of economic tranquility followed the war, corporations thought of themselves as guardians of the public interest and accepted new regulation. As conditions tightened from inflation, import competition, and a weak stock market, at the same time as the pace of regulation intensified, their cooperative attitude changed. Fighting back, they found right wing organizations eager to help. Think tanks assisted business lobbies and advocacy groups were formed to support individual right wing projects. The Business Roundtable was formed in 1972, including the heads of most major corporations. Although nothing new, business lobbying began to grow. Early efforts were aimed at trimming environmental and safety regulation. Ralph Nader's popularity as a consumer advocate inspired resistance and ended up as a political liability for liberals. Corporations stepped up political contributions, established lobbies, and learned how to influence legislation.

Later, business oriented governments supported a broad based corporate strike against all forms of regulation. In addition to a comprehensive effort to uproot regulation, lobbyists developed pork barrel legislation that brought business to companies they supported. These efforts led to a flood of campaign funds for conservative champions of big business, providing right wing candidates the money to win elections. In time the nefarious activities of business lobbies poisoned the legislative process and virtually ruined the Republican Party and the conservative movement.

Changing attitudes and resistance to the Vietnam War among students created what became known as the counterculture, a rejection by a large group of the young of conventional social mores. As post depression children brought up to greater affluence, they were less oriented to convention and sought a freer life of greater leisure. Its outward manifestation was support of better race relations, women's rights, distrust of authority, freer sexual relationships, and above all protest of the war. Backlash to the counterculture made moderates more receptive to right wing propaganda. Supporters of the war, which included most Americans until fairly late in the game, were especially appalled. The counterculture became a useful tool for alarmists exaggerating the Soviet threat and seeking to increase defense spending. They claimed the Russians were winning the Cold War because Americans were being ruined by luxury and incapable of defending themselves.

The stars were aligned for the right. The search for a following had barely begun when the Johnson landslide reversed. A revolution in American politics took place between 1965 and 1968 for three principal reasons. First, protest against the Vietnam War was largely identified with Democrats. Protesters were correct that this was not a winnable war and we never should have become involved, but the disorder turned off many Americans. In the World Wars, in Korea and Vietnam, Democrats had been the party of defense. Now they were being identified as soft on communism. Making themselves champion of defense became one of the right's chief underpinnings. Decades of political disadvantage from the soft image was to play out badly for Democrats again in 2002, when many felt politically trapped and voted for invasion of Iraq under circumstances they would never have previously gone along with.

The most immediate factor in turning the tables on liberals was objection to civil rights. Just as the new conservative effort was getting under way, race riots, the black power movement, and civil rights enforcement provided an emotional issue for bashing liberals. If the law itself was accepted, enforcement measures such as busing and quotas were not. Although the wealthy right was unaffected by these problems, they recognized the opportunity. A strategy was quickly developed for blaming racial outrage on liberal Democrats and the institutions of government.

3

Setting the Stage for Reagan

WITH THE DEMOCRATIC PARTY TORN by Vietnam and rising inflation, Richard Nixon slipped into the White House in 1968. The vote was close only because George Wallace, the third party candidate, took more votes from Nixon than Humphrey. Grounded in established ways, the new president continued with liberal programs. The Environmental Protection Agency, Occupational Safety & Health Administration, and various forms of minority capitalism were begun, but Nixon seems to have backed them to build support for a second term. Although Goldwater conservatives were not strong for Nixon, he made a substantial contribution to the their cause.

Nixon was a strange man. He trusted no one, nor the institutions of government, including the now established spy satellite information that provided an accurate picture of the Soviet military. Absence of faith in this data and in any information coming out of the CIA was exploited by conservatives eager to gain political advantage out of exaggerating the Russian threat. Negativism hung like a cloud over Nixon, making leadership difficult.

By the 1972 campaign, civil rights had turned strongly positive for Republicans. If Nixon's first term had been marked by not getting out of Vietnam and politically oriented economic policy that added to the rate of inflation, the failures were more than made up by running against busing and affirmative action. The strategy paid off with a smashing victory over liberal George McGovern. Nixon had found the political soft spot. Putting aside the Klu Klux Klan hoods, he built a backlash anti-black vote fertilizing resentment against civil rights enforcement and its liberal supporters. Enforcement laws could be assailed as undemocratic to pick up the anti-black vote without appearing bigoted. Race became the most important means of building the right's political strength. Reagan was to finalize the strategy by creating the impression that liberalism was coercive and non-egalitarian because it supported special privileges for a few that were costly to freedom and to the Treasury.

Later presidential campaigns by unworthy candidates such as Jesse Jackson and Al Sharpton helped maintain the feeling of resentment. Support in the western states was picked up by playing on regional dislike of eastern liberalism, a stronger spirit of rugged individualism, and directing the race tactic against Hispanics. The right's ability to take advantage of race was buttressed by failure of the Great Society to elevate minorities as much as had been hoped. Some African-Americans were uplifted, but too many were not, and the feeling was that they deserved their fate. Since the dregs helped keep the issue in the forefront, the right had no plan for helping them. Chastened by conservative success, Democrats also gave up. A segment of African-Americans became a permanent drag on society and an ongoing boost to the right.

Nixon also popularized another theme that third party candidate George Wallace had used in 1968 to attract a surprising number of votes from working class whites in the north: associating liberalism with out of touch eastern intellectual elites. This became a favorite theme of right wing think tanks. Astoundingly, they were calling down a war on knowledge, deriding professionals, professors, and judges as snobs lacking understanding of the real world. The wealthy elitist right was transferring its lack of interest in the common man onto those who cared about democracy and fairness. Irrational, but it worked with many southerners, northern working class whites, and westerners. The anti-intellectual story line remains a favorite right wing talking point.

Behind the anti-intellectual message was the aim of creating doubt about the factuality of news information. It marked the opening salvo in a remarkable campaign against legitimate news sources as biased. While Goldwater had griped about media bias, Nixon was paranoid on the subject. Ugly portrayals of him as vice president culminated in losing the 1960 presidential race. Nixon gave his vice president, Spiro Agnew, one principle assignment, rallying support against the media. Although the effort was fueled by Vietnam War protest, its intent was broader. From here on discrediting liberal positions and trashing news that reflected badly on the right became one of the chief occupations of their think tanks. So persistent was the attack that by 2000 a majority of Americans distrusted standard media news sources. Neo-conservative intellectuals, who originally bet on Hubert Humphrey to gain entry into government, were attracted to conservatism partly because they were so effective at this kind of propaganda.

The media strategy was based on confusing fact with opinion. The new right wing was firmly rooted in ideology rather than history or common sense or fact. The ideology was unequivocally supported, regardless of the evidence. Maintaining a position in the face of contrary facts required denigrating factual information, much like a lawyer with a difficult case to defend. The guiding light of the media storm was Edith Efron's 1971 book, The News Twisters. It argued for pursuing media support by using opinion to overcome fact. The Accuracy in Media organization started about this time, pitching into the free press as communist influenced. Later, the Media Research Center opened an all out assault on so-called liberal bias.

Nixon's greatest contribution to the right was his own disastrous first term. By failing to wholeheartedly pursue peace in Vietnam and expanding the already lost war, he perpetuated the anti-war sentiment that ended in Democrats being perceived as weak on defense. War spending contributed to deficits and inflation, spoiling the economy. His economic policy, aimed at getting re-elected, combined price controls with loose monetary policy, taking advantage of going off the gold standard. The system of government participation capitalism that had worked so well appeared to be at fault, opening the door for a return to free market capitalism.

Nixon's disastrous economic policy was quickly reflected in the second term. After price controls came off in January, 1973, inflation took off. The stock market went into a slump that was to end two years later in the largest decline since the depression. Stagflation and the disappointing economy of the 1970s was largely Nixon's legacy, but the right wing's new media organization seized the opportunity to identify the troubles with Carter and excessive government.

Nixon's smashing 1972 victory is credited to George McGovern being too liberal, but McGovern was one of the most impressive men of the day and not so easily defeated without Nixon having other advantages. Detente and recognizing China gave him an aura of diplomatic expertise and suggested that the American people were ready to end the Cold War. Gerald Ford also pushed detente and Carter was enthusiastic.

Not so the right. Peace threatened one of its primary underpinnings. In response they marshaled forces against accommodation with the Kremlin. Doing so attracted another group to the gathering coalition, neo-conservatives. Leading neo-conservatives were former Trotskyites, that is to say Marxists fervently opposing the U.S.S.R. Although they had dropped communism, visceral hatred of the Soviet Union continued. Long time pamphleteers and book writers, ideology was their strong point, making them perfectly cast for right wing think tanks. Formerly gathered in the liberal Humphrey camp, his melt down after 1968 left them adrift. In search of a base for exerting political influence, they managed to set aside communist feelings toward wealth. Becoming an integral part of the fight against detente led neo-conservatives to positions of importance in the conservative movement.

The new Democratic president, Jimmy Carter, turned out to be perfect for playing up the Soviet threat. Carter was indecisive in dealing with changing times and tended to make snap decisions that got him in trouble. The economy was in transition following abandonment of the gold standard, upset by increases in the price of oil and the beginning of a permanent trade deficit. Right wing think tanks and media critics were honing their skill at the blame game and Carter had a way of positioning himself as an ideal target. All the accumulated troubles of the 1970s were fixed on him, though most were Nixon's fault. Carter appointed Paul Volcker to head the Federal Reserve Bank and his inflation fighting tight money policy led to a struggling economy in election year. Trying to tack back and forth against the headwinds, Carter looked indecisive.

The right continued to use Carter as an example of bumbling liberalism long after his departure. In fact, Carter was something of a visionary. He was the first to act on energy conservation, establishing automobile mileage standards and pushing solar and wind energy. He faced the greenhouse effect with air pollution requirements for utilities. Reagan threw out or weakened all of these moves, to our present regret. It was Carter who pushed development of high technology weapons, the only positive side of Reagan's military build up. In his famous at the time malaise speech, Carter warned against exactly the kind of self-absorbent overspending that has placed the nation in trouble, but it was a loser politically to Reagan's cheerfully indulgent no sacrifice avoidance of problems.

Despite the promise in detente, Cold War episodes broke in favor of the right. Cuba was lost to communism and anti-colonial outbreaks in Africa encouraged Russian intervention. Brezhnev began talking about gaining an edge in the Cold War and the nuclear threat seemed to worsen as they exceeded the U.S. in number of ballistic missile launch sites. The armed services began planning for a staged nuclear war with a surviving winner, a ridiculous notion that intensified fear. The Russian invasion of Afghanistan was the final blow. It was the first move against a territory not taken during World War II. Suddenly those claiming the Soviet Union sought to conquer the world had something concrete to point at.

Afghanistan led to sanctions, withdrawal of food support to the U.S.S.R., and boycott of the Moscow Olympics. An oil embargo arising from another Arab Israel war added to Carter's woes. He committed a serious blunder letting the former Shah of Iran into the country for medical treatment, leading to the Tehran embassy being stormed and hostages taken. These incidents played into the right's hands. They pictured detente as appeasement in the face of communism on the march. Their claim that the Soviets were winning the Cold War seemed plausible.

The Carter years saw the emergence of two factors that lifted the right - identification of a strong military with the Republican Party and religion as a factor in politics. Democrats had led the country into Korea and Vietnam, but Vietnam taught them a lesson. For their part, conservatives had championed a military approach to the Cold War all the way back to 1948. Resistance to peace was undertaken through the Committee on the Present Danger, formed before Carter became president, but especially effective during his tenure. The group's purpose was fostering alarm about the Soviet Union. It included Reagan and many others who were to gain high position on his team. Although the military danger was refuted by over fifteen years of spy satellite information, they took advantage of the doubt Nixon had created about intelligence. The combination of the old argument about Democrats losing China, a pacifist image coming out of liberal protest of Vietnam, and Carter's fumbling, placed conservatives as champions of national defense. An alarmist group exaggerating threat for political advantage and expert in the art of propaganda played a crucial role in Reagan's election.

Religion had not been important in American politics until the combination of disgust with Nixon and Carter's ministerial demeanor helped him win the presidency in 1976. Carter was against abortion and busing and for re-establishing school prayer, stands that were probably responsible for winning the presidency. This support was lost for a number of reasons. An Internal Revenue Service inquiry into the tax free status of non-integrated private schools, many founded by religious organizations in response to forced integration, infuriated politically oriented evangelicals.

Of greater importance was the right's vocal stance against communism. Evangelical churches responded to fighting the evil of communism and supported Reagan's plan for a military build up. They were alarmed by the counterculture and outspoken about what they saw as decaying moral standards. The Soviet threat and morals were joined in a number of books about the coming day of reckoning in the form of defeat of the United States. The aggressive anti-Soviet position led to alignment with the right wing, a deal sealed by the right's adoption of moral concerns, a position that went all the way back to Bill Buckley.

Religious groups concerned about growing secularism in America began to thrive in the 1960s. Their political focal point arrived in the 1973 Roe vs. Wade Supreme Court decision legalizing abortion. Banning religious services in public schools followed. While some of the most popular televangelists were caught in actions that disgraced evangelicals, others like Jerry Falwell and Pat Robertson turned to political activity. Robertson established a connection with Nixon, but neither Nixon nor Ford cared much for this kind of assistance. Then the 1976 election demonstrated that religion had become a political force.

Evangelicals tended to preach the Puritan ethic of asceticism, thrift, and hard work, rather than traditional Christian values such as help for the poor. To them, poverty was evidence of sin, worldly success a sign of virtue. Fundamentalist preachers, who interpreted the word of God for their congregation in unequivocal terms, were sympathetic toward the right's forceful interpretation of economics, politics, and international relations. Although money centered right wingers were far less virtuous than most liberals, they were looking for support wherever it could be found. In time evangelicals became the right's most outspoken supporters, including playing down traditional democratic values, sharply biased forms of nationalism, certainty of doctrine, and denouncing independent thinking. The politically active religious movement was added to the Reagan coalition.

Since past reactionary movements had often had a religious tone, right wing leadership was on the lookout for such a connection. They were aided by many evangelical churches being profit making business enterprises. These churches resembled the right in use of fear for gathering a following. Salvation was achieved through a form of Christianity that had little to do with the Biblical teachings of Jesus Christ. Like the democracy of the founders, Christ's religion involved purity through good thoughts and deeds, but evangelicals taught salvation through following the word of their worldly leader. Giving themselves to Christ often led to being relaxed about un-Christian ways, such as admiring money and saving souls by means of war.

With this background, coming together of the intensely secular right wing with evangelical churches was not as surprising as it seems. The practical right, eager to build a following from wherever it could be found, jumped at the opportunity to embrace right to life. Think tanks went to work on the use of values as a theme and turning it against liberals.

Reagan's record with religion and family values was poor. He is still the only divorced president, was indifferent to his children, and rarely went to church. On the other hand, he had the manner of an evangelist and his all-American demeanor was attractive to religious sects. Vocally advocating right to life and religion in schools, Reagan earned their enthusiastic support. He perfected the saintly lingo to such a degree that the religiously inclined never noticed the failure to deliver on his promises. Other than the wealthy leadership, evangelicals were to remain the hardest core of the right wing.

Religious support was invaluable because voters focused on abortion, secularism, and school prayer, were not concerned by the right's economic policy and were enthusiastic about its aggressive foreign policy. Recruited from among members of the middle and lower classes, these supporters failed to notice that reduced business regulation and tax breaks for the rich did nothing for them. Although the free market was to develop in a way that harmed their economic interests, they fell for the argument that the shortcomings were the fault of godless liberals. Blind faith among religion based voters was decisive in winning the 2004 election for George W. Bush in the face of a poor economic record and the worst foreign policy boondoggle in American history.

The most intriguing aspect of religious support was its backing of the armed forces. As the Cold War ended and a large military was no longer necessary, the services and the right wing fought against cuts. Evangelical churches might have been expected to embrace peace, but they responded to the idea of spreading democracy by militarily aggressive foreign policy.

Forced to reach out for support from any source because of its tiny base, conservatives were asking for trouble allying themselves with the rigid ideology of fundamentalist religious extremists and warmongering neo-conservatives. Religious support upset the political process through election of unworthy candidates using close identification with religious matters having nothing to do with governing. Abortion, gay rights, and the like became more important than they deserved, rendering right wing governments less effective. Neo-conservatives encouraged Reagan on unnecessary defense spending that was costly to the economy and distracted attention from unfavorable economic trends. In the end, neo-conservatives led the right into a war that destroyed their power, but in the late 1970s, their backing helped capture the White House.

Another factor blossomed in the 1970s to boost the right. High costs and lack of innovation in domestic manufacturing were expressed in Japanese inroads into our automobile and television set markets. By the time Reagan came to office, a history of trade surpluses had turned into deficits. Imports were beginning to threaten the jobs of working class Americans. Government was already blamed for giving blacks special advantages and for inflation, now the right attempted with some success to pin the loss of blue collar jobs on liberal government. Democrats for Reagan were working class Americans voting Republican for the first time as an expression of their economic insecurity. The loss of high paying industrial jobs worsened during the Reagan presidency and beyond, but the right effectively sold the idea that liberal government was responsible. Logic did not deter a right wing exercising its standard practice of tarring liberals with every complaint in sight. Ceaseless attack was all the more effective for liberal failure to counter-attack. During the sixteen years between Goldwater and Reagan, the combination of all these factors melted away the old liberal Democratic base.

In addition to riding the wave of reaction to excessive liberalism, court based rulings not supported by the majority of white voters, and effective right wing propaganda, Reagan was a born vote getter. Rather than a strong leader, Reagan was an able politician embracing help from wherever it could be found. He provided marketable softness by clothing elitist economic ideology in populist rhetoric. Reagan had a gift Goldwater lacked, a gift George W. Bush was to share, the ability to appear as a nice trustworthy person. His special personality attracted extremists, from evangelical Jerry Falwell to the violent National Rifle Association bloc to anti-commie witch hunting members of the John Birch Society, while still leaving moderates comfortable. He followed Goldwater's two basic premises: less government, expressed in the belief that private industry always did better than government, and aggressive foreign policy, including avoidance of foreign treaties and the UN. No one was more talented at picturing big government as a hopeless lumbering fool.

Reagan arrived at the presidency as the most practiced political charmer in U.S. history. He had long ago turned from Hollywood to political actor. By 1980 he had perfected presentation of the rich man's line in a way that appeared to include the general public. Although the communist threat was far reduced from its early days, Reagan talked as if the Cold War had just begun, with no progress over the last thirty-five years.

First as a spokesman for General Electric and later as governor of California, he developed the themes that lured the public to vote against their interests in favor of the rich: law and order, moral decay, the magic of free market economics, the evils of big government, and the need to defeat the Soviet Union. The modest acting talent had been turned into a polished political professional of wit and assurance. No president arrived with a more complete and convincing message and the presidential bully pulpit provided a perfect stage.

Reagan was just what the right was hoping for. There was a definite unreality to their doctrine and as a movie creature, he lived in a space where fact and fiction melded. His way of always seeing the bright side seemed to transform mistakes and failures into successes, without appearing to be covering up. Reagan's convincing sincerity and personal conviction overcame the fact that he was a front man for a movement that was out to destroy American tradition and hand over government to those measuring in terms of the thickness of a wallet.

4

President Reagan

IF RONALD REAGAN'S CHEERFUL NATURE instinctively responded to visionary promises of free market capitalism and supply-side economics, his enthusiasm was strongest for fighting communism. Hollywood had a large communist element that he fought as head of the Screen Actors Guild during the harshest part of the communist scare, 1947-1952. Direct exposure led to zeal for the fight. Reagan's personal feelings were so strong he seemed to overlook that by the time he arrived in the White House communism was dead in America. Although the United States had proven otherwise, in the back of his mind was the concept that liberalism led to communism, with stops along the way at the welfare state and socialism. Reagan's colorful anti-government statements fell out of anti-communism. He saw active government ending in something resembling the Soviet system.

Not only was this nonsense, it clouded his views in unfortunate ways. For example, Reagan missed one of the founder's central concepts, that militarism rather than liberalism was the primary threat to a democratic society. The Roman republic, a model for our system, fell to militarism. Many of the founders opposing a peacetime army, thinking its existence could develop into despotism. When George W. Bush used the war on terror to advance executive power and build up the military, the founders groans could figuratively be heard. If the president of the United States on September 11, 2001, had been Julius Caesar rather than Bush, the country might have ended up far more authoritarian.

Unlike his fellow members of the Committee on the Present Danger, Reagan did not think we were losing the Cold War. He recognized that containment had worked, but he was impatient. Dreaming of himself as the marshal arriving in town to slay the bad guys, he was determined to push the tottering Kremlin over the cliff. His push was a military build up, not to fight the Russians, but to induce an arms race that would ruin them economically. Reagan did not disapprove of detente out of the usual fear of being taken advantage of by evil communists, but because it eased economic pressure on Moscow by reducing their need for military spending. Although the right was to claim the strategy worked, there is no evidence the Kremlin responded.

If building a large military to defeat a staggering foe appears inconsistent, more generously Reagan can be said to have recognized that containment was no longer necessary, permitting an immediate attempt to bring down the foe. In command of intelligence his fellow anti-Soviet group had rejected, he became more convinced that the enemy was on the ropes.

Conviction about Soviet weakness left him free for his specialty, verbal attack. Although unlikely to influence Moscow, it was a winner politically. Belligerence worried the State Department and others who thought he might be wrong on Soviet weakness, but Reagan was confident that retaliation was unlikely. He stirred up trouble in Poland and applied economic pressure, notably encouraging Saudi Arabia to oversupply the world with oil to depress prices (cut in half in early 1986). At the time, the U.S.S.R. was a larger exporter of oil than the Saudis and oil was its main source of foreign exchange.

The Reagan arms race strategy would never have been used by Truman, Eisenhower, and the following presidents, for they recognized its negative effect on the economy. Typically of the right, Reagan was unruffled by the fact that combining major tax cuts with a tripled defense budget did not make economic sense. Blinded by the opportunity for immediate victory, Reagan refused to worry about the budget. He seems to have bought into the concept it was just another hurdle the free market would take care of.

Truman and Eisenhower were aware of the spendthrift habits of generals and admirals, Reagan viewed them romantically. Now their wish lists were fulfilled. That many of the new weapons were no longer particularly useful was irrelevant, the idea was to induce a reaction from the enemy. Costs, carefully supervised in earlier days, were not controlled, contractors were inadequately supervised, and generals and admirals were permitted to make changes that added significantly to original cost and subsequent maintenance requirements. With a plan simply to spend, waste was rampant. In terms of its affect on the Cold War, the entire effort was a massive waste of money.

While it is accepted today that the Russians did not take the Reagan lure, at the time CIA data supported the plan. Its estimates were as follows.

	Military spending		GNP	
	U.S.	U.S.S.R.	U.S.	U.S.S.R.
1969	81.4	68.1	939	463
1974	86	105.7	1,420	781
1980	134	201	2,732	1,541
1985	253	275	4,010	2,197

Accepting that the U.S. was spending more than the Soviets during Vietnam (1969), the estimates go on to claim that soon thereafter the enemy forged ahead and, while they did not increase as much as the U.S. during Reagan's time, remained ahead with a substantial increase. The data corresponds with detente and growing economic troubles in the Soviet Union. We know they were anxious to cut military spending, yet the CIA claims they were rapidly increasing. The estimate reflects Soviet engagement in Afghanistan, but the forces there were never large.

Other than spy satellite pictures that closely monitored Soviet nuclear capability, CIA intelligence was sketchy. The estimates appear to be mere guesses and recent studies agree that there was no reaction to the Reagan build up. The GNP reading, for instance, is used as the basis for a fairly fixed estimate at 13.5% defense spending, but the estimate is highly suspect. According to the CIA, the U.S.S.R. grew more rapidly than we did between 1967 and 1985 and it began the period at about half our GNP. Both the beginning figure and the growth estimates are unlikely. U.S. GNP was probably at least four times the Soviet at the end of World War II. Coming from a low base, they probably grew at a faster rate for a while, but by the 1970s their economy was struggling. Population growth had slowed, while the U.S. advanced. Some authorities feel they were devoting 25% of GNP to arms, but from a much lower base.

An alternative method based on manpower and equipment suggests that Soviet military spending remained fairly stable after the big missile build up in the 1960s. Manpower remained constant at about 4.1 million. While ours declined after Vietnam from 3.5 to 2.2 million, in terms of cost our manpower undoubtedly remained higher. Our naval expenditures far exceeded theirs. While the Russians were known for large tank production, the machines were relatively low cost, particularly as they were produced in government factories using government provided materials. They never developed a first class long range bomber and fell far behind in guided missiles. If the Russians spent $275 billion on defense in 1985, as the CIA claimed, a larger amount than the gold plated U.S. armed services, they got amazingly little for the money. Considering the relatively low cost of their operation, it is doubtful they spent $100 billion, still enough to discomfort a GNP that was probably half the

CIA estimate. There is no physical evidence in the form of new weapons that the Russians responded to the Reagan arms race. The reason is simple - their defense was an established nuclear ICMB system.

If the Reagan military build up was based on false assumptions, there is evidence it was not directed solely at the Soviet Union. That the Russians were fading was not a mystery. Moreover, in forty years the only times they moved aggressively against the west was the Berlin blockade and Cuban missile crisis. They backed off both times. The invasion of Afghanistan, much touted to justify higher arms spending, was recognized as inconsequential relative to us and likely to be negative for the Russians. Because of Afghanistan's reputation as the graveyard of great powers, it was immediately seen as their Vietnam. Many members of the Committee on the Present Danger may have been alarmists, but others were realistic. The Russians provided a convenient excuse for other initiatives.

Influential supporters of a greatly enlarged military seem to have been thinking beyond the Soviet Union toward broadly expanding U.S. influence overseas. Democratizing the world was becoming an idealistic theme for expanding U.S. power. The existing worldwide infrastructure of military bases stood ready to serve a more powerful conventional force. The business community, the controlling segment of the right wing hierarchy, was aware that America's economic dominance was fraying. Japanese and German products were making inroads and the two oil embargoes were a wake up call. Oil was absolutely vital to the economy and all of the major non-western fields had been taken away from American and British corporations.

Then there was politics. With the Soviet threat a key to the right's political rise, for them peace was not good. When the end of the Cold War suggested cutting defense spending, the right was prepared to resist. The modest Clinton cuts were trumpeted as exposing us to great danger. If no one could define that danger, Americans have always reacted to such suggestions.

Reagan himself did not indicate a desire to expand U.S. power militarily and after early exercises in Grenada and Lebanon did not use the armed forces offensively. The key event for Reagan came out of proposed development of the multi-headed MX missile and deployment to Europe of intermediate range missiles as part of a plan begun under Carter to eliminate short range at the front atomic bombs. The resulting worldwide protest got through to the President. It happened that the massively excessive supply of nuclear weapons appalled him and here he was expanding the nuclear race. As early as April of 2002 he spoke out for arms control and the following month proposed START, Strategic Arms Limitation Talks. While protest took the form of a nuclear freeze, the President was already thinking about reduction. These feelings induced him to begin talking to the Soviet premier.

With the start of negotiations, the war circle screamed that a freeze was Russian propaganda. Although Gorbachev was to get an equal or greater share of the credit for ending the Cold War, Reagan began negotiating in terms of a nuclear reduction before Gorbachev became premier. Believing his arms escalation had already gained an edge for the U.S. (it had barely begun, but Reagan was an optimist), he was ready to talk from a position of strength. When Gorbachev became his opposite number, for the first time an American president was talking to a Russian premier who did not take the old Stalin stance that we had aggressive intentions toward them and accepted that the Soviet Union was in trouble. The traditional defensiveness of both Russian and American leaders no longer stood in the way.

The October, 1986, Reykjavik agreement called for complete elimination of intermediate range nuclear missiles and they nearly agreed on getting rid of big intercontinental missiles, while setting the stage for substantial reduction. If Reykjavik was not enough, the Cold War effectively ended in September of 1988 with Gorbachev's unilateral arms reduction, including removal of forces from East Germany, Hungary, and Czechoslovakia. Though right wingers had trouble giving up the threat and the following President Bush was suspicious, fall of the Berlin Wall late in 1989 was the final signal. The 1991 break up of the Soviet Union was an unexpected bonus. Although the Soviets lost by the economic failure of communism, Reagan hastened the demise by combining a liberal view of Russian weakness with right wing aggression, an achievement that would not have been possible if he had stuck with right wing orthodoxy.

While Reagan was wrong about the arms race, military spending did influence the outcome indirectly. By the 1980s the Soviets were aware of falling behind industrially. Lagging badly in technology, they were going to fall back even more. The technology gap was especially worrisome as related to arms. Gorbachev's alarm about the Strategic Defense Initiative (Stars Wars) was an expression of worry about high tech weapons in general, which they knew to be an important component of the U.S. military build up. These concerns led directly to perestroika, Gorbachev's attempt to modernize the Soviet economy. It was perestroika that brought down the Soviet Union. Although the economy was not doing well, it was getting by. The old system might have lasted for many years if left alone or only gradually changed. By this indirect route, the arms build up made a contribution to the unexpected break up of the Soviet Union.

Reagan may have been inspired in dealing with the Soviets, but his arms race strategy was a costly miscalculation. The tripled military budget was an economic tragedy. A military-industrial complex was created, a political monster demanding to be fed regardless of defense requirements. It also significantly influenced future foreign policy. The nation was committed to a policy of militarism that went against the principles of the founders. Americans found that they liked muscle flexing. They took pride in being the sole superpower and relished frequent military interventions abroad. These sentiments played into the hands of the right by providing a substitute for the Russian threat.

Other than dealing with the Russians, Reagan foreign policy was a farce. The most important foreign policy area after Russia was the Israel-Arab conflict. Fixation on the Soviets led to neglect during the Reagan presidency. Al Haig, Reagan's first Secretary of State, put a stamp of approval on Ariel Sharon's invasion of Lebanon, a miserable embarrassment that stirred up terrorism against Israel in fractured Lebanon. The U.S. embassy was blown up and 1,800 U.S. peacekeeping troops had to be withdrawn after 241 lost their lives in a terrorist bombing. Putting so few troops into a cauldron made no sense. Reagan never made a serious effort to understand the Israel-Arab conflict, a disappointment after Carter had played a tough and important role in achieving peace between Egypt and Israel.

If Lebanon was bad, the Iran-Contra affair was worse. The U.S. backed Iraq in its war with Iran, though Iraq was the aggressor and repeatedly used poison gas. After Shiite terrorists, over whom Iran was believed to have some control, took U.S. hostages in Lebanon, the administration arranged to trade arms their release, meaning we switched sides for a while. The proceeds were used to buy arms for the Nicaraguan contras, though a specific law had been passed to prevent such activities. These arrangements were made by members of his poor quality National Security team and Reagan appears not to known what was going on, a reflection of his general disinterest and lack of control over his staff.

Later, when Iran appeared on the verge of winning the war, the U.S. sent advisors to Iraq with a plan developed out of satellite observances to help reverse the tide. The scheme succeeded, with the help of massive poison gas attacks, and Iran was forced to sue for peace. This extremely questionable performance had the consequential downside of making Saddam feel the U.S. was a friend unlikely to interfere with his invasion of Kuwait in the summer of 1990. That led to the first Persian Gulf War and the chain of events that subsequently caused such great troubles.

Although the President's attention was on the Kremlin, the economy was the real issue during the first term. Reagan arrived at the White House determined to change the economic course to a degree not seen since Franklin Roosevelt. A troubled economy provided the opportunity. A recession had begun in election year and the deficit hit a record $73 billion. The rate of inflation exceeded 10%, leading to tight money despite the recession.

Reaganomics proposed to solve the deficit by slashing government spending and stimulus from large tax cuts. Friedman-like control of money supply would defeat inflation.

Supply-side failed, becoming something of a joke, however, it does work if tax cuts are not repeated and spending is controlled, as Clinton was to demonstrate. The Reagan team's romantically ideological view of supply-side and the free market led them to assume the big 1981 tax cut would quickly reverse the recession. Instead, the economy got worse and the deficit soared. For the first time the deficit exceeded $75 billion and projections showed it running over $200 billion in 1983, at that time a frightening amount. It was to reach $221 billion in 1986 despite three years of recovery. Republicans, formerly champions of a balanced budget, needed an excuse.

The think tanks went to work and blamed it on Carter. He was cast as a modern Herbert Hoover and they were valiantly picking up the pieces like Franklin Roosevelt (incongruously, Reagan liked to associate himself with FDR). During almost two years of economic agony, only Reagan remained calm, living out the dream. Then the Fed eased, the stock market took off, interest rates declined, and happiness reigned. Rigidly ideological as ever, the right learned nothing from these early shortcomings.

Taking government off the backs of the people was Reagan's rhetorical ideal and his most effective theme. The magic of a laissez faire marketplace would then accelerate growth and create eternal prosperity. The crusade for less government had two main targets. One was elimination of the welfare state through a substantial reduction in government services, the other was freeing up industry by eliminating regulation. Despite the already high deficit, a planned 30% tax cut, and a major increase in defense spending, the budget would be balanced through supply-side stimulus and major cuts in spending. That was the dream.

Government waste was a juicy target. The table below reflects growth in the "other" category of government spending (in billions), representing overhead, government assistance programs other than Social Security and Medicare, other medical, and pork barrel spending.

	federal receipts	"other"	%
1955	$65.5	$ 8.9	14
1960	92.5	14.4	16
1965	116.8	25	21
1970	192.8	37.2	19
1975	279.1	74.8	27
1980	517.1	131.3	25

A basic premise of conservative ideology was that the benefits of most government programs did not offset their cost, while the necessary ones like Social Security and Medicare should be self-funding. Many government employees would lose their jobs in a serious cutback, but re-deployment into productive work would lift rather than weigh on the economy, particularly as privatizing government functions would improve efficiency and provide replacement jobs. Cutting government would unleash a burst of capitalism from more productive direction of capital and labor. Conviction about the virtue of less government did not extend to the military, as wasteful a use of government funding as could be imagined. Had their actions been consistent with their principles, they might have succeeded.

As the Reagan presidency began, reducing government held the spotlight. The leading part was played by Office of Budget and Management head David Stockman, a brilliant young former congressman and rabid believer in supply-side economics and the wonders of the free market. A prodigious worker, he saw the way to victory, when suddenly the dream fell apart. First, his detailed projections fell victim to recession. That made spending cuts all the more necessary, but no one would go along. If resistance from Democrats was expected, the heads of the federal agencies, now conservatives, balked.

One of the President's most effective lines was that government was the cause, not the solution to our problems. It turned out to be all talk. Once in office he lost interest and did not back Stockman. Reagan might be a magnetic speaker, but as governor and president he had a practical streak. The rare reduction in overhead and pork from $133 billion to $118 billion in the three years 1982-84 that Stockman accomplished was inconsequential related to the deficits from tax cuts and defense spending.

Conservatives had backed down. When the time came to fulfill the promise of less government and fiscal responsibility, support was lacking from conservative congressmen and intellectuals who might have shamed others into toeing the line. The long campaign against excessive government and liberal extravagance, the heart of right wing doctrine, was lost to conservatives with their own special interests. An important slice of right wing doctrine proved to be hot air. Not only did they fail to cut, they were soon working government for their own benefit. Under the next conservative president, George W. Bush, rather than reducing government, the system was degraded until breaking into open corruption. Conservatives did exactly as doubters expected, allowed their intense focus on making money and lack of interest in the public good to feather their own nest.

When the chips were down, what they cared about was tax cuts for themselves. They grabbed the money and ran from the responsibilities. Considering that the ideology was merely a political tool for those seeking to preserve and enhance their own economic well-being, it was not surprising that money prevailed over principle. The power to lower taxes was the guiding light, not responsible economic policy. That focus never changed over the years, it only became more pronounced. Added tax cuts were always the emphasis, regardless of economic conditions. The ideology was vigorously defended, but nothing counted other than a reduced top tax bracket.

Immediate troubles with the economy seemed to be overcome by the end of 1982 and the following year GDP jumped 7.2%, but the deficit persisted and the advance merely returned growth to the level of the 1970s, meaning it was below prior decades, despite the boost from deficits and defense spending.

GDP Growth by Decade
(inflation adjusted)

	% change	
1950	1329	
1960	2502	79
1970	3772	51
1980	5162	37
1990	7113	38
2000	9817	38

Though the right persists in saying otherwise, the record shows that taxes have little influence on the long economic cycle. Keynes tried to influence the severity of economic setbacks through tax policy, though he recognized that the business cycle could not be eliminated. Keynes thought tax increases (actually elimination of recession fighting cuts) would not hurt the economy during an expansion and he proved correct during the 1990s. The right hated Keynes because they wanted to use each recession to step down taxes. Their claim that temporary tax cuts did not work was based on the thirst for permanent cuts.

The top bracket tax increase from 28% to 39.6% carried out by Bush I and Clinton generated a bonanza of revenue during the stock market boom, producing a surplus years ahead of expectation. Strong growth suggested that the Clinton top rate did exactly the opposite of the right's claim. Rather than inhibiting growth, it helped the economy by balancing the budget. Despite two substantial tax cuts by George W. Bush, it now appears that the rate of growth for the present decade will drop almost to 20%. The verdict of history is that tax cuts carried too far harm the economy.

While Reagan was not particularly concerned with the deficit, he did react. The right was infuriated when a small upward adjustment to income taxes was made in 1982, plus an increased gasoline tax. In 1983, effective in

1984, Social Security was overhauled through a tax increase on the middle and lower classes (the rich got off mostly free). The 1986 Tax Reform Act raised taxes, except for the top bracket, which was lowered all the way from 50% to 28%. This remarkable stunt was pulled off by pointing out that various forms of tax evasion reduced the top bracket to about that level anyway, and some of the evasions were eliminated. By this time it was becoming clear that the original cuts had been excessive and the aim of the 1986 law was reform rather than reduction, yet the right managed a 44% cut for its top bracket clientele. These changes reflected both Reagan's practical side and his absolute devotion to lowering the top bracket, the result of a 90% rate during his peak earning years in Hollywood. This was an extraordinarily narrow perspective, since at that time Hollywood stars were about the only people in the country making big money, but Reagan's views were always heavily impacted by personal experience.

At this early stage of power the right was not as rigidly doctrinaire as it was to become. After Bush I reneged on his campaign promise of no tax increase, the famous read my lips line, the right made a pledge of no tax increase a requirement for anyone running for office with its backing. Oddly, Reagan's greatest domestic accomplishment was saving Social Security, a New Deal holdover the right hated. The revision converted Social Security from pay as you go to amassing funds to meet future obligations (except that deficits, largely resulting from right wing tax cuts, ate up the funds). On returning to power in 2001, the right would attempt to correct that Reagan heresy and destroy Social Security.

Although Stockman made minor progress in reducing government, by Reagan's second term non-defense spending was advancing rapidly. Never mind, the right continued to pay homage to the ideal of getting government off people's backs, only now the effort was directed at eliminating regulation to boost business. Spending restraint in an effort to tame the deficit was pursued during the moderate Bush I presidency and under Clinton until the deficit was eliminated, but it was a matter of holding the line rather than cutting. When the right regained the White House with Bush II, spending went off the deep end (the record of "other" spending since 1964 is shown in the table on page 158). The less government thesis, so fundamental to right wing doctrine, turned out to be no more than vote gathering sweet talk to obscure what they were up to with the tax code.

That the less government crusade was a letdown under Reagan and completely dropped with Bush II suggests it may be politically impractical. Once begun, a government program is extremely difficult to let go. That reality did not phase Reagan or the think tanks. They went right on blaming high spending on the federal government. Arch conservatives conceived that in time government would drown in its own excesses and that would be great. Rather than seeing this as irresponsible, it was considered the natural order. Tax cuts that produced larger deficits were good because they hastened the drowning.

In 1981 Reagan's momentum was such that a strong effort to reduce government might have succeeded. Stockman believed major cuts were close, but he needed Reagan's support and the President lacked the stomach for overcoming obstruction. It would also require patience and ideologues were not inclined toward slow progress. Reagan expected supply-side and the free market to take care of the economy. Disinterested in details and determined to see only the bright side, he viewed tax cuts as a great achievement and did not worry about consequences. Revolution was in the ideology, not corrective actions that might undermine the doctrine. Although government continued to grow, and grow significantly when counting the military, the progression of government regulation of business was reversed and that was the right's primary interest.

By the second Reagan term the down side of a low top tax bracket was beginning to show. An orgy of dazzling corporate executive and Wall Street compensation had begun, encouraging practices that led to the economic crisis of 2008. Wall Street was going crazy in speculation and corporate takeovers, many by raiders who tore apart companies for personal gain at loss to the economy. The crash of 1987, when the market dropped a record 22% in a single day, was a sign of instability. Some of the most prominent names in finance ended up in jail. The new age of unregulated buccaneer free market capitalism had quickly developed a greed for immediate rewards that was worrisome at the time, later became accepted as normal, and ended in the debacle of 2008-9.

Reagan boosters claim that he restored the country's pride. To the extent this was true, it enhanced the feeling of exceptionalism that had unhappy consequences in subsequent years. The idea we were somehow better, that everything we did was divinely inspired, that economic and foreign policy rules did not apply to us, was dangerous. It led to complacency about high trade deficits and high handed foreign policy that wasted America's position of honor and trust in the community of nations.

The right was not fazed by failing to meet its promises. Rather than adjusting after the disappointing first two years, once the rebound began, think tanks orchestrated a chorus of agreement that everything had gone according to plan. When the economy slumped again in 1990 after their promise of everlasting prosperity, they again were not bothered. Ongoing deficits meant supply-side was a hoax, but with the economy growing again they celebrated free market ideology. Reagan went along with the theory that eventually deficits would end up forcing a serious cutback in government programs.

The presidency had been gained by putting together many disparate parts, so that when plans went awry, the coalition might have been expected to fracture. Surprisingly, setbacks led to growing stronger. Carefully drawn plans for governing had never been advanced, the right wing movement had always been more ideologically than practical. Think tanks controlled the ideology and they declared victory and manufactured studies to "prove" the case. Being wrong was never a concern, they were always right if the public could be convinced. Rather than being discouraged when the ideology proved impractical, think tanks were invigorated by defending the faith. By their interpretation, the country had been pulled back from the brink, a national emergency avoided. The original frustrations were excused as being forced to start with a Carter created mess. Rather than a problem with the doctrine, difficulties were caused by ongoing big government. Think tanks stepped up the propaganda, hitting liberals all the harder. Truth had always been of marginal interest, now they abandoned it entirely, claimed victory, and went on about the business of selling the public.

5

The Reagan Legacy

FOLLOWING HIS DEPARTURE, CONSERVATIVES ATTEMPTED to spread Reagan's name on schools and roads throughout the country. They were thinking of Mt. Rushmore. After announcement of his Alzheimer's in 1994 things calmed down, but in 1997 Reagan was rated far down the list of presidents by a distinguished group of historians. The right went nuts, launching an amazingly exaggerated view of him and his presidency that continues to this day. His memory is evoked in a saintly manner, as if all that he did was divinely inspired. Right wing ideology became the Reagan doctrine so as to give it a favorable look. He became a kind of store front mannequin to beguile the public. George W. Bush was carefully modeled on Reagan, presented as a nice simple-minded straight shooter who spoke of freedom in a religious way and defended the nation from its enemies. Each of the 2008 Republican presidential candidates went out of his way to identify with Reagan, trying to take advantage of the fictional character created out of the ashes of his presidency. Prostrating themselves before the Reagan god has become a Republican ritual.

Adoration of Reagan was part of an effort to create the appearance of success for right wing policy that ultimately proved a miserable failure. That failure is Reagan's failure and eventually he is likely to be rated far lower than the 1997 ranking that so upset the right wing.

On a personal basis, Reagan's role in bringing the Cold War to an earlier end deserves high marks. Former Russian satellite countries found freedom and the Soviet Union broke up more rapidly than otherwise would have been the case. It should be kept in mind, however, that this triumph was accomplished by going against right wing doctrine. In addition, Reagan did not win the Cold War, as the right claims, the Soviets lost to a seventy year internal struggle with an economically fatal communist system that could not compete with capitalism.

Not only did the Soviet success fall out of going against right wing practice, Reagan was far from the ideological icon painted by the right. His glowing rhetoric about the benefits of less government and embrace of the free market should not disguise that in practice he was a moderate and in international relations he was cautious. Whatever success Reagan had was because he broke from right wing rigidity and adjusted to events.

From the perspective of the wealthy and business leaders, Reagan deserves the hero image. His tax cuts went beyond their fondest hopes: a top bracket reduction from 70% to 28% and a corporate tax rate cut from 48% to 34%. The outsized annual income and opulent life style of corporate chieftains, Wall Street traders and investment bankers, hedge fund managers, and private equity capital groups were great for them, but came at the expense of the large majority. Unleashing free market capitalism had the same consequence as previous such experiments – a burst of prosperity followed by a wrenching economic decline.

Early in the Reagan years the sincerity of right wing doctrine came into question. No serious attempt was made to downsize government, tax cuts prevailed over fiscal responsibility, economic growth did not accelerate. As it came up short, no adjustment was made. Instead, the right hardened its position, stepped up the use of propaganda, and assaulted all things liberal. Failed ideology became ever more revered. The hardened positions led to the nation floating along in disregard of mounting economic problems and overreacting to international difficulties.

Rather than a sound leader, Reagan was a performer luring popular support through feel good rhetoric. And it was not all feel good. Nixon is credited with the strategy for picking off southern states, but in the north the race card required a more conscious effort. The Great Communicator was the master of playing that game without appearing racist. Reagan glorifiers had a fit when he was called a racist. The accusation was harsh, but no one was better at inciting black backlash. He could make a position against any form of racial preference sound like democracy's last stand and at the same time give racist followers a feeling of being on the side of God.

The law and order theme worked. Casting himself as champion of equality, he backed up the talk by refusing to enforce integration laws. Who wanted to believe dear old Ronnie was not quite a saint? Republican candidates were forever wedded to the disguised race card. By 2000 it had became so habitual no one noticed.

Reagan's greatest claim to fame, of course, was "winning" the Cold War, but was the win in fact his? The positive case rests on the policy of peace through strength. Reagan would admit that his timing was right, allowing him to accomplish something his predecessors could not have done. He recognized that the communist regime was crumbling and that added pressure might produce a win. His harsh rhetoric was aimed at stirring up trouble in the satellites, adding to the pressure. In these ways he was visionary.

However, the arms build up in the peace through strength policy was just the opening salvo. Only after Reagan pulled back on the nuclear threat, moderated his language, and talked seriously with the other side, all against right wing practice, did progress unfold. The credit Reagan gets for ending the Cold War was earned because he diverged for right wing policy.

The true test of greatness is in the long term. In Ronald Reagan's case, the evidence weighed more heavily against him with each passing year, until the right wing movement self-destructed in Iraq and economic collapse. The policies that ruined the economy and placed our international position in jeopardy were set in place by Reagan. George W. Bush had such extreme limitations that he never should have been president, but his failures were the consequence of directions set by his predecessor.

For about twelve years after Reagan, the large majority of Americans did well, then the historical inequities of free market capitalism began to show up. A few at the top monopolized the gains while the middle and lower classes lost ground. A tiny right wing minority had been placed in position to reward itself inordinately at the expense of the middle and lower classes and that is exactly what it did. The practices that provided fabulous rewards for a few harmed the rest of society and the economy. Prior to Reagan, making $1 million a year was a dream. Today a few winners make over $1 billion in a single year. Democracy gets a black eye when the majority is squeezed while a few take home unimaginable rewards. It is all the worse when many of those rewards were gained in activities that were detrimental to society.

Reagan's installing of free market capitalism led to a massive shift of wealth to a few, but contrary to promise the rate of growth did not accelerate. Instead, as the longer term effects of free market capitalism took hold, growth slowed. The present decade has been marked by a dramatic slowing in the rate of growth, despite vigorous Fed pump priming, low interest rates, another round of tax cuts, big deficits, and a jump in military and "other" spending. GDP growth in the present decade now looks as if it will come in at about 20%, the lowest since the 1930s and eighteen percentage points lower than the prior two decades. Most telling of all, incomes for most Americans have declined since 2000. Tax cuts, sold to the public as the key to more rapid growth, did not prove a magic elixir for the economy. A rising trade deficit was the consequence of corporate freedom to engage in activities that undermined the U.S. economy. The banking system got lost in a maze of deregulation. The economic mismanagement of the Bush II years was not peculiar to him, it reflected an approach put into operation by Ronald Reagan.

Free market capitalism might normally have taken more than a generation to evolve into the kind of economic inequality that becomes democratically objectionable. Aggressive tax cuts at the highest bracket shortened the cycle. They led to an orgy of activity on Wall Street that undermined our industrial base. Capital came out of productive pursuits and went into speculation, encouraged by new forms of indirect investment that bet on short term price movement. Wall Street was where the big money was. It attracted the brightest talent attempting to get rich quickly performing activities that ended up negative for the economy. In the rush to get rich no one seemed to notice that the underpinnings of the American economy were eroding.

Bad as the long term effect of Reagan economic policy proved, the apparently great foreign policy triumph had equally adverse repercussions. The plan for victory through an arms build up appeared successful when the Soviet Union collapsed, except the arms race was not the reason, for the Soviets never joined the race. Reagan's enthusiasm for the non-existent arms race led to spending far beyond need in the misplaced hope the Russians would follow. Much of the money was wasted in programs that were obsolete or of little use. The deficits that financed an unnecessary military helped undermine the economy. If defense spending had continued at the level prevailing through most of the Cold War, foreign policy would have been conducted in a different manner. As it was, arms based aggressive policy led to mistakes. The money could have been more beneficially used to strengthen an economy suffering from old age.

The effect of the arms spending orgy was creation of a politically powerful military-industrial complex that could not be stopped once it gained a foothold. Foreign policy relied on military solutions. As America emerged in a unique position of power, it had the opportunity to create a peaceful, more prosperous, more democratic world, while preserving its economic power, but resort to military solutions led to throwing it all away. Militarism encouraged the spread of nuclear weapons, with unknown complications for the future. The requirements of hegemonic foreign policy were not thought through in terms of manpower, financing, and the attractiveness of alternatives. A world dominated by U.S. military power was never possible without higher taxes, probably a draft, and restrictions on the freedom of Americans, none of which the right wing or the public was prepared to accept.

American tradition is to be wary of the military. Prior to the Cold War the standing force had been limited to what was necessary to expand the frontier. America's post war international commitments called for a larger force, but defense spending remained closely controlled until the Reagan build up that took place as the Cold War was ending. After the Cold War, in a world of nations bent on economic rather than territorial expansion, no effort was made to determine the practical requirements of the new conditions and spending near the Reagan levels continued. We should have conducted an assessment of our requirements, as Eisenhower would have, keeping in mind that the recent build up had proven unnecessary and that international rivalry was becoming economic rather than territorial. The analysis undertaken was conducted by the military, not the proper source for determining the nation's overall needs.

In exercising the arms race ploy, Reagan had taken the annual military budget from $100 to $300 billion, leaving America at the end of the Cold War with far more arms than necessary for defense. What were we to do with the no longer needed force? The answer was to find a use by deciding our borders were no longer limited by the oceans. A modified form of imperialism was adopted that called for mastery of the entire world in the name of preserving peace and spreading democracy.

This grand new role of military dominance meant that Reagan's military build up changed our way of dealing with the rest of the world. The power bestowed by vastly superior arms was tempting and Americans responded by going onto the offensive. The concept of unilateralism was developed, or making certain through military strength that we remained the sole superpower. Always expressed in benign terms of peacekeeping and democratization, the revolutionary nature of unilateralism was not appreciated. The public did not realize what a massive task it would be. We were drifting toward a serious mishap.

If the economic benefits of Reaganism went largely to a small group of the wealthy, how could the right hold onto power over the vast majority not sharing in the gains? In part the answer is that the economic negatives in a large trade deficit, declining middle class incomes, and Wall Street speculation rather than investment, took time to develop. Keen observers recognized that we were headed for trouble, but in general Americans took to Reagan optimism and the propaganda machine was effective in covering up the negatives.

Since Goldwater, and pointedly under Nixon, the right had set upon the media as biased, using the strategy of trumping fact with cleverly stated opinion. As they fell back on propaganda to obscure the Reagan shortcomings, a foundation had been laid. By discrediting the factual record and claiming over and over that they were right and liberals were wrong, public support was maintained. The right wing learned how to play on emotions, so that a small ruthless group could foist off its beliefs on the public.

Reagan was the flag bearer and supreme performer at this effort to propagandize the citizenry and fool them into voting for those harming the nation economically. No one was cleverer at making selfish right wing economic policy sound good for all and covering up the bad side. As the propaganda campaign continued after his departure, his memory was continually evoked in its support. Right wing propaganda was effective because it was built on the emotional foundations of race, religion, militarism, and fear. The public was distracted by attention getting attack on liberals. Many Americans were induced to believe theories that defied fact and to not noticing that the right was stealing away with the economic rewards.

Rigidity and unwillingness to compromise poisoned the political climate. Business became a significant factor in legislation, often with undemocratic results. The Republican Party sold out for money. As corporate magnates became extraordinarily wealthy, their sense of civic responsibility was lost at the same time as their influence on national policy corrupted the political process. Blaming Reagan for all that subsequently happened may be unfair, but he put the train on the track.

Two instances during the Reagan years illustrate the strange combination of delusional noise in misguided directions. Consider Star Wars, the proposed massive laser shield to protect against nuclear ICBMs. Reagan was typically enthusiastic about an idea that scientists said was either impossible or so expensive that implementation would bankrupt the nation. Perhaps he shared the skepticism and pushed Star Wars merely to induce the Russians to spend (as the right claimed after the fact), but he sold the idea to Americans and committed massive amounts of money. Public optimism about the crazy idea led to Star Wars becoming a political force, with the result that successors continued the spending, though Clinton redirected to a more practical downsized program. For the expenditure of about $200 billion, we now have a limited radar based system that still may not work.

Star Wars was symptomatic of Reagan: his dreamlike impracticality, disregard of economic factors, and ability to sell malarkey to the public. If Star Wars had been possible, it would have been duplicated by our enemies, as advanced forms of warfare always have been. It would have been immensely cheaper to ban nuclear weapons.

The other event was the effort by one of his closest and least able advisors, Ed Meese, to change laws in favor of right wing ideology. Meese was one of Reagan's long time aides. Part of the original chief of staff triumvirate, he proved ineffective in the White House and was given a variety of other jobs until named as Attorney General for the second term. Meese immediately set out to change the law of the land to favor right wing ideology. The strategy was to claim resurrection of the original meaning of the Constitution and challenge the legitimacy of modern jurisprudence. The concept implied eternal constitutional precepts immune to modernization. The specific target was the ruling legalizing abortion, Rowe vs Wade, but a much broader interpretation was the real intent.

The problem with the argument was that the Constitution did not set out the law of the land. The founders recognized that this would be impractical and followed the English principle of common law, or law made by judges in court following common sense and legal precedent. As a result, instead of involving specific law, the Constitution lays out the procedures by which laws are made. The Constitution is concerned with the details of establishing the executive branch, the legislative branch, and the courts, with their various responsibilities, through which laws would be made. Meese's theory of original intent was bogus. It was nothing more than a disgusting effort to rewrite the rules in accordance with right wing doctrine.

The effort left an overhang of disrespect for the law. If some of the early Reagan and Bush I appointees had not been reasonable men, the Supreme Court might have fallen into the hands of ideologues trying to undermine the basis of established law. As it was, the Supreme Court's Republican leaning led to appointing the worst president in history. Who knows what might have happened with a few more Antonin Scalias.

If the wheels came off the right wing monster under George W. Bush, why did it not happen earlier under Ronald Reagan? First, time was required for free market economics to undermine the economy. Second, misuse of the military only occurred later.

Then there was the vast difference in personality. There are similarities between Reagan and Bush.

- They were lazy, with little interest in detail and rarely probed.
- Neither controlled their subordinates.
- They made no effort to understand the complicated Middle East and allowed Israel to run wild, setting set back the troubled situation in the Holy Land.
- They had a tendency to be innocent of practicalities.
- They talked tough, but were usually cautious.
- They lacked the intellect to form policy.
- They had an attitude of entitlement that led to a lack of interest in the common man.

On the other hand, Reagan was a competent and Bush was not. Reagan compromised right wing doctrine to create a successful presidency, Bush was all over the place, directing the government in an ever more ideological manner while spending liberally for votes. By Bush's time, business and its lobbyists had thoroughly infested government, making it seriously corrupt.

After starting with questionable people in important positions, the Reagan government shaped up with able experienced people, practical doers rather than right wing fanatics. Bush was taken over by ideologues and had relatively incompetent people in high positions. He had an uncanny instinct for selecting the wrong people, whereas Reagan's instinct with personnel was good.

Under Reagan right wing doctrine was implemented in trial fashion. The right was still feeling its way and had not yet established itself throughout the Republican Party. Under Bush moderates were gone, Democrats had lost their spark, and the right was completely in charge. Finally, the passage of time worked against Bush. He was paying for the economic decline and militarization of foreign policy that began under Ronald Reagan. The reign of George W. Bush had the effect of making the Clinton and Reagan administrations appear better than they were, but Reagan and Bush are inextricably linked.

6

Imperialism and the Military-Industrial Complex

REAGAN'S RECOGNITION THAT THE RUSSIAN bear was dying did not alter the strategy of gaining political advantage by scaring the public. A no longer imperiled nation was neither good for their defender aura nor helpful in keeping the public in a state of accommodating fear. As the Cold War ended, they tried to hold history at bay. Despite Gorbachev's pull back in 1988, the threat mode was perpetuated for three more years until the Soviet Union fell apart. At that point they had a problem. With every defense program in sight delivered or on order and no enemy to scare the public, they faced a reduced defense budget. Two factors sustained them. Without quite realizing it, the United States was rooted in imperialism. With unquestioned leadership both economically and militarily, the imperial impulse was irresistible. Secondly, a powerful political force had been created during the Reagan years, the military-industrial complex, more accurately a political union of the military, defense contractors, and the right wing.

First, consider imperialism. Although they object to the term, Americans have always been imperialistic. Pre-Revolution maps have a horizontally stretched look of claimed territory, despite population being clustered along the coast. At the time of the Revolution, only a few settlements stretched over the Appalachians, yet in negotiating peace in Paris at the end of the war, Benjamin Franklin was determined to gain recognition of rights all the way to the Mississippi River. Although he succeeded, the triumph was not enough. Franklin also wanted Canada and the Canadian dream persisted. Attempting to take advantage of England being tied down fighting Napoleon was the reason behind the War of 1812. The attempt to take Canada failed when the U.S. military was not up to the job. Anti-American feeling coming out of this effort helped create Canadian nationalism separate from our own.

Many of the founders were thinking beyond the Mississippi all the way to the Pacific. Taking advantage of Napoleon's need for cash to conduct his wars, in 1803 Jefferson made a giant leap in that direction with the Louisiana Purchase. It included all the land from waters draining into the Mississippi River, which meant the top of the Rocky Mountains. Lewis and Clark, dispatched by Jefferson, went all the way to the Pacific.

At the time of this massive land grab, only a few Americans had reached the Mississippi. The interests of several hundred thousand Indians physically in possession were not given the slightest consideration. Spain, France, and England, the previous absentee "owners", had never taken possession with settlers, but Americans flooded the lands with reproductive farmers, who forced out the Indians with help from the army.

From the beginning, Americans saw themselves in the grandest terms. For men who had barely managed to gain their freedom, the founders were not lacking in ambition. John Adams, Thomas Jefferson, James Madison, and many others foresaw the United States transforming the world. They thought of an America destined to become the most powerful of nations. From the beginning, endless growth was part of American ambition.

Florida, for three hundred years a Spanish colony, had been another War of 1812 goal. Its takeover became official in 1819. Looking west across the continent, Texas was next. Part of newly independent Mexico, it was mostly occupied by Indians before Americans moved in. Although the addition of Texas was delayed by slavery considerations, it was accomplished in 1836. The Oregon territory was next, becoming formally part of the Union in 1848. England sought a natural Oregon border on the Columbia River, but the U.S. insisted on an extension of the 49th parallel earlier agreed to west of the Great Lakes, adding what became the state of Washington.

American diplomats dealing with England, Spain, or France over these lands were consistently aggressive and they always won. To the Europeans, the territory was only good for trapping fur and they supervised with a handful of temporary governors. Americans, on the other hand, cared deeply. Settlers gave us a direct interest and they kept coming, reproducing at a remarkable rate. Opposing forces lacked the will to ward them off and mushrooming settlements created an inevitability of triumph. Settlers provided legitimacy. America did not see itself as colonial, like Europeans, because we used the land productively. As a result, most of the new lands were gained by negotiation, with fighting involving only Indians.

The exception was the Southwest, owned by neighboring Mexico. Mexico was not on the other side of an ocean, but it had few settlers in Texas and on into New Mexico and California. Although early opposition in Texas was Indian, Mexico also objected. A war began in 1846 and an American army marched all the way to Mexico City. Consideration of annexing the entire country fell apart when Mexicans resisted the occupation. President Polk settled for his primary objective, California, together with the lands in between. The coast to coast nation was complete in 1848.

Would that be enough? Between 1848 and 1865 the nation was engaged in controversy over new states: would they be slave or free? The fight that became the Civil War was less about slavery than preservation of the union. If the Confederacy had been allowed to break away, as in theory it had the right to do, the dream of Manifest Destiny would have been shattered. Lincoln, like the founders, saw the fate of the nation in the grandest terms.

After the war, expansion began again. The purchase of Alaska from Russia in 1867 was different from the others. It was not contiguous and farm settlements were not a prospect. Nevertheless, Alaska represented a big chunk of the North American continent they still hoped would be one nation. It also represented an indirect advance into the Pacific. Ocean to ocean America being complete, expansionists searched for further opportunity. Europe offered no realistic prospects, but the undeveloped Pacific and Asia did. Commodore Matthew Perry had opened up Japan in 1852 and China, with its vast land expanse and large population, was a dream land for selling American goods and saving non-Christians. At first efforts in the Pacific were limited. What was to become American Samoa was added as a coaling station. Midway Island was claimed in 1867 and occupied in 1871. Missionaries arrived in the Hawaiian Islands in 1820 and gradually assumed control of the best land. Disease wiped out much of the population and contract labor was brought in. The weak monarchy was brought under control and the United States annexed the islands in 1898.

The vast Pacific was slow work, however, and the expansionary instinct became concentrated closer to home, in the Caribbean. Spain, the weak European country from which the U.S. had already stolen so much, was the target. Cuba's fight for independence from Spain provided the opportunity. Washington manipulated the Spanish American War, gaining control of Cuba and Puerto Rico. Annexation of Cuba was prevented by a law guaranteeing its independence, though the U.S. remained in control for about twenty-five years. Puerto Rico became part of the U.S., along with Spain's Pacific possessions, Guam and the Philippines. Puerto Rico and Guam went peacefully, but the Philippines resisted and the U.S. engaged in old fashioned European style colonialism. A cruel three year war followed and sixty years later the U.S. had to give up the islands.

Why the far away Philippines and Guam? There are two reasons. China was seen as the growth outlet for excess American goods. Secondly, an American naval theoretician found a ready market for the idea that worldwide control would be achieved by the nation controlling seaborne commerce. Alfred Mahan believed that a fleet of warships capable of destroying an enemy's main force could dominate world trade and thus become the most powerful nation. His leading book, published in 1890, was probably a factor in kicking off the battleship race of subsequent years, principally involving England, Germany, France, Japan, and the United States, with Russia and Italy as secondary players.

As far back as the War of 1812 the United States had hatched plans for a larger navy. The original excuse was threat of invasion from Europe (militarily based fearmongering has a long history). Invasion was becoming less and less likely as the country grew, but Americans reacted to threats, however far-fetched. Through the nineteenth century a variety of plans for a greatly expanded navy were held up for lack of money. Teddy Roosevelt got into the battleship race and paraded the Great White Fleet around the world as a reflection of American power. Our rivals laughed, not only because white was the worst possible color to paint a warship, but the fleet had already been rendered obsolete by the rapid advance in technology, notably greater fire power and speed due to conversion from coal to oil.

A few years later the United States arrived on the world scene through participation in World War I. In 1919 President Woodrow Wilson arrived at the Paris peace talks with the Fourteen Points (he had laid out the points shortly after entry into the war), his moralistic plan for remaking the world. France and Britain thought of him as an impractical fool and some of the treaty's less permanent results came out of Wilson's approach. His efforts were significant as our first venture into setting standards for the rest of the world and remaking it in our image. The time for territorial expansion had passed, however, particularly after the next war when the U.S. pushed for European countries to give up their colonies. After the end of the Cold War, Wilson's image was revitalized as right wing leadership adopted the idea of democratizing the world.

The military-industrial complex was formed out of the desire of the military for as many new toys to play with as it could get away with in cahoots with the toy manufacturers. Both had access to Congress and money to spend on favors. When it came to lobbying, the armed services were second to none. Represented in all fifty states, they were a significant employer in many. The defense industry also had facilities all over the country. Any proposed base closing brought anguished cry from the home state and defense contracts were loudly proclaimed prizes. Arms manufacturers added to their clout as mergers produced large companies. Their influence with Congress blossomed, supported by the growing power of corporations under the right wing.

The end of wars had always led to difficult economic adjustments and the right was willing to do anything to keep the economy going. This time they were able to avoid economic consequences by going ahead as if the war had not ended. Funding released by the end of the Cold War could have been employed more productively, but the military-industrial complex offered continuation of the good times. The country had grown accustomed to the military and was reluctant to give it up. Defense was a growth industry when so many others were dying.

The complex was also served by capitulation of Congress to corporate interests, perhaps better expressed as corporate interests electing more and more representatives to government. Harry Truman made his reputation as guardian of the nation's finances against defense contractors. Now the relationship between the buyer (the government) and the seller was transformed, with the selling corporation holding the upper hand. The defense budget had been converted from careful review to the ultimate pork barrel project. Just as the enemy was fading, the spending spigots were opened. Even after the U.S.S.R. broke up and former satellites became democracies, funding was maintained. Cuts were largely in the military labor force, in which contractors had no interest. The uniformed personnel reduction from 2.2 to 1.4 million was partially offset by outsourcing that swelled the volume of support from private industry.

Preserving its business required the military-industrial complex to scramble. At first they clung to the Russian threat. While some contracts were cut back, defense spending merely leveled off in the immediate post Cold War years of the Bush I presidency. Then the Kuwait War came to the rescue. Sufficient momentum was sustained so that under Clinton spending declined only from $298 billion in 1992 to $266 billion in 1996, however, that encompassed a 15% reduction in carrier groups and 40% in divisions, air wings, and ships. The 11% decline was less than Eisenhower's 18% cut after the Korean War. In 1997 pressure from the right led to a spending advance, despite the fact that the Balkans problem had been largely solved and none of the disruptions ballyhooed by the right came about. By the end of the decade, the few minor skirmishes engaged in revealed that the plan for capability to fight two simultaneous major wars was excessive. The Clinton Secretaries of defense put the savings from downsizing where it belonged, in high technology.

The term military-industrial complex originated with Dwight Eisenhower in his farewell address as president. His words: "We must guard against the acquisition of unwarranted influence by the military-industrial complex."

Eisenhower knew about the inefficiency of military spending and that inter-service rivalry led to excessive requests. As a former general, then president during the most intense phase of the Cold War, he might have been expected to favor a large defense budget, but Eisenhower was a traditionalist. For him militarism went against American beliefs. He was charged with defending a way of life as much as territory and uncompromising anti-communism could distort American values. Permanent mobilization would lead to seeking out conflict and military solutions replacing diplomatic. Eisenhower approached the Cold War more calmly than his successors. He appreciated that nuclear bombs meant that the conflict was unlikely to become hot and also made conventional weapons of little use.

Eisenhower saw what Reagan missed - the link between security and fiscal responsibility. Excessive military spending was wasteful for the economy. America's leading position was not based on arms, but the ability to provide for its people and set an example for the rest of the world. Military power was less important in fighting communism than the example set by a successful democratic capitalistic society. The essence of containment was economic rather than military.

While succeeding presidents wandered from the Eisenhower strategy in varying degrees, limited conventional forces remained the policy, except during the Vietnam War. By the time of Reagan, the strategy had defeated communism in most of the world. Reagan's impatience to undo the Soviet Union by resorting to militarism, combined with absence of concern about fiscal responsibility, was the opposite of Eisenhower. In his hurry, Reagan blanked out the progress of the previous thirty-five years. On the one hand he recognized we had won economically and on the other hand he could not resist hurrying things along by a military push. Presidential rankings that place Eisenhower well below Reagan hardly make sense.

The sudden rush at the end of the Cold War to build a conventional military force changed America's approach to international relations. It was accomplished by a carefully planned assault on the American consciousness. End of the two supreme power Cold War stand off was presented as removing peaceful equilibrium and leaving a less stable world. The supposed instability was pictured as an opportunity to intervene in trouble spots to preserve peace and spread democracy. Interventions, which became more frequent, had the effect of making the military seem necessary. Most of the new threats were not serious and could have been handled diplomatically. The only consequential event in the twenty years since the end of the Cold War was Iraq's invasion of Kuwait in 1990. Not only could it have been avoided by prompt action when Saddam moved an invasion force to the Kuwait border, it was quickly solved by gathering a large international force. Despite the easy win, Iraq remained in the forefront of pretend threats because the warmongers had nothing else to rely on.

A nation founded on the belief that military power could upset democracy and had fought all its wars with citizen soldiers responding to an emergency changed for two reasons: 1) a flush of nationalism deriving from becoming the sole superpower just after having created an all powerful modern military force, and 2) the influence of the right wing. If defense spending had been based on need, as it had until Reagan, the U.S. would have approached its role as sole superpower in a far less military way. Reagan's original justification for tripling the defense budget had nothing to do with need, for a conventional force was unlikely ever to be used against Russia. Since it made almost no contribution to ending the Cold War, as a practical matter the new military was a colossal waste of money. When its presence encouraged military solutions to international difficulties, the country was moving from the traditions that made it great. Overwhelming military power probably also contributed to complacency about maintaining our economic power.

That the business oriented right would abandon sound economic policy in favor of militarism seems peculiar. The reason was partly political and partly due to inclusion in the coalition of neo-conservatives and religious elements anxious to push democracy around the world. These groups considered leading by example too passive. The special leadership position provided by our non-military tradition did not impress them. A plan to expand our world domination by military means had been part of neo-conservative thinking from the 1970s. Now the wheels of aggressive unilateralism were grinding and there was no George Washington or James Madison or Dwight Eisenhower to keep the country on its traditional course.

The end of the Cold War in combination with the impracticality of major warfare in the nuclear age marked the most militarily significant occurrence in the history of the world, yet the great moment was missed. Elsewhere it was recognized that economics had won the Cold War and the future standing of nations would relate to their economic rather than their military power. Secure in victory and with by far the largest economy, the United States failed to recognize that its own economy was showing signs of age and the burden of supporting a large military was an economic disadvantage.

Eisenhower would have seen that the vastly changed circumstances called for a new master plan. He would have considered that great military power is an easily misused drug and detracted from more economically beneficial uses of the money. America's unique standing in the world owed more to the soft power inherent in its democracy and capitalistic prosperity than military power. Temptation to use the military to force our will on others was bound to create resentment and lead to a mistakes. Not only was a unilateralist guardian of peace based on military power dangerous, it was impractical without a vastly larger force.

The special opportunity in a new world order had to have occurred to Reagan, Bush I, and Clinton, but Reagan was drawn to action themes and he was not a planner. Bush might have responded, but he was a reacter with little faith in long term planning. He seems to have been searching for answers, but was content to accept a reduced military without considering major overhaul. Clinton was the most likely and he did respond with a plan to spread American power through internationalization of trade. Foreign policy intellectuals were intoxicated by ideas of transforming the world through free trade. They assumed this would be favorable to the United States by giving our corporations greater scope for expansion, never suspecting it would lead to loss of large numbers of higher paying jobs.

Clinton seems to have felt that American trade leadership would be aided by continuing to have armed forces all over the world to assure a peaceful environment for the growth of commerce. Planning specific to the military was limited to a cutback within the boundaries of maintaining the existing worldwide force structure. He compromised by reducing troops in Japan, Korea, and Germany, avoiding consideration of closing most of the no longer needed bases. Madeline Albright, Clinton's Secretary of State, referred to the indispensable nation, a grand illusion that implied a military more powerful than needed for current threats.

Imperial thoughts of worldwide dominance through overwhelming power led to missing the opportunity to replace military spending with more economically productive uses of the money. The country was pushed in this direction by a series of episodes that played to the militarists' concept that the post Cold War world was less stable. At the beginning Bush I could not break out of the Cold War habit. He had been enmeshed in the conflict for too long to accept that it was over. Busy helping create the new governments in Eastern European, Iraq's invasion of Kuwait came as a surprise less than a year after fall of the Berlin Wall. If Saddam had been firmly warned when dispute arose over a joint oil field and Mesopotamia's historical claim to Kuwait, the trouble would probably have been avoided. There was ample reason to be alert. Saddam was known as one of the world's most ambitious despots and unlike others he was located in a vital area. Distracted in Eastern Europe, Bush failed to react when Saddam gathered a large force on the Kuwait border. The President had only two weeks before Saddam moved and it seems likely he was relaxed about Saddam, the U.S. having backed him in the recently closed Iraq-Iran war. In some ways the situation resembled Korea in 1950, when an insufficiently worldwide view and concentration on Russia led to neglecting the trouble spot. Secure in military power, carelessness was often to mark U.S. management of world peace.

Having failed to react, a military solution seemed the only answer. The coalition and quick victory made a worldwide champion of Bush and seemed to verify arms as the best way to achieve peaceful ends. Though it could barely be described as a fight, Kuwait raised American confidence, still suffering from memories of Vietnam. Foreign intervention and wider use of aerial bombardment seemed the most effective instrument of foreign policy. Such thinking was a trap. Beginning at the moment of triumph in the Kuwait War, Bush committed one error after another. Turning back Iraq became a watershed in the future course of foreign policy.

Another mistake was leaving peace negotiations to General Schwarzkopf, resulting in a largely military rather than political settlement. Iraq's claims to Kuwait were not renounced and the border and jointly owned oil field remained disputed, giving Saddam the means to embarrass the U.S., if insufficiently provoking to recall an invading army. Saddam remained a thorn in our side, creating a contentious aftermath that played out perfectly for right wing militarists. During the Clinton years ongoing concern with Saddam became the foremost vehicle for promoting the need for a larger force.

A number of other consequences of significance to the coming terrorist attack fell out of the suspended muddle in Iraq. Although it was necessary to use Saudi Arabia as the launching platform for driving Saddam out of Kuwait, the Saudi king encountered strong opposition to foreign troops on sacred Moslem soil. Despite repeated promises to leave, the perceived requirement for maintaining troops in the area and the air base to support the southern no fly zone led to remaining, though bases could have been established elsewhere, as they were in 2002. In the meantime, Osama bin Laden was provided with his most important talking point in developing terrorist sentiment against the U.S.

Saddam's presence also created the perception that sanctions were necessary, and they led to starvation in Iraq, adding to animosity against the U.S. Enemies were made of people we later expected to greet us as saviors. In addition, maintaining the no fly zones was expensive. To the Arab world, it looked like we were using Iraq as an excuse for maintaining armed forces in the Middle East.

None of these developments would have been significant except that they happened in oil country. Oil was finite, one day it would run out, and Middle East oil would probably last the longest. The most significant future events fell out of oil, notably the invasion of Iraq in 2003 and insistence on remaining in a politically hopeless country. Fear about a regional blowup leading to interruption of oil supply was the soundest reason for remaining in Iraq. A continued large military was not only related to a vague theory of fighting two simultaneous significant engagements at the same time. At least one of those contests was bound to be in this area.

7

Militarism and Bad Decisions

KUWAIT ENDED UP AS A minor battle, but it was revolutionary. The long sought goal of bombing accuracy was finally achieved, greatly altering tactics. In the fall of 1990 a just retired Air Force general said that I would be amazed how fast the coming encounter with Saddam would be over. I scoffed that the Air Force had been talking bombing accuracy before World War II without ever producing. He was right. Accuracy was exaggerated, with less than 10% of the bombs being technologically directed, but the future had been previewed. Vast improvements were made in subsequent years, along with specialized missiles and launch platforms. The appalling data on bombing accuracy from World War II and Vietnam was obsolete. The terrible killing of civilians, so marked in Vietnam and the later stages of World War II, was no longer necessary. War could be surgical, with few troops in the field.

This meant that the Powell doctrine of massive force was dated, yet the flush of victory led to an opposite conclusion. Unable to throw off the ghost of Vietnam, small engagements were seen as requiring major force. Clinton understood the revolution and employed bombing accuracy to accomplish small tasks, drawing contempt from the right and the armed services, who considered them distractions. So determined were militarists not to consider small commitments that sending a few thousand troops to keep peace in the Balkans was seen as wrecking readiness. Big war thinking led to a planning void in precisely the kind of missions undertaken after Kuwait and likely in the future. The Iraq disaster came out of the army's unwillingness to take responsibility for peacekeeping.

Bombing accuracy was the signal achievement of the Reagan military expansion. Eight years later we were to win a small war without putting a single soldier on the ground or losing a single man. In 2001 Afghanistan was taken with the tiniest of forces backed by precision air power directed from the ground. If targets could be hit, many types of conventional weapons could be reduced or perhaps eliminated. It was time to overhaul strategy, except that the generals did not want to give up their traditional toys. They managed to avoid a thorough reassessment.

The revolutionary possibilities included a high technology information centered battlefield that removed the necessity of having to guess. With information, coordination could be carried out on a higher scale that might eliminate much of the costly duplication in the multi-service approach. Such ideas were not welcome to the old regulars. They were still resisting when Secretary of Defense Don Rumsfeld tried to get them moving.

With its compulsion for ever more equipment, the military-industrial complex had so corrupted Washington that insufficient attention was paid to the potential high technology offered for a more efficient and less costly military. High tech weapons reduced the need for manpower in the offensive phase, at the same time as their use resulted in greater need in the aftermath, but post action was dismissed as not the army's duty. The military refused to accept that its highly professional fighting army was unlikely to be used, at the same time as mundane peacekeeping missions would increase in frequency.

If technological advance had insufficient influence on the military, it did on the civilians directing foreign policy. War was now a more attractive option. The U.S., already by far the strongest militarily, was stronger than ever, creating a feeling of invincibility and strengthening the trend to a more assertive role in trouble spots. Sophisticated weapons gave a remoteness to war and a surgical quality involving fewer casualties, especially for the home team. The terrible consequences of the past no longer applied to a swift conflict. Without the human slaughters of the Civil War and the World Wars, war lost its ugliness. Only 147 U.S. troop deaths were reported in Kuwait and most of these were not on the battle front. War was fun. A mere 1.4 million servicemen, only modestly larger as a percentage of the total population than the pre-World War isolationist services, could still be the most powerful ever known.

New weapons not only outdated the large force concept, they obsoleted many conventional systems, yet planning continued in the same old way. Traditional weapons such as tanks and aircraft carriers were reduced in number, but the transformation called for by forward thinkers was not undertaken. The M-1 tank, for instance, was an anti-Soviet weapon. Under the new conditions it was overlarge, expensive, and immobile. Gold plated stealth aircraft (each B-2 bomber cost in excess of $1 billion and is extremely expensive to maintain) were not required against realistic opposition and a sophisticated opponent could probably overcome their confused radar image. Despite only a few fighters having been shot down since Vietnam, a new stealth class was developed. The military-industrial complex lies behind this waste. Ever more advanced weapons are its bread and butter.

High tech weapons also made the military more acceptable to the public. Historically, the United States had a small permanent force dwarfed by conscription that fought the great wars and returned to civilian life. As Vietnam drew to a close, the draft was abandoned and a larger permanent force established, supplemented by a volunteer reserve. The limited force gained added strength from high tech weapons, meaning that the elites, the Bill Clintons, George Bushs, Dick Cheneys, the right wing and neo-conservatives as groups, who had never served and had no desire ever to, were free forever.

Bush I overlooked the change, with tragic consequences. If he had prolonged the Kuwait War another day, Saddam's army would have been surrounded and going to Baghdad would not have been necessary. While Bush wanted to eliminate Saddam, some of his advisors saw the dictator as a stabilizing force. After all, maintaining kings and dictators in power had been American Middle East policy for a long time. With his army not only defeated, but captive, Saddam was unlikely to have survived. As U.S. troops stood by in Southern Iraq, Saddam immediately began misbehaving. He crushed a Shiite revolt, then moved on against the Kurds in the north, events that could have been avoided by use of the new weapons. It was the beginning of a series of embarrassments that made the U.S. look weak and Saddam an ongoing threat, all of which played into the militarists hands.

Then Bush hesitated in the Balkans over unwillingness to make large Powell doctrine commitments. Balkan instability helped make the case for an ongoing large military, but Clinton cleaned things up without ground fighting by U.S. troops. The warmongers responded by belittled him for showing them up. Clinton's most remarkable success, completely discounted by the right wing, was Operation Desert Fox, a four day campaign of air strikes against Saddam in 1998 (the President was accused of authorizing the raids to distract the public from his Lewinsky troubles). With UN inspectors having eliminated weapons of mass destruction and fearful of more strikes, Saddam decided on complete elimination of all traces of weapons of mass destruction. Proud as ever, the policy was never announced and the CIA dreamed up the theory he was reconstituting all its phases, again serving the interests of the militarists. If Bush had used the new weapons to suppress Saddam's comeback and in the Balkans, Clinton probably would not have been president.

Another missed Kuwait lesson was the example it offered of an appropriate post Cold War international system. In earlier days, the U.S. was isolated by oceans and economic self-sufficiency. Now the oceans were shrunk and the world was becoming a single economic unit. Always in the background in considering the armed services was its importance to enforcing peace. A cop would be helpful in maintaining order in a worldwide economy. The appropriate charge for the U.S. military was as glue for an international peacekeeping force. The Kuwait coalition was largely ours, but most of the cost was refunded, a neat trick that should have been tempting to a deficit country with a rising trade imbalance.

As part of the new world order, formal proposal for an international peacekeeping force led by the U.S. was a logical step. A multilateral worldwide system might have been welcome. The role of world policeman could have been undertaken through the UN, though that might have involved too much shared leadership and the UN was probably too quick to step into humanitarian cases. More practically, NATO could have been converted to an international peacekeeping force. NATO expanded into Eastern Europe to give former Soviet satellites a closer unity with the rest of Europe and with the United States. The right thing to do with NATO was convert it into a truly international force for peace. Although the U.S. was an important part of NATO, it did not want a broad international commitment that limited its flexibility.

Any chance Clinton had for a pragmatic military reassessment was probably lost by his stumbling start on peacekeeping missions in Haiti and Somalia. Adding to his reluctance was the unfortunate gays in the military issue that began his regime and his draft dodging reputation that made him defensive with generals. Part of conservative political positioning was identification with national defense, so that after the Republican win of the House in 1994, any inclination Clinton might have had toward reduction of the military was no longer possible. By the second term the President was being hammered for supposedly letting the military run down after a mere 11% reduction in the defense budget from the fevered Reagan levels. Peculiarly, it was the very man they were devoted to criticizing who showed conservatives how to use force effectively and at little cost. Clinton had enough trouble with the right over military reductions and bucking the establishment on the issue was chancy.

The public had come to accept a large armed force and the military-industrial complex had established itself as a political force. Prior to Clinton's departure, defense spending started up again. As long as the right controlled a portion of government and could hold the public's attention with trumped up foreign dangers, military spending in line with practical defense requirements was politically difficult.

Right wing pressure to take out Saddam during the Clinton years was overdone, but neo-conservatives leading the effort had more than Iraq in mind. Not only was the Middle East a focus to protect the primary source of oil, but neo-conservatives were emotionally attached to Israel. For them Israel was our permanent Middle East outpost in the most important part of the world.

The military cause was also bolstered by longstanding international commitments. Forty-five years after the end of World War II, the U.S. retained what could be considered occupying armies in Japan and Germany. Although the German force could be justified as confronting the Soviets, an important reason behind both "occupations" was discouraging former enemies from developing a comprehensive military of their own. A bear hug policy of providing security for potential rivals had become the established way of doing business. A network of foreign bases was justified as aiding friends and keeping a close presence with possible enemies. The European force also served as glue for the Atlantic Alliance, which had an international military in the form of NATO. These established commitments were worth preserving for their peacekeeping ability, but now that the Soviet threat was gone it was time for allies to assume their own defense. Germany and Japan had been fearsomely talented military powers, but had aging declining populations and mature economies.

In the Far East, ancient animosity between Japan, Korea, and China was something to guard against, but the number of troops retained in Korea and Japan was excessive now that the rivalry was economic. One of the few things Bush II did correctly was engage China, South Korea, Russia, and Japan in mediating nuclear bomb development when North Korea wanted to deal only with the U.S. China kept negotiations going when we proved too brittle and eventually progress was made.

After World War II American imperialism's territorial expression was the establishment of foreign bases. The Philippines, Cuba, Puerto Rico, Guam, and Panama had become military bases early in the century and after the war wherever our troops visited, bases were set up. Over 700 exist around the globe, not counting some operated by NATO and, other than a cutback at the end of the Cold War in small listening posts monitoring the Soviet Union, the number goes on increasing. Some of the military cutback during the 1990s came out of the beloved bases, but reduction could have been far greater. The bases may actually diminish readiness, for manning all of them requires a lot of men and equipment. Although personnel in the Iraq theater amounted to only about 10% of our total force, the military was strained because of the breadth of commitments elsewhere.

Sometimes the push for more sites has an unnecessarily adverse influence on relations. The already declining relationship with the new Russia was further soured by the effort to establish an anti-missile system on their doorstep, a system that did not function. Claims that it was aimed at Iran were hard to sell since that country lacked both nuclear weapons and the missiles to deliver them.

Afghanistan opened up the possibility for bases all over central Asia and the plan for Iraq was a series of outposts to serve as the nucleus for controlling the Middle East. At the rate the U.S. was going, bases would have been so thick throughout the world that virtually nothing would have been left for a ready strike force. Not merely a seeker of bases, the military is extremely reluctant to give them up, regardless of changed circumstances. When thrown out of Spain and the Philippines, the generals' feelings were hurt. Pushed out of Saudi Arabia, the U.S. countered by setting up air bases all over the smaller Persian Gulf countries. These bases are more than enough to service the area, yet a second aircraft carrier group is often sent to the Gulf in addition to the one stationed there in showy belligerence toward Iran.

The defense budget was also preserved through a major political effort from the armed forces. Following a low point after Vietnam, a determined effort was made to sell themselves as an unqualified benefit. The ham-handed generals that turned off members of Congress during Vietnam were replaced by men with political skill. Appearances before congressional committees were carefully structured. A process began of always praising the troops, a practice that went to extremes to cover up the embarrassment of Iraq. No general, or retired officer, or politician, ever referred to the troops as anything less than magnificent, all part of a campaign to keep the public behind a no win war. The troops were terrific, but the inevitable murdering of civilians, misdirected missiles, deaths by friendly fire, and torture had to be covered up to maintain the image. Relief from not having to serve left the many beholden to the few and the Joint Chiefs knew how to take advantage.

As Chairman of the Joint Chiefs of Staff at the end of the Cold War, Colin Powell was the most influential among those selling an ongoing large military. Powell was the right man. Being black and thoughtful added to his already high credibility. He was also cautious about employing force, conveying the impression it would never be used unwisely or without international cooperation. While a unilateralist, Powell's was different from neo-conservatives. He had no thought of committing to questionable ventures in nation building and democratization. Being practical and non-idealistic added to his credibility and was helpful in selling the military.

Considering their conflicted position, the testimony of Powell and other generals before congressional committees about post Cold War requirements was accepted much too readily. The Powell doctrine that any form of intervention required a large commitment continued to be accepted long after indications that it was dated. Lacking a Russia, military planners substituted capability to handle two simultaneous imaginary threats of semi-major proportions, both larger than anything likely to occur. Assuming each conflict took a minimum of 200,000 men, the number usually bandied about, several hundred tanks, naval and air support, plus the new high tech weapons, any thought of a cut back could be pictured as dangerous, exactly the intent of the two war premise. This unlikely scenario went largely unquestioned. After the easy victory in Kuwait, a burst of chest thumping carried the public along. The hangover of Vietnam, including its invaluable lessons, was forgotten, setting the stage for an equally foolish venture.

Congress went along not merely because of right wing support. Democrats failed to question the two conflict scenario and the need for so many overseas bases. They accepted the generals biased assessment rather than tying military spending to current need. During the following twenty years, we never came close to a single necessary major engagement, much less two at the same time.

Claims of a more chaotic world never came true. Other than Kuwait, post Cold War perils were small engagements of minor consequence, easily handled by a smaller force. The war on terror brought a series of responses to trouble spots, mostly involving insertion of small groups of special forces to work with local armies. There was no mass move to terrorism and al Qaeda was soon in hiding. No one wanted anything to do with them. After a revival in Iraq, their Sunni supporters deserted them. The distracting quagmire of Iraq provided an opening for troublemakers elsewhere, but nothing happened. In an indirect way, the long engagement in Iraq proved once again the absence of need for a large military. That did not stop the militarists from continuing to play up the rogue threat concept. If not tied down in Iraq, the militarists would have invented excuses elsewhere.

No one sat down and thought about the fact that defense spending had risen from under $100 billion in 1977 to $304 billion in 1989 and the reason for the 1977 amount had disappeared. America had an important role as keeper of peace and it could not all be done with soft power, but cutting back to the pre-Reagan level on an inflation adjusted basis was easily possible. The large inventory of conventional weapons, the now demonstrated ability to hit targets accurately and avoid commitment of a large force, and the potential in peacekeeping alliances, provided a basis for reduction in the defense budget. In a nation beginning to struggle economically, that savings would have been helpful.

Consider what an evaluation of our future military requirements at the end of the Cold War should have reviewed. Since action against a major power was no longer on the horizon and we already had plenty of tanks, ships, and planes, there was no need for more, other than replacements. For those intent on spreading democracy, a thoughtful process would have concluded that it was not a military project. In many parts of the world, notably the Middle East, pushing for democracy was going to create more problems than it solved.

The greatest misjudgment was the failure to evaluate requirements for the unilateral plan of advancing American interests militarily. Guarding the entire world was an irrationally open ended commitment. Careful consideration of its requirements would have revealed the need for fundamental change in national policy and greater commitment to force. That meant more manpower, a draft, and higher taxes. Was this what Americans wanted? Unilateralism became policy because it was the only plan out there. Its proponents sneaked it into national policy without review and it just hung there, similarly to NSC-68.

Over-confidence and lack of planning led to a casual attitude toward intelligence. In retrospect the oversight in not making a major effort to gain better intelligence about Iraq, a country we had focused on for twelve years, seems incredible. The key to peacekeeping was cutting off trouble before it broke out and that depended on information. Our CIA was prone to gadgetry and covert operations, its intelligence capability was minor. Keeping the peace meant turning the CIA into a source for better understanding of other nations. Information could offset the efforts of those who would take us into unnecessary hostilities by misleading the public.

Behind the specifics for why the armed forces were not cut to a greater degree at the end of the Cold War is a crude intangible, the siren song of power. Vast worldwide military power is intoxicating. Sacrificing military predominance would have been historically unprecedented. It would have been possible without the Reagan build up, but the vast quantity of resources, the new high tech weapons, the highly trained condition of the personnel, the jobs and the profits in defense plants and military bases, were hard to give up. The founders, Abe Lincoln, and later Dwight Eisenhower, were not in a similar position. They might have been willing to give up military predominance in favor of a sounder economy and American tradition, avoiding the temptations of armed power, but the sacrifice would have been unusual. Americans like to think of themselves as exceptional, but their instincts are normal. Despite a history of peace loving, giving up such a strong hand would not have been natural. By 1991 Americans had grown fond of the military.

High sounding rationalization covered up the efforts of militarists. Human rights and democratization became feature issues late in the Cold War. They were particularly popular with the right's religious backers and with neo-conservatives. Continuing the crusade was instinctive to religious elements, while neo-conservatives, forceful leaders in pushing to expand rather than contract the military, recognized the help humanistic elements provided to their cause.

Times had changed. Patriotism had become more overt and criticism was suppressed. America was moving away from its ideals in new ways. If the peace dividend drew some commentary among Wall Street stock promoters, otherwise potential uses for the money released by reduction in the armed services never got much attention. Liberalism was in such a weak state that the multiple alternative uses of military funding never got on the agenda. Crucially, the right wing, in command through most of those years, never took the economy into consideration, a dumbfounding oversight when their primary aim was more tax cuts.

Instead, the argument went that we were not doing enough. Clinton was accused of wrecking military capability by carrying out the downsizing proposed under Bush. After the Somalia debacle, Clinton used the armed forces carefully, but still actively. He took on small tasks one at a time, living by the foreign policy dictum of not getting exposed on too many fronts, but he was relentlessly criticized for excessive caution. As it became clearer that peacekeeping would be the armed forces major role, both the right and the military resisted. Training for a major peacekeeping emergency was not undertaken, with fateful consequences. The military was not reconstituted in terms of post Cold War conditions, it continued to operate in the old mode of major conflict.

While the size of the post Cold War force was under discussion in congressional budget committees during the Bush I years, neo-conservatives at the Pentagon trotted out a new policy of using military power to dominate the world. It was probably only part of an effort to prevent cuts, but there was a failure to recognize how thoroughly un-American it was. In the public state of triumphalism, it was easy to overlook that such a policy had the potential for serious damage, particularly in the Middle East, where messing around with democratization was asking for trouble. Years ago we had intervened in Iran, with disastrous consequences when the Shah was overthrown, but the lesson was missed by those who thought arms could overcome all obstacles.

No one seems to have considered that a large military force cannot lie idle, it craves action. The mere possession of a superior military creates bias toward armed intervention. This was not a garrison force, it trained all the time in exercises geared to the possibility of North invading South Korea or the Chinese attacking Taiwan. World War III was always a looming presence, played out against a variety of alliance and enemy combinations. Although mock battles kept the military sharp, they helped create paranoia about foreign risks and those views transferred to the political arena through support from right wing think tanks such as the American Enterprise Institute. Presidents seeking to impress voters had an instinctive tendency to show off with live exercises such as Grenada and Panama. Showing off led to mistakes in Lebanon and Somalia and more were likely, perhaps on a grander scale. Military mistakes can become especially costly. Peculiarly, generals are probably safer than presidents, for while they like the toys, they have a keener sense of consequences. Sooner or later overeager civilians were going to commit the army to a Vietnam-like operation.

A professional army's affect on decision making at the civilian executive level made a misstep all the more likely. Presidents and their advisors were acquiring a more cavalier attitude toward committing to war. Loopy politicians like Newt Gingrich claimed military expertise just because they took an interest in the new weapons and were fellows at the American Enterprise Institute. Idealistic impractical intellectuals like Paul Wolfowitz and Douglas Feith could hold high positions at the Defense Department. The professional military was a branch of government in a way that a draft based force could never be. It could be used to serve the ideological or political ends of leaders knowing nothing of the horrors of war.

In 2006 Representative Charles Rangel proposed a draft, not out of feeling it was necessary, but to create a keener sense of national responsibility for the exercise of military power. With a draft, operations like invasion of Iraq would be held to a higher standard. Rangel had experience with military blunder, having gone through the horrible retreat from North Korea in the winter of 1950-51. He was aware that two of our most famous generals, Washington and Eisenhower, expressed fear about the consequences of the U.S. becoming militaristic. The Reagan military build up was almost bound to end in tragedy.

A powerful military as an expression of U.S. power led to not noticing that international rivalries were no longer based on the size of armies, rather they had taken an economic form. We seemed to forget that the Cold War was not a military struggle, it was economic. In the economic contest among nations, Japan and Germany arrived in second and third place partly because they had not wasted resources on a strong military. A costly armed services was a disadvantage in an economic war. The security blanket system had already proven economically harmful. Japan had leveraged its willingness to be defense dependent to keep out our goods, as had South Korea and others. India reversed the process, leveraging our push for closer economic ties to add to its nuclear capability.

By 1990 the U.S. industrial lead was shrinking, but command in high technology seemed to assure continued predominance. Both Bushes and

Clinton saw the United States as the primary beneficiary of globalization. Military power was viewed as an aid to building our economic power, though the former was actually a drag on the latter. Military power made the U.S. overconfident about globalization and complacent about the threat from the rising trade deficit.

As the country's attitude toward the military changed, it rejoiced in using armed force at times that could have been solved peacefully. Consideration for other nations played less and less a part in our decisions. The culmination was Bush II's expounding about perpetual war to address a tiny group of terrorists and a problem whose solution was non-military. No other nation saw terrorism as a problem to be dealt with by overwhelming military force. Overreaction to terrorism led to suppression of democracy, supposedly a wartime necessity, though a genuine war was hard to find. Truthfulness was shredded in propaganda. The administration was fulfilling the worst fears of the founders. With militarism taking hold, the greatest danger to the nation became internal rather than external. The sum of these activities threatened the American way of life.

8

The Post Cold War Years

BUSH I WAS A PROBLEM for the right. It hated moderate Republicans, sometimes seemingly more than Democrats. The dislike took the form of non-support and fostering a wimp image. The contrast in treatment of George senior, a man of ability and principle, with George junior, a man of little talent or conviction, by the right wing media is remarkable for the perceptions created. Senior, a hard working intelligent war hero, was a wimp, and junior, a lazy non- thinking draft dodger, a powerhouse. The difference was in one being subservient to the right and the other not. Father Bush's failure to gain a second term was due to a combination of Ross Perot, a recession, and absence of support from the right wing propaganda machine.

Although Bush had problems in his last two years, they were minor compared to the last two of his son's first term, yet the propaganda machine covered up the latter and did nothing for the former. Reagan had raised taxes several times, but Bush's deficit fighting tax increase was on the top income bracket and the right would not stand for that. The Bush loss sent a message - being moderate was a death sentence for Republican politicians. The loss left the right in complete control of the party.

With the popular Reagan gone and his economic policy in disarray, the right needed to hustle. It had been too depend on Reagan's vote getting talent and key elements of the doctrine were not working as planned. In response they became highly organized down to the grass roots. The electoral process was altered by bringing professionalism to the local level. Nationally directed campaign strategies were launched, candidates were selected for their devotion to the right wing, and lots of money was spent in their support. Strategists brought forth focus groups and detailed polling. The single minded message and depth of support for their selected candidates grew into a national chorus. Karl Rove was only the most successful of a new breed of political manipulator running circles around candidates relying on old fashioned methods of personal appeal. Think tanks and marketing organizations constructed politically popular wording for all contingencies. Policies boosting the wealthy were phrased in ways that made them appear good for everyone. In time all Republican congressmen had the same monotonous answers to questions.

Politicians found getting on the bandwagon and adopting right wing positions a great help in winning elections. Free market fantasy and military glory have a built in popularity. Winners using the right wing organization were left dependent and never allowed to forget it. Congressional representatives were guided and disciplined into a closed team of true believers, while life was made miserable for moderates. Right wingers in Washington did not so much represent home districts as provide unified support for conservative causes. Independent thinking was not countenanced, block voting was expected, tactics that added force to the group. If a few concessions might alter the vote of Democrats, right wing members could be counted on not to waiver. Moderates were defeated in primaries or became disgusted with the new ways and quit. The atmosphere in Congress changed to poisonous partisanship, which they promptly blamed on Clinton. Nothing got done that did not come from the right. Politics became a crusade, a war where fighting fair was for losers. How a win was accomplished was inconsequential. No one seemed bothered by the resemblance to authoritarian forms of government.

By the end of the century, the campaign to win the hearts of the general public by bashing blacks, gays, and liberals, while appealing to national pride, had gone on for three decades. Sheer persistence had made it effective. The appeal to nationalism after 9/11 had been years in preparation. Real men were with the hard right.

At first Clinton's liberal leanings played into the hands of his opponents, for the trend was still conservative. Secretary of the Treasury Lloyd Bentsen and chief economic advisor Robert Rubin persuaded the President to build an economic policy around eliminating the deficit. Their remarkably balanced tax plan, loudly proclaimed by the right as disastrous economic policy and drawing not a single Republican vote, produced a wonderful economy and after a few years surpluses. The rich prospered as never before, allowing the deficit to be cured several years in advance of plan. To their surprise, the right was better off under Clinton than it had been with Reagan.

Both Bentsen and Rubin were wealthy men who understood that the rich could easily afford the tax increase and would probably gain from it. Democrats were confirmed as the party of fiscal restraint and right wing

Republicans as selfish spendthrifts. By enforcing the policy of pay as you go (no increased spending without offsetting revenue increases or cost cuts), higher taxes did not mean greater spending, as the right always claimed. Unlike Reagan, Clinton actually cut government, or more correctly reduced personnel through efficiency.

Clinton chose health care as his signature starting point, about as brave a choice as possible, but unwise for that reason. Later ridicule of the plan obscures that it was welcomed by the the public, moderate Republicans, and big corporations looking to lower costs. That the U.S. did not have such a program was a disgrace and the fractured system in place led to rapidly rising costs that were negative for business profits. As the plan stumbled over its complicated nature and Congressional desires for amendments, the right wing media gathered its forces to savage the proposal. They succeeded to such a degree that few recognized that it was not the fault of plan, but right wing propaganda that buried it. More desperately needed each year to bring some control over runaway medical costs, no one had the nerve to mention the subject until Bush's weakness permitted it to be resurrected by Democratic presidential candidates in 2007. Right wing media dogs had damaged the nation once again.

The attack on "socialized medicine" was well financed by interested parties that might have been negatively affected by the legislation. One of the reasons for its complicated nature was keeping insurance, drug, and medical care companies in the picture and avoiding the most efficient solution, a single payer system managed by the government. No matter, the vicious media campaign hardened Republicans and some Democrats against the plan and it was defeated. Seeking to cover up that special interests and reactionary ideology had defeated something the country needed, the defeat was blamed on a highhanded Hillary Clinton operating impractically in secrecy.

Other than fiscal responsibility, defeat of Hillarycare turned the first two Clinton years into a bust. Loss of the House in the 1994 mid-term election seemed to doom the Clinton presidency, but the politically astute President figured out a way. He adopted portions of the right wing program that were acceptable and made them his own. Clinton recognized that liberalism was dead. A born compromiser, he was willing to make whatever he could out of the primacy of conservatism.

Economic interests and foreign policy had always been closely tied in the United States, a joining that became more pronounced as declining growth at home induced industry to seek expansion abroad. America did not become the champion of free trade by accident or economic theory, it did so out of the desire of our corporations to go abroad for growth. George Bush and Bill Clinton saw opportunity in free trade, both for American business and to expand American power. The end of the Cold war seemed to open up the world to capitalism and they were determined that the U.S. seize the opportunity to expand its dominance through trade. Despite warning in competitive shortcomings relative to Japan that went back two decades, they were confident that free trade would work to our advantage. Expanded trade seemed to offer the added benefit of spreading democracy and boosting peace, allowing the most powerful country militarily and economically to become all the more dominant.

Clinton jumped enthusiastically into the free trade issue. Though Ross Perot got a lot of votes running on the sucking sound of jobs lost to cheap Mexican labor, Clinton was not concerned. He bought into the concept that the United States would be the biggest gainer from free trade. The trade deficit fell during the early Clinton years due to rapid growth in U.S. dominated high technology industry. Later, when the trade deficit reached a new high in 1998, setting the stage for a huge increase under Bush II, he did not react to the rising tide of downsizing and elimination of portions of American industry.

Complacency about the trade deficit was partly the result of being the sole superpower and partly the high technology information revolution. High technology made globalization all the more real, it was a force of nature. Moreover, it was our force of nature, we owned it, we could not be stopped. The decline in manufacturing employment was not a worry because it was old fashioned heavy industry, whereas we owned high technology. As it happened, high technology proved easier to outsource than heavy industry and modern communications made possible a wide variety of service business abroad at much lower cost. After the trade deficit fell from $152 billion in 1987 to $31 billion in 1991, it began moving up again.

The rising trade deficit and beginning of a downward trend of middle class income after the turn of the century indicated that free trade was not working as expected. Globalization was great for China, India, Russia, Brazil, and others, but not for the U.S. Countries with government backing were winning over a U.S. devoted to free market ideology regardless of the cost.

The twin avenues of imperialism, a strong military and free trade, turned out to conflict with one another. Truman and Eisenhower would have seen that heavy military spending was wasteful and inhibited the ability to win at free trade, but such was the hubris of winning the Cold War that the danger went unseen. Large military budgets and free market theory precluded assisting domestic industry, as our rivals were doing. A much lower tax rate on manufacturing and a national health care program would have helped, but complacency because of our supreme power led to a lack of concern.

Meanwhile, the right was building its political power. As propaganda and political campaign professionalism lifted Republicans into control of the House of Representatives in 1994, conservatism had taken a more aggressive form under the leadership of Newt Gingrich. He was a grandstander who considered himself more powerful than the President, when foisting off the reactionary dogma on the American people required subtlety. His Contract with America was a strong program. It was idealistic (term limits), but practical in leaving out abortion. It called for a balanced budget (which Clinton achieved more quickly than called for), line item veto (passed, then declared unconstitutional), welfare reform and more crime fighting (both delivered in cooperation with Clinton), various tax cuts (at cross purposes with budget balancing and successfully resisted by Clinton), and a serious effort to roll back regulation and reduce government spending. The only unreasonable part was the typical call for greater military spending, at cross purposes with cutting taxes and balancing the budget. Both parties joined in reducing regulation, with unfortunate consequences to come.

The heart of the Contract with America was resurrection of the anti-government stand. The newly empowered Gingrich felt Clinton was so weakened that Democrats could be steamrolled. To further diminish Clinton, he was denounced as no other president since Truman. Immediate adoption of a right wing program of steep cuts in government was demanded and the government shut down for lack of funding. Clinton was already operating on the principle of matching increases with cuts; Gingrich was asking too much.

The Contract with America was the last gasp for less government. When the right regained the presidency in 2001, no effort was made at reduction. By that time conservatism was so much in control and so corrupted by power that government was turned into a feeding trough. The high principles of the pre-Reagan days and of The Contract With America were lost in greed. The revised anti-government approach undertaken by George W. Bush was to wreck government with a slew of unqualified political appointees in charge of agencies and undermining the civil service with bad leadership and outsourcing the most interesting work.

During the Clinton years the right marshaled its ideas from the free form Reagan period and organized an attack on the public consciousness. The number of think tanks increased and their activities were coordinated into a powerful propaganda machine. Leaders such as the Heritage Foundation directed less attention to policy and more to co-opting the media. The mid-1980s had seen the rise of a powerful new form of propaganda, political talk radio, led by a humorous bigot by the name of Rush Limbaugh. He was to become perhaps the single most influential man in the movement and much honored by the right, though any resemblance between what he said and the truth was twisting current news for use as background material. Limbaugh had hundreds of copiers, so that AM talk radio became a snake pit of bile against blacks, gays, women, liberals, and anyone speaking out against not lowering taxes or criticizing George W. Bush. While most of this ranting seemed deranged, it swelled the tide of opinion that standard news sources were biased, creating a more receptive environment for propaganda.

If legitimate sources of information from universities to the standard media could be viewed as biased in favor of liberals, then history could be rewritten and current events interpreted to support right wing doctrine. Rewritten history could turn the principles of the nation's founders into right wing principles. The shortcomings of the Reagan years could be blamed on liberal obstruction and successes for the wealthy as triumphs for all.

The right also began to exercise control over information through publicly held companies that controlled large chains of newspapers. News staffs were reduced and the news homogenized, where it was easier to influence from the editorial page. Talk television began at CNN and grew with the addition of more cable news channels. Talk shows thrived on opinion, the right's specialty. Unlike newspapers with standards that separated news and opinion, television bowed to the cry for balance, when balance meant equality between the right and news reporters, providing tilt to the right. For a while talk TV fell almost completely to the right, as panels were loaded and liberal talk show hosts were replaced by right wingers.

1996 saw the beginning of Fox cable news, devoted exclusively to cultivating right wing views and advancing the Republican Party. A private news television channel doggedly repeating the motto, fair and balanced, vociferously denying that it was an organ of the right wing, but directed toward promoting right wing views, was a triumph. Fox news was sufficiently careful about its presentation that many listeners did not realize they were being subjected to distortion. Newspapers devoted to a particular cause have been around for a long time and have never been broadly effective, as remained true of the right wing New York Post and Washington Times. On the other hand, a national television channel posing as a news source was a breakthrough. It provided much broader exposure and television was the most effective means of spreading propaganda. Staging and personal appearance by so-called "experts" made TV the most effective way to manipulate factual news.

Fox's success influenced competitors to adopt the formula of less factual news and more background. As cable networks developed the talk show format, right wing hit men scored a breakthrough by being entertainingly confrontational. The strategy was to overwhelm by theatrical belligerence, insistence, and doggedly interrupting other views. Television discussion was often between a right wing diehard and a straight reporter, with the diehard's efforts directed at casting doubt on the reporter's factual news. Any points made by the opposition were immediately condemned, for alternative possibilities were not acceptable. The methodology was to subordinate straight news to political strategy and popularity of the individuals involved. Avoiding facts and coloring the periphery allowed what passed for information to reflect well on right wing causes, while condemning liberals.

Condemnation, avoided by standard news organizations, made TV programming attention getting. The public did not understand that it was listening to commentary in which the "reporters" and "guests" were not providing disinterested news or opinion. I often wondered if Hume, O'Reilly, Barnes, Kristol, Hannity, and other Fox regulars realized how similar they were to Nazi and Pravda broadcasters. The television talk show circuit became so brutal and intelligent discussion so unlikely that the programming cooled.

After years of effort, many Americans accepted that factual news was liberal biased, giving the propaganda machine greater control over public perceptions. Clinton's winning personality allowed him to survive, but Al Gore was the first major victim. Gore was pictured as a bizarre liar based on fictionalizing his statements (notably that he started the internet) and John Kerry faked war wounds and engaged in traitorous anti-Vietnam activities that made him unfit for the presidency. Swift Boat Veterans for Truth was an utter disgrace, but the right wing media provided coverage that made it seem legitimate. It probably tipped the 2004 election to Bush. The worst propaganda crime was the Iraq War, which the right wing media helped Bush sell. Post invasion horrors were covered up long enough to re-elect Bush. America was living on failed doctrine, oblivious to the fact that its leaders had no regard for the truth.

Liberal bashing became more sophisticated. Liberals were pictured as soft-hearted, their open-mindedness equated with standing on the sidelines while a desperate battle was fought between good and evil. Liberal pantywaists deserved to be pushed aside, America was too precious to be left in the hands of weaklings, even as the tactics used to pursue glory defied our founding principles. Gore deserved to lose because he was not tough enough to prevent being ridiculed and strong armed in Florida. Gore continued to be treated as a kind of simpering coward who would have had no idea what to do about 9/11 (his reaction is apt to have been less political and more seriously focused on terrorism). Liberalism began to acquire an un-American flavor. The right won completely on the defense budget. No voices were raised against rising defense spending and the effort against terrorism was entirely military.

The campaign of falsehoods against Gore and Kerry benefited from eight years of practice beating up on Bill Clinton. The right used Clinton's political talent as evidence of being slippery and untrustworthy. The senselessly partisan attack on a sitting president culminated in the silly impeachment. The House of Representatives had become less a responsible governing body than an agent for a fanatical right wing. Meanwhile, an unknown terrorist group had bombed two American embassies and was planning bigger actions, but the President was distracted and in no position to react. No democratic president could hope to accomplish much with one of the legislative branches under control of the right.

In its control of the House of Representatives the right began to resemble the Soviet Politburo. By the time of impeachment, Gingrich had tripped himself up and was gone, but a bullet-brained fanatic by the name of Tom DeLay had taken over. DeLay was not a money bags aristocrat, he was a mean little prick with a thirst for power. This was a man on a mission, if not one familiar to the public. He rarely spoke openly and it was obvious why when he did. DeLay lived in a beastly world of lies, with a Nazi-like demeanor indicative of a determination to take the country in a reactionary direction. As the law caught up with him in 2006 and he resigned, the doleful record of the House under right wing control finally led to defeat at the polls.

The last vestiges of honor had faded with The Contract, leaving the right ever more Machiavellian. The executive branch had to be captured and the innocent appearing, apparently moderate George W. Bush, personally an inconceivable presidential candidate, began to look attractive. The right was lured by his devotion to cutting the top income tax bracket. A man clearly ill-suited to the post of president was merely another challenge for the propaganda machine. He was turned into a reincarnation of Ronald Reagan, with a flavor of Jesus Christ thrown in.

By 2000 the right wing media had gained immense power over public perceptions through what became known as the echo chamber. An obscure blog or one of the more violently pro-right publications might come up with a clever liberal bashing idea or a dirty rumor on a well known Democrat. The idea would be spotted by the New York Post or Washington Times, up the chain of respectability from the originator. A number of organizations specialized in spotting juicy tidbits, so the papers did not have to work hard to find the material. Limbaugh and other talk radio hosts, always under pressure for more dirt to feed their non-stop talk, were also eager for garbage. Upgrading gave the material enough legitimacy to be used by Fox news and the story might make it to a respectable source. If the originator happened to be the office of the President of the United States, it was almost guaranteed to be floated as a true story.

The best example was the Swift Boat Veterans for Truth strike against John Kerry just prior to the 2004 election. Not only was the attack prominently mentioned in the national media, but the main accuser appeared many times on cable television. This man had been selected by Nixon years before in an effort to discredit Kerry following his anti-war appearance before Congress in 1971. His claims were refuted by all reliable sources, but appearance on national TV had the effect of putting the burden of proof on Kerry.

Like previous elitist authoritarian groups, the right would have preferred an all powerful leader as the best means of dominating the public. After Gingrich fell, the job description for public face of the right became a passive man voters liked, not identified with acrimonious anti-social right wing policy, and above all controllable because of buying into the party line. Bush fit the bill. He ran as an old fashioned Republican and never spouted right wing causes. As president, he provided matchless concealment. The emphasis on tax cuts was not directed at the principle of less government, but as a public dividend on the surplus. The strategy was to avoid identification with the right and build on the nice guy, highly respectable, Reagan-like trustworthy persona. This disguise remained throughout the first term and into the second campaign. Only after re-election did Bush come out and publicly embrace right wing policy.

9

Capturing the Public Mind

THE ELECTION WIN IN 1980 caught the reactionary conservatives only partially prepared. They believed the dream that the free market would solve the economic problems, government would be downsized, and the economy would benefit. Reagan's vote getting talent had been vital to selling the story. Dependent on his captivating personality, when Reagan compromised the ideology and the ideology itself had mixed results, they had reason to worry. Reagan's popularity dropped in the second term and the new found power of the right seemed to be slipping away. To make matters worse, his successor was not one of them.

Looking to secure the future, the right took lessons from the master. Reagan had been vague on the facts and he forged ahead with the same rhetoric regardless of how things worked out. He had demonstrated that emotion and personal stories could prevail over fact. Reacting to these examples, the right chose not to adjust to the failures of the Reagan presidency. They went with what they had and organized more rigidly behind the ideology. The religious aspect of the movement was moved up to a more conspicuous spot, especially abortion and secularization of society. While liberals persisted in the belief that religion should be kept out of politics, the right captured the high moral ground. A vague nationalistic imperialism was brought in as a substitute for the Soviet threat. Another tactic was indirect, an intensified attack on liberalism and personal vilification of Bill Clinton. By the time George W. Bush ran for president in 2000, they had built up a well organized assault on the public consciousness.

In planning the attack, they considered how a rich man's perspective could be sold to those with different economic interests. Propaganda alone would not do, basic human traits had to be exploited. Studying what made people become conservative, they found a number of characteristics that could be broadly applied.

Conservative attitudes are based on the most natural of human instincts, self-interest. Resistance to progressive liberalism derived from fear of change that might upset an established position of superiority. Since liberals sought to limit that superior position, they were the enemy. The right wing legislator had greater motivation than his liberal counterpart as he defended his own turf, whereas the liberal is merely driven by generosity and idealism. High motivation led to a willingness to stretch the truth in defense of their territory, something the liberal had difficult duplicating. Inequality was acceptable to conservatives because their wealth creating economic policy dragged along the lower classes by increasing their income. Conservatives thought achievers ought to keep the full fruits of their accomplishments and have the right to pass them on to their children, while liberals felt this led to an undemocratic society. Without progressive taxation, both income and inheritance, compounding would place the rich in almost complete control of the nation's resources within as few generations.

The protective desire to maintain a superior position led to being fearful about liberalism to the extent of not drawing a distinction with socialism. Conservatives emphasized socialism's failure, overlooking that American liberalism had remained distinct from socialism.

Conservatism comes naturally to those in an established position of power and wealth, but how do the tendencies translate to the general public? The answer lies in the fact that most conservative inclinations involve fear. Fear is an easy emotion to convey and the right simply used it in other ways. They pictured the world as a dangerous place of evil and violence through emphasis on the black problem, crime, the Russian threat, job security, terrorism, secularism, and moral decay. At the same time the right was built up as moral, upstanding, and the defender against these fears. Rigid ideology, black and white views of people and life, close-mindedness, and militarism, provide simple answers that give comfort to the fearful. Those beset by anxiety seek a protector and the right set itself up as filling that role. This was the reason it was so important for them to be perceived as the defender against the Soviet menace and liberals as soft on communism. The same perception was later applied to terrorism. Civil rights laws, busing, and affirmative action coming out of the liberal sense of fairness and democracy created the original opening that allowed the movement to progress so rapidly.

The military and its adherents play the fear game through sensationalizing minor international episodes as broadly threatening. The resulting fear leads to overlooking that greater military spending may increase danger by ruining the nation's finances and inspiring enemies. Right wing Republicans had used Iraq as a source of threat throughout the 1990s, making an invasion easy to sell after 9/11 added a sufficient level of fear. The invasion was not sold on the basis of bringing democracy to Iraqi, a relatively nebulous thought, but as an imminent nuclear threat. Preemptive invasion would have been resisted without persuasive presentation.

While blacks and the Soviets were the most important fear inducing factors prior to 9/11, others helped built support for the right. Loss of high paying work in the industrial heartland generated insecurity. Losing what was believed to be lifetime employment at good wages and secure retirement, millions of blue collar workers had to accept lower paying higher turnover jobs. The heart of democratic progressive America was turned into an anxious, fearful group as a result of the corporate search for low cost foreign labor. The right knew how to take advantage of the misery. Workers fell into the arms of those who were taking away their jobs. Throughout much of the period of decline in higher paying manufacturing jobs, Republican presidents were in office, but the right succeeded in placing the blame on liberals. Unions were costing jobs, not management. Plants closed not because of the pursuit of low cost foreign labor, but high taxes, mandated pensions, health care costs, environmental regulations, occupational safety standards, and union restrictions. The argument contained enough truth to play well with the fear ridden. The Rush Limbaugh redneck was born out of race baiting and economic insecurity.

When the Russian threat disappeared, minor foreign upheavals were exaggerated until 9/11 came to the rescue. Since its following had been built playing on fear, the right knew exactly how to capitalize. The opportunity was exploited by home security alarms and a loud chorus of nationalistic propaganda. The deficits, the failure of the economy to produce more industrial jobs at better pay, and the debacle in Iraq would have meant certain defeat for Bush in 2004 except for the terrorist threat. If the right had been more practical and focused on Osama bin Laden rather than going into Iraq, Bush would have been a landslide winner. The right could have dominated government, but their nature was to overreach and the long campaign to use Saddam for political advantage led them astray.

Despite the foul ups, Americans remained in a sufficient state of fear for Bush to be able to obscure the seriousness of his mistakes long enough to win the 2004 election. The indignity and fear coming out of the terrorist strike meant that the unilateral approach that led to the invasion could be interpreted as the only alternative and the resolution of a determined leader, rather than the fiasco it was. The right recognized that failure is something the public would rather not think about, so an optimistic picture could be painted and critics accused of lacking patriotism. Fear induced ignorance made it possible for Cheney, Rumsfeld, and Bush to sell the idea that Iraq was necessary, would succeed, and we would be safer with President Bush in command, despite all the evidence to the contrary.

The right wing form of reactionary conservatism diverges from the norm. The Burke view was that progressive solutions tended to be utopian and amounted to unproven tampering with what was known to work. Separation of governmental power was especially important in a democracy, for great power was never to be trusted. Diffusing power was the reason states rights was so important to the founders. Old fashioned conservatives opposed as foolhardy concepts such as a national destiny to democratize the world, for conditions in foreign countries could not possibly mirror our own.

The new conservative movement originally followed these guidelines, except for the desire to turn back the economic clock to the 1920s. As they tampered with the economy to gain a larger share of the nation's resources, greed took hold. After gaining control over the federal government, they lost interest in states rights and sought to upset separation of powers to strengthen the executive branch and influence the courts. While claiming to be strict constructionists, they tried to reinterpretation the Constitution to suit their aims. As for militarism and thoughts of democratizing the world, these are completely foreign to traditional conservatives. The new right radicalized standard conservatism for two reasons: 1) to use government power for nurturing additions to their wealth and 2) willingness to do whatever it took to remain in power.

In capitalizing on conservative inducing practices, the right was subverting democracy so that an elite group could dominate society politically and financially. The key was preventing lesser folk from recognizing what was happening. To accomplish these ends, the right established a variety of lavishly supported think tanks that hammered on the evils of the labor movement, civil rights, big government, and all forms of liberalism. Excessive government was blamed for all the nation's ills, a message that remained unwavering when the right was in control. Individually the issues were not as important as the uniformity of message and the cumulative effect of the attack.

Think tank position papers merely provided the raw material, they could not directly influence voters. Assault on the public consciousness required modern communications. The right moved into a variety of media sources, most notably television, where the majority of Americans got their news in short gulps subject to emotional presentation. The shallowness and short attention span of TV provided the opportunity to manipulate news in a manner that had not previously been possible.

Media experts were brought in to disseminate the party line, plant propaganda in the news media, and become professional TV "guests". The hit men and women were effective on television, where extremism was found to be entertaining. A strategy of vitriolic opposition was developed to counter reasonable argument and monsterize liberals, making the word a subject of contempt.

Wealthy backers financed newspapers like the Washington Times and New York Post, along with such influential publications as Bill Kristol's Weekly Standard, a mouthpiece for neo-conservative foreign policy. Kristol and Fred Barnes, also of the Weekly Standard, were regulars on Fox TV news, hawking right wing causes with an apparently even-handed expertise. The fact they usually proved to be wrong never swayed their opinions. Ideologues are impervious to events that go against them.

Through incessant repetition and assertive presentation over a long period of time, many questionable and false themes became accepted as common wisdom. The contest between fact and dogma began swinging in favor of dogma. To get a sense of the reliability of media news and opinion, the source had to be known.

At the beginning, think tanks put out reasonably sound position pieces. African-Americans could not be openly hit, but blaming bad feeling toward blacks on excessive government social services created animosity toward liberals. The law and order drive, championed by conservatives after black rioting, was another form of indirect attack that discontented working class whites responded to. As deficits grew from tax cuts and high defense spending, position papers proclaimed that the fault was with social services. Defense could be supported by exaggerating the Russian threat, later by our "necessary" role as the world's policeman, and still later by terrorism.

In the initial phase, think tank ideas seemed fresh. Nothing can be made to sound better than the invisible hand of laissez faire economics. When tax cuts did not modify the business cycle, deficits piled up, government was not cut, and defense spending turned out to be unnecessary, modifications seemed to be called for. Instead, common sense and the truth were simply abandoned. The goal of enhancing the wealth of the rich remained the same, so the ideology had to as well. Some slight alterations in rationale were concocted for following exactly the same course. The distinguishing feature of think tank position papers became defense rather than development of right wing doctrine. Information was used not to inform, but to indoctrinate by twisting news to reflect well on the cause and blaming shortcomings on liberals. Fact based journalism was set upon as biased and opinion employed as a substitute.

Think tanks proliferated during the Reagan presidency, some in support of all aspects of the cause, others directed at specific segments. Since taxes were the chief concern, specialized advocacy groups were developed for virtually every form of taxation. Volume offset factuality. Special interest groups set up their own think tanks to gain funding. Never concerned for reasoned truth, they developed emotional response by clever wording and incessant repetition. Play books were made up for all contingencies. Focus groups were developed. All drew on the propaganda talent of the think tanks.

The most prominent think tanks are:

American Enterprise Institute - the pioneer think tank now specializes in foreign policy. The $25 million annual budget is mostly picked up by corporations, especially those in defense, on whose behalf it acts as the Washington lobby for the military-industrial complex. Home for neo-conservatives, especially now that they are disgraced, AEI bears primary responsibility for the Iraq debacle, only the worst in a series of foreign policy miscalculations brought to us by Bill Kristol, Richard Perle, Jeane Kirkpatrick and others. AEI also houses Newt Gingrich and Lynne Cheney.

Was it appropriate for the wife of the Vice President to be part of a right wing propaganda organization, especially one helping to ruin our reputation all over the world with a militaristic policy of world domination? No, but in this gang her presence is viewed as an honor and right wingers always consider themselves above the law.

Mrs. Cheney might have been wiser to have thought twice about boosting the credibility of an organization whose focus became a variety of conspiracy theories, false propaganda, and helping known liars spread their fiction about Iraq on the Hill. Confident as ever despite Iraq, AEI has taken to blaming Bush and Rumsfeld for messing up its brilliantly conceived war. AEI was helpful in getting Bush to hire General Petraeus and attempt counter-insurgency on a broad scale in Iraq, which brought a measure of calm to the country.

Heritage Foundation - founded in 1973 by several wealthy backers of Goldwater, including the arch conservative Coors Family and Richard Mellon Scaife, who made a name for himself attempting to destroy the presidency of Bill Clinton by underhanded methods. Heritage is less a think tank than a packager of advocacy reports and lobbying efforts directed at current issues. Although under election laws think tanks are not supposed to engage in lobbying, Heritage is closely tied with them. Despite a degree of partisanship that should have destroyed its credibility, Heritage is still able to present itself as a Washington heavyweight. Partly this is because it has acted as a recruiting department for placing arch conservatives and its own members in government jobs, where they unfailingly undermine the department, most famously when Paul Bremer and many key members of his Coalition Provisional Authority wrecked any chance for calm in Iraq during the year following the invasion.

Cato Institute - founded in 1977, Cato is loaded with Ph.D.s and makes an effort to be perceived as a kind of advanced institute of the highly intelligent. Its $15 million annual budget is directed at championing libertarianism. Cato specializes in free market philosophy, supporting corporations, and providing bogus economic rationalization for lowering taxes. Unlike other think tanks, it does not consistently follow the party line, being critical of Bush spending and opposed going into Iraq.

Hoover Institute - the west coast think tank, home to George Schultz, who held many cabinet positions under Republican presidents, the most important being Secretary of State under Reagan. Schultz is a solid man and gives Hoover credibility. Previously a rare common sense right winger, as the movement's basic underpinnings failed, he grew rigid, including putting a stamp of approval on the clueless George W. Bush before he ran for president. Hoover became a refuge for some of the most ignominious architects of the Iraq disaster, including Don Rumsfeld.

Hudson and Manhattan Institutes - known mostly for the now disgraced neo-conservative views that dominated George W. Bush. They are also identified with the theories of Leo Strauss, a mild mannered scholar of Greek philosophy, who questioned democracy and spoke of Machiavellian methods of gaining cooperation of the masses. Feeling the masses should be ruled by intellectual elites, Strauss was popular with neo-conservatives, who thought they were the most qualified. Strauss followers choose to overlook that he thought little of those devoted to the accumulation of wealth. The Hudson took on the convicted perjurer Lewis Libby, formerly chief disrupter for Vice President Dick Cheney and a founder of unilateral doctrine. Think tanks and lobbying firms make well paid resting grounds for disgraced right wingers or those who can no longer find legitimate employment because of being consistently wrong.

Except for Heritage, all of these organizations put out thoughtful unbiased work, though it is a lesser portion of the total. Hundreds of other think tanks cover all facets of public policy with a huge aggregate annual budget directed at creating a favorable view of right wing doctrine. While these organizations are legally separate, their coordinated effort to disseminate the party line and consistent support of the same arguments were vital to making repetitive propaganda effective.

Absent from the right wing propaganda onslaught was the man who made extreme conservatism respectable, Bill Buckley. Buckley was early in emphasizing the free market, traditional American and religious values, and strong anti-communism. He was also the first to go after middle of the road moderates as politically, intellectually, and morally repugnant. Buckley was different, however, his mind was never closed. He remained intellectually honest, leaving him no room on the political side of a movement built on twisting fact. He could see that businessmen were not always right. Loud mouth money grubbing exploitive conservatism for personal gain was not his way. Unlike the new mob, Buckley did not lose his soul.

As the ultra conservative movement developed after the propaganda level was turned up when the doctrine either failed or was not followed under Reagan, the same old tax cut songs persisted and the practice of blaming all troubles on government. With the passage of time, persistent hostility to all things liberal gained ground. The right built what Tom Frank describes in What's the Matter With Kansas as a panorama of madness and delusion. Fixing the attention of the downtrodden on religion, virtue, blacks, and trumped up foreign threats allowed liberal Democrats to be blamed for the discontent felt by many. The working class was led into cheering policies harmful to its own way of life. Liberal Democrats were so stunned at the crazy logic that they sat and watched, unable to comprehend what was happening. Eventually, right wing propaganda infiltrated everyday life so thoroughly that many preposterous misconceptions became accepted as common wisdom.

The most important of these was bias in the media. To cover the shortcomings of the Reagan Revolution while not changing their ways, fact based information had to be discredited. The means was to undermine the credibility of information based media by accusing it of bias. According to the right, all information is suspect until run through its own filter. Saying anything to the contrary is bias. This effort extended to rewriting American history back to the Revolution. False history and opinion passed off as fact was aimed at making right wing propaganda look true and debunking genuine information.

The campaign extended to discrediting informed people. Since the well educated tended to be progressive, universities and intellectuals were presented as impractical head in the clouds elites betraying the common man. Of course, it was the right wing leadership that considered itself elite and was giving the shaft to plain people, but by relentlessly directing attention elsewhere and persuading that troubles were caused by liberals, they succeeded in converting many to their way of thinking.

The tactic employed a devilish device used again and again: take their own worst faults and forcibly identify them with liberals. Reverse themes are favorites of right wing television news, panel shows, and talk radio. Apparently people are sufficiently informed to know of things like media bias, so the label is hung on liberals and genuine news sources to obscure the true guilty party. When in power the right relentlessly clung to the fantasy that liberals controlled government and so were accountable for current miseries, while conservatives remained an oppressed majority. Any shortcomings during right wing rule were explained as ongoing subversive liberalism overcoming the will of the people. The Supreme Court was pictured as a nest of vipers because it had not rid the nation of abortion and gay marriage or allowed Christ into public schools, though a majority on the court was appointed by Republican presidents and this very court gave the presidency to George W. Bush under questionable circumstances. More of these reverse themes are examined in later chapters on the media.

Even at its peak, the size of the core group of the right was hard to determine. Although carrying on ceaselessly about the country being equally divided, the core remained a tiny minority of wealthy reactionaries and corporate executives, probably less than 2% of voters, though increased numbers of wealthy and those buying into the elite superiority concept might lift the total to 5%. A surprising number of not particularly wealthy people were able to ignore the dishonesty because of supporting the idea that the country should be run by elites, with elitism expressed in monetary success. Interestingly, many of the new rich who made their money doing something productive rather than on Wall Street recognized the falsity of the right wing movement and became liberals. Their inheritors, however, will provide a useful future pool for the right.

Election wins came from enlisting those who failed to understand the true nature of the program. Some of these were old line upper income traditional conservative Republicans fearful of losing their economic advantage and attracted to less government and lower taxes. This group had always been Republican, could not imagine voting Democrat regardless of the right's poor record, and as a practical matter voted its wallet. A strong desire to believe left them easy prey to propaganda. These devoted Republicans refused to condemn the selfish mean spirited nature of the right and its heavy reliance on lies and misrepresentation, for they wanted to believe in the party, had a near-wealth affiliation with the leadership, and therefore dismissed the nasty stuff as mere politics.

The opportunity for a small group to rule over the many lies in relatively few voters, generally estimated at 15%, understanding the issues well enough to make intelligent decisions. The rest are believed to be more or less random voters, the explanation for polls varying so remarkably over a short time during campaigns. Many of the matters that caused the uninformed to lean one way or the other traditionally favored Democrats: anti-big business, anti-foreign involvement, employment and economic worries. The right addressed these areas in order to reverse normal perceptions. Though Republicans are not stronger than Democrats on national defense, by playing up foreign threats and championing an overlarge military, they were able to gain a conceptual edge.

Making liberal a dirty word changed voter attitudes toward government. All economic woes were blamed on liberal government interference with the free market. They worked on racial prejudice, turning many industrial workers in the north in favor of the party of wealth. Religion was added to the fold. All were emotional issues selected for their appeal to uninformed voters. Public perceptions were confused to induce enough random voters not to notice they were electing a right wing that was only interested in using their vote to gain tax advantages.

The right's ability to obscure its intentions was built on the public's lack of understanding of the ideology. There is no Communist Manifesto or Mein Kampf establishing a clear cut plan. Goldwater's Conscience of a Conservative is long out of print and the movement diverged from his standard. Obscurity was not coincidental. Since Americans would have been shocked if they understood, effort was directed at masking what they were up to. Absence of a manifesto allowed the aims to be covered up and support gained from those influenced by the high sounding concepts, but failing to understand their ramifications. Less government, tax cuts, privatization, the free market, and not allowing others to inhibit our international goals, were attractive ideas to those with little understanding of their consequences.

Citizens of the U.S. are assumed to be on the same democratic team, the differences no more than variations on the same theme, but the right's aims were not democratic. Fairness is part of the definition of liberal. It is also limiting, an inhibitor to the kind of ambition that leads to the biggest accomplishments. To the right fairness is weakness, something to be turned against the opposition. Reasoned truth underlies morals and goes to the foundation of democracy. The problem with the right wing can be summed up in a dislike of democracy. They do not care about justice, or goodness, or being right, money is their god, their measurement of worth. The right excuses subversion of the truth by claiming a new form measured in terms of exercising influence. Factual information becomes liberal artifice. Their world of intensely advertised ideological theories aimed at benefiting themselves would have appalled Adams, Jefferson, and Madison.

The right never lost sight of the goals, they were merely gradualized and obscured out of political necessity. A remarkable example of this was lowering taxes, mostly for the rich, in the midst of what they claimed to be the war of the centuries. Any diversion or toning down was temporary acceptance of the handicaps of the moment. Although the right used obscurity and gradual steps to shroud its intentions, the goals were clear to those willing to look beyond the propaganda.

The structure of the right wing was built to defend and enhance its position through lies and misrepresentation of the real world. Detached from reality, it was inevitably destined to break down as they were unable to react to what was happening. Their actions frequently went awry because they were looking at things through the distorting prism of their ideology. Dependent on propaganda, they began to believe in their own advertisements.

One of the manifestations was a group of legislators in Washington incapable of governing and determined to undermine those who could. The result was appearance of religious freaks like Senator Rick Santorum and power crazed unethical types like Tom DeLay who were incapable of sensible decisions. Bitter ideologues led a disgraceful impeachment of the President of the United States. An unqualified president carried right wing policies to conclusions that spoiled the nation's credibility and ruined its economy. A stampede of Republican presidential candidates in 2008 showed not the slightest inkling of the nation's problems and tried to tie themselves to the myth of Ronald Reagan.

The shortcomings of the right are revealed in studying its professed ideology, including anti-government, the free market, unilateral foreign policy, militarism, and religion, but first a more complete review of the right wing propaganda machine.

10

The Media Attack

OF ALL THE STRATAGEMS FOR deceiving the public into going along with creation of an aristocracy of wealth, the most brilliantly conceived and carried out was media support. The sort of lightweight immediate response advertising normal to political campaigns would have had little effect. The long term campaign sought to infiltrate all media sources. The plan behind think tanks was less the intellectual quality of their product than having a renewing source of copy for infiltrating right wing doctrine and anti-liberalism into newspapers, television, radio, books, and later the internet. The effort was not directed at assembling facts, but overwhelming sources of information with propaganda. In the Soviet Union and Nazi Germany propaganda was force fed to the public through a controlled media, but the right had to compete with established free press sources. Despite this high barrier, enough Americans were won over to gain control of the federal government, while so many voters were left confused and unsure about their sources of information as to be susceptible to suggestion.

How did they do it? The right came up with an inspired approach - discrediting legitimate news. The standard news media was repeatedly accused of bias in favor of liberalism in order to create doubt about news information and a state of mind that was more receptive to propaganda. Since those involved in legitimate news uniformly opposed rigid ideologues attempting to twist information to their advantage, the trick was to build on the idea this unity represented bias.

On one level the news profession's purpose was to disseminate information and on another level the ideologues purpose was to sell concepts. The design was to join the two for the public as one level of information. The plan was carried out by making the news less about factual information and more about politics, personality, polls, and opinion. To the extent news can be turned into opinion, fact can be avoided and bias becomes more of a factor. In such an atmosphere, the well organized propagandist using facts as something to be twisted in favor of their side has the advantage. The right assailed one of the foundations of democracy, an informed public, to foist off its theories by creating confusion about what information was real.

One of the tactics was to use adherence to professional standards against the straight media. News reporters were devoted to verifiable information and avoided supposition, while the right operated with no such limitations. They were especially effective using a position of power. When the primary source of information on national events was a right wing White House with no compunction about lying, perceptions that bore little relationship to the truth could be pawned off on the public. Reagan was a delightful spinner who enjoyed creating false impressions, but he avoided outright lies. By the time of George W. Bush, the right had lost all regard for the truth. As right wingers openly stated, the reality based community had been bypassed by those able to create their own perceptions. A trick brought to them by Reagan, they went on to make it a vital element in dealing with the public.

The bias argument was aided by centralization of newspaper and television ownership. Local newspapers tended to be fact based and therefore by definition liberal. As they were acquired, their news became homogenized in the interest of earning the profits that justified high purchase prices. Then newspaper profits began to slide as circulation and advertising was lost to new media sources. Declining fortunes added pressure to reduce the number of reporters and avoid expensive time consuming investigative reporting. Increasingly dull newspapers fostered the trend to consumers getting their news from television, with its quick once over lightly approach. Conservative management of large publicly held newspaper chains dominated editorial pages and sometimes broke into the news room. At one time the right seemed on the verge of capturing television as well, but the major channels fought off the attack and poor ratings on some cable channels allowed fair reporting to stage a comeback.

Less independent reporting led to greater dependence on official sources as a substitute for expensive direct investigation. When official sources were connected to a right wing with no compunction about manipulating its side of the story, the press became more susceptible to mis-information. George W. Bush controlled the news to a greater extent than any other president. An inaccurate picture often emerged from stenographic repetition of statements coming out of the White House. Willingness to accept the official word reached an extreme when the press went along with the absurd Iraq threat claims. The far-fetched idea that Iraq constituted a nuclear threat should have been alerting, but the weakened state of the legitimate press led to an absence of response. With foreign correspondents eliminated by the new economics, no one was out there to set the record straight. In the end, Bush so overused the power of the executive branch to create favorable impressions that he lost credibility.

Fading local newspapers provided an opening for The New York Times and The Wall Street Journal to become national in scope, with much greater influence than any past publications. The Times has always been relatively dull and not inclined toward opinion or investigative journalism. It was distinctive because of detailed news, making it tough to victimize, but discrediting it would be a major victory in creating the impression that straight news was biased. The Times had the advantage of being a focused target. In another triumph of persistence, the right wing won over a shocking number of people to its view.

As to The Journal, its national news coverage is a secondary function for an essentially financial publication. The Journal editorial pages are another matter. They became the premier cheerleader for the right and the most widely read vehicle for aggressive right wing propaganda. Staff work was frequently supplemented by material from think tanks. The fanatically biased editorial pages were expanded and became widely read in business and conservative circles.

The future of newspapers is not promising. The ranks have been thinned and circulation goes on declining. Survival required more local news, entertainment, lifestyle, sports, and features such as how to get rich. Political coverage became more about polls and personality. The winner was television, where news is characterized by sensation, personality, opinion, and absence of unbiased analysis. The public knew far more about Clinton's personal problems than his politics. The evening television news consists of hurricanes, kidnappings, steroid investigations, the O J Simpson or Scott Peterson trial, overseas disasters, trapped miners, the president's daily appearance, with the result that significant events become lost in the shuffle. The high volume required to produce all day television news led to a multitude of irrelevant stories that deemphasize important news in a swarm of trivia. The search for sensation helped sell militarism and unilateralism by showing foreign news as turmoil, when most of the upheaval was localized and unimportant to this country. Television news is about ratings, not relevance.

The right was ready when cable television presented new opportunities. With the big three networks afraid to tamper with the feature evening news, cable channels opened up a new venue. As discussion groups became standard fare on cable, they took a strong tilt to the right. MSNBC, for instance, originally balanced liberal and conservative leaning moderators and panelists, then the liberals were let go, though their ratings were often better than replacements. The reason may have been that advertising was easier to sell for right leaning shows. Only after right wing positions became too obviously wrong did the channel swung to the left. Fox news, owned by far right Rupert Murdoch and led by former Republican campaign advisor and fake programming expert Roger Ailes, was a special triumph, as already noted.

At one time TV political talk shows were dominated by confrontational discussion having nothing to do with analysis. Extreme points of view were the stock in trade and rarely did discussion take place among reasonable people. Right wing loudmouths became well known personalities and fame provided legitimacy with the public. It also led to the lucrative lecture circuit and an opportunity to spread the right's poison. The downfall of extreme conservatism under George W. Bush ended the worst of this programming and most of the extreme voices have been thrown off the air.

The right's tactic was to control discussion. In the Social Security debate, for instance, the President was able to steer attention to private accounts and avoid the crucial point that privatization would greatly increase an already high deficit. The Social Security argument should have been about rising deficits, the real source of concern about ability to fund the program. With the right controlling the discussion, the deficit was never mentioned.

Media objectivity also suffered from operating on doubtful assumptions, such as corporate power is benevolent, capitalism is synonymous with democracy, and the U.S. is always a force for good in the world. The nationalism aroused by the Bush team made it difficult for the media to take up important issues, like our loss of international legitimacy from high handed foreign policy or the alarm raised around the world by preemptive invasion. The ambitious plan to dominate the entire Middle East starting with Iraq was not revealed and the administration never owned up to it. Bush's simplistic and uninformative interpretation of why terrorists were going after the U.S. was accepted without consideration of the real reasons.

The right sells the bias argument in an extraordinarily brazen manner, literally defining fact based news as liberal and opinion based news as fair and balanced. Mildly liberal leanings are wildly exaggerated and a single segment reflecting badly on the right condemns the source to the purgatory of everlasting bias. Several right wing sources scavenge the news for mild incidents of liberal leaning so that its media sources have a stream of fresh talking points, most blown out of proportion by presenting them as major issues. All the major television network news chiefs are labeled as biased because of their refusal to deal in right wing bilge. Spokesmen for right wing think tanks are portrayed as experts, while non-right wing think tanks are automatically liberal, and therefore biased. The process seemed irrationally overdone, except that a winning momentum was established, until failed economic and foreign policy exposed the false positions.

There is liberal bias, of course, but not of sufficient importance to be worth talking about until the right began relentlessly harping on the subject. Persistence made liberal media bias virtually an accepted fact among the less informed and for those wanting to believe as justification for their leanings. One fact dominates the argument - to the degree there is liberal bias, it pales beside the acute bias of the right wing. By the dictionary definition of liberal - free from prejudice or bigotry, open-minded, tolerant, and willing to give - liberal is exactly what the media ought to be.

Let me clarify the bias argument. What are we talking about? Liberal bias within the standard media largely involves social matters, such as abortion, race, the environment, the death penalty, gun control, gay rights, campaign finance reform, free trade, and the like. Most people agree a clean environment is a good thing, but to the right efforts at clean up, or any form of control, are governmental intrusion harmful to business. The public good be damned if it gets in the way of corporate profits. Pro-environmental positions are biased, but the bias is on the side of the common good, rather than corporations trying to add a few pennies per share to their earnings by avoiding their public responsibilities. The point is that the environment is a judgmental matter, not news. The standard media usually takes a progressive position on these matters and that bias can be reflected in news stories, though rarely in the crusading manner of the right.

Most of the specific right wing claims of bias involve these judgmental issues, not hard news information, yet discrediting hard news is the right's aim. These matters are not nearly as important to reporters as getting genuine information out to the public. Liberal bias is hard to find in reporting daily economic, political, national, and international events, yet the right has somehow convinced its followers, while confusing many others to its advantage, that such publications as The New York Times are nothing more than liberal propaganda vehicles.

The straight media's effort to be fair minded by making a conscientious effort to be balanced has been used to build the bias case. Making certain the conservative point of view is represented often means pairing a right wing advocate with a genuine reporter, with the effect of creating legitimacy for the propagandist. The argument that there were two sides to every story and both sides deserved to be heard was false when the subject involved information. In those circumstances, the truth and a lie do not deserve equal representation.

Standard media fairness is never reciprocated. In our system, the unscrupulous have an advantage. Propagandists have an ideal environment to ply their art. Persistent demand for equal representation in all forms of the media overlooks that the legitimate side is rarely partisan, usually concerned with fairness, and representative of fact based news rather than opinion.

The right wing uses the media to sell its creed aggressively and unabashedly, with a degree of restraint only when it seems advisable. It was astonishing to see a man of the cloth, Jerry Falwell, holding forth in the most un-Christian manner for the wealthy and against Democrats. On the other hand, the so-called liberal press was not a defender of Bill Clinton when he was beset by the right. It was also generous to George W. Bush, despite socially and financially questionable tax cuts and ill-advised foreign policy. The calamity in Iraq drew remarkably little criticism for its first two years, an embarrassment that would not have been reciprocated if Democrats had made such a mistake.

An example of how far this argument went was Bernard Goldberg's book, Bias, a best selling account of supposedly liberal bias at CBS. Worried by acceptance of the book, two authoritative journalistic institutions looked into the charges and found virtually nothing. The book consists of charges that are easy to disprove, misinterpretations that when straightened out suggest an opposite conclusion, and a personal vendetta against a former employer. The arguments are directed at judgmental issues, not hard news. Goldberg used the typical right wing contention that selling so many books indicated he was correct and sudden fame allowed him to sell more books of biased garbage.

If some bias inevitably creeps into the standard media, with the right there is no creep. The small degree of liberal bias pales in comparison to the right's organized campaign of misinformation. For such violent partisans to call the enemy biased is ridiculous. For them news is not news, but an opportunity to massage the dogma. When facts get in the way, the message is always overriding. The line of attack is to assume they are correct, never permit discussion of their rationalizations, and concentrate on assailing the position of moderates and liberals. They pull phony tricks like asking reverse questions and insisting on yes or no answers. Criticism of Iraq was assaulted as traitorous, supportive of terrorists, a slur against our noble troops, and favoring terrorism over democracy. They claimed the standard media was biased because it only reported bad news out of Iraq, when good news was rare and not particularly significant.

Such tactics are emotion enhancing diversions aimed at cutting off criticism and diverting attention from information that is negative for their point of view. Those not thinking Bill Clinton should have been thrown out are classified as biased. A brain-washed friend of mine asserted that Clinton's social indiscretion in the oval office was far more serious than taking the country into an unnecessary and ill-conceived war by lying to the public and members of Congress. Those questioning tax cuts are evil people out to ruin the economy. An account of Ted Kennedy's senatorial career is biased when it fails to mention Mary Jo Kopechne. The right's ability to get away with these highhanded tactics is testimony to the gullibility of the public. Calling the rest of the spectrum biased because it is to the left of right wing extremism is preposterous when the right itself shapes the bias by taking intemperate views and treats common sense and moderation as bias.

Under relentless storm about liberal bias, the standard media buckled. Major outlets took on right wing pundits under pressure for "equal" representation and outstanding publications such as The Washington Post a cautious tone domestically and a hawkish position internationally. The right scored its most improbable triumph over the biggest target, The New York Times. Where was The Times when Bush was advocating the Iraq War on false pretenses, covering up a dreadful blunder in Afghanistan, and selling tax cuts with one-sided information? In fact, the White House used The Times as its leading source of bogus stories about weapons of mass destruction and the Saddam-al Qaeda connection. It featured propaganda and buried on the inner pages later information that the stories were not true. The Times White House correspondents regularly served up softball front page stories making President Bush look grand and abstained from the kind of reflective critique or investigative journalism expected of the nation's number one newspaper (this has never been a Times strength, other than on the op-ed page).

The secrecy employed at the Bush White House was like nothing ever seen before. A regime striving to keep as much information as possible from getting out screamed for greater effort from leading media sources. Secrecy opened up a mother lode for investigative reporting. A revealing story would end the author's career with the President, but where were the devoted truth-seeking journalists willing to fall on their swords? Instead, journalists were content to work with propaganda handed out by the White House communications staff.

For presidents, shaping the news has become a major part of governing. Clinton's influence was undermined by portraying him as a womanizer and a compromiser. He became identified as a person the media could safely have at. The right hit Carter hard without getting completely disrespectful, but Clinton was subjected to never ending attack. Having gained momentum, slamming Clinton became acceptable and the legitimate media pitching in. The New York Times came up with the Whitewater story by mistakenly assuming the land investment was connected to the savings and loan scandal. The story was kept alive so long that most Americans were unaware that it had been thoroughly debunked, and The Times never apologized.

The Bush people were intent on avoiding Clinton's extremely negative press. With backing from the right wing propaganda machine, Bush immediately mastered the standard media. Manipulation was turned to art. The White

House staff concentrated on the press, crafted stories, and focused attention on Bush doing relatively harmless things. An absence of hard news made spin more effective. They played favorites with sympathetic news sources, to the point where others hustled to get on their good side. Some critics felt so isolated they capitulated and looked for excuses to praise the President as a way of getting in the door. Personal interviews with Bush were granted on condition of no follow up questions and no laughter or vexation at answers that avoided the subject. The thoroughness of the campaign was dictated by the fact that left unguarded, Bush often embarrassed himself. They blitzed the Sunday political talk show circuit and got away with evasions that would not have been accepted a few years before. Information was lost in the combination of aggressive propaganda and a timid media that did not know how to deal with a presidency bent on concealment and willing to say anything to achieve its ends.

The plight of The New York Times was interesting. With Paul Krugman and Maureen Dowd blasting Bush twice a week, and Frank Rich once, in order to appear balanced Elizabeth Bumiller regularly wrote sympathetic stories. It was a good trade for the White House. Her articles were on the front page and the others were op-ed writers read only by those interested in public affairs, who tended to be against Bush anyway. Krugman's op-ed pieces were more likely than the business pages to reveal news about business affairs related to the administration, but he could be ignored.

The combination of secrecy and manipulation created vulnerability if newsmen had been willing to work at exposure. An illustration was the Bush AWOL charge. The White House staff's fevered indignation legitimized something that would have been passed over and suddenly Bush was scrambling. The staff examined his service records, meaning that if something negative was there it was removed. Not surprisingly, the portion of his record relating to the period in question has never been found. The right would have screamed to the heavens about the missing documents, but the standard media was left high and dry by its need for verification. The press ran off and hid when CBS News used recopied or abridged documents that could be called fake because they were not originals.

An example of Bush media manipulation was the appointment of a hand picked presidential commission to study the failure of intelligence in the pre-Iraq invasion period. Naturally the commission blasted the intelligence, helping to excuse Bush-Cheney-Rumsfeld. The real story, selective use of intelligence to justify an invasion that had already been determined on, only gradually leaked out.

One of the reasons political interplay overwhelms significant matters is the importance of White House correspondents to perceptions of the national scene. This is a prized position for reporters, yet it is difficult to think of a more boring chore, especially under a predictable leader like Bush who spent most of his time politicking. The answer to boredom was the personality contest, as opposed to analysis or digging for the story behind the news. Boredom was accompanied by the problem of access, with its limitation on critical analysis. With access restricted to accompanying Bush on one meaningless political jaunt after another, desperate reporters were easy marks for planted stories developed by the political staff.

A well presented article on who got what in the Bush tax cuts would have been interesting, all the more so from honing in on what the President said to cloak the large share going to the top tax bracket, but the preliminary work would have been extensive and the media no longer wanted to make that investment, particularly with Karl Rove threatening to cut off access. A news agency undertaking a major project would be investing too much in a single story when there are scores of others daily and the assumption is that all will be forgotten tomorrow.

The biggest question about the press during the Bush years was how it missed the story of post invasion conditions in Iraq and failure to deal with the deterioration. There was more to it than being fooled by White House cover up. The press appears to have felt that criticizing the war was unpatriotic. Wars have long been popular with newspapers, probably because the abundance of interesting stories sells the product. Critical Vietnam reporters were not listened to until the TET offensive revealed we were losing the war. Harsh treatment of the President over the non-defense hurricane Katrina demonstrates that wars are treated differently.

A secondary factor restraining the press is unwillingness to admit mistakes. The New York Times introduced the Whitewater story, but never recanted its claim that Whitewater was connected to a failed savings & loan association, helping to perpetuate the myth that Whitewater indicated corruption by the Clintons. Human nature works in media organizations just as for individuals. Plenty of reporters on The Times would have liked to set the record straight, but it was the original reporter's story and as long as he refused to recant, no changes were made. As The Times expressed regret for not calling the White House to task for the fake stories that took us into Iraq, reporting on conditions there remained sketchy. An avid reader, I did not know until my daughter went there that explosions went on all day in Baghdad.

The legitimate press has a responsibility to the nation. Democracy is harmed when an administration can get away with leading the nation to war under false pretenses and tax policy devoted to the rich. The right wing's winning of the bias argument led to otherwise avoidable mistakes. Pressure on the media became a means for the wrong people to perpetuate themselves in power and lead the country in the wrong direction.

11

Personalities, Reversals, Words and Myths

ONE OF THE RIGHT'S MEDIA control methods was the creation of personalities who gained credibility from becoming well known. Media personalities took advantage to write books, many of which made it onto best seller lists. The aura of a book created legitimacy and the opportunity to spread propaganda. Some right wing authors had legitimate publishers, others used a string of specialized houses. Right wing books are sometimes so outrageous as to be funny, sometimes so strange as to be unreadable. All have little connection with fact.

The most dramatic personality is Ann Coulter. She was a regular on the TV talk show circuit until becoming so outrageous the invitations no longer came. An attractive blonde of undeniable intellect, her style is bizarre overstatement. In the hands of a skilled moderator able to play back her far out positions in a way that revealed their absurdity, she smiled coyly and seemed to admit that it was a game of earning spots on talk shows in order to sell books and gain a position on the lecture circuit. Her books are a jumbled avalanche of accusatory emotion against liberals and out of context quotes to prove her points. They quickly become repetitively unreadable, except apparently to far righters reveling in bunk. Writing such outrageously fulminating books (there are six) was no mean feat and most of them spent weeks on best seller lists as a result of being bought up by right wing organizations and handed out free. Coulter justified overstatement as satire, though the raw meanness overwhelmed the humor.

Right wing personalities specialize in the game I have identified as reversal. Areas where the right is especially off base are smoke screened by pointedly accusing liberals of that fault. The leading example, media bias, has been discussed. Another reversal was going after liberals as mean spirited, when the right is heartless toward ordinary people and ruthlessly attacks anyone not agreeing with its point of view. Right wing personalities grimly concentrate on messages of hate. The king of talk radio, Rush Limbaugh, is a volume producer of bile. He is imaginative, sometimes funny, and his material so far out and full of innuendo and lies as to be entertaining. Somehow his audience takes him seriously. Limbaugh overwhelms with solo spinning (no guests to counter the flood of talk, interrupted only by filtered call ins from supporters). I once heard Limbaugh sound off in the early part of his show about liberals always damning good people, then shifting in response to a phone in to Hillary Clinton and viciously wading into her for the next two hours. Limbaugh has no positive message, it is all hate.

No better indication of the nature of the right and its success with propaganda can be found than that such an extreme liar as Limbaugh can be regarded as one of the country's most influential formers of opinion. This is a man who had a book written about him, Al Franken's Rush Limbaugh is a Big Fat Idiot, that became boring as the well documented lies went endlessly on. Liberal bias claimants think Limbaugh should be given a prime time network news program, but his only connection with news is as a feeding ground for bizarre commentary. Anyone claiming Limbaugh does news lacks understanding of the distinction between propaganda and information. Since hate is the basis of Limbaugh's popularity, he rants about liberals being haters.

Like Coulter and many others, Limbaugh overdoes it to sell his show to disgruntled rednecks by making it more controversial. Acting like a reasonable human being would not be good for his net worth. The right's true nature is reflected by his high standing in their circles.

Politically based talk radio is dominated by reactionary froth at the mouth right wingers. Attack sells. Discontented blue collar workers and religious nuts respond to the message. Liberal efforts to restore balance collapse in dullness. Talk radio involves long sessions of non-stop monologue, making it difficult for anyone limited by fact.

Talk show success is taken as indicative of the correctness of the right's positions and that liberal views are dying, but the attraction is similar to pornography. Although the mixture of far right positions, conspiracy theories, and overstated malevolence toward liberals is amusing to listen to in short bursts, on a regular basis garbage smells. Limbaugh's claim to twenty million listeners seems doubtful since it is unlikely there are that many angry idle rednecks out to sink their country. If the estimate is correct, it reflects the power of the anti-black vote and depressed state of the right's lower income victims. Still, his popularity and that of scores of other off the wall hard-case broadcasters suggests an abundance of resentful people who enjoy running down minorities, gays, foreigners, feminists, environmentalists, and liberals. Down on themselves Americans evidently get a lift from this sort of madness.

Another Coulter reversal is claiming intellectual superiority by saying that liberals are unwilling to debate, though the right's absolute immovable positions makes debate futile. Anyone trying runs into a stone wall, including so many interruptions their points cannot be made. Right wing practice when participating in panels is non-stop attempt to monopolize the allocated time. The over-talk tactic no longer worked when the indefensible policies of George W. Bush made them look foolish.

Another clever reversal was developed in the counterattack to protests about tax cuts favoring the rich. The right cried class warfare, exactly its own mission. Inclusive liberals were engaged in class warfare against those attempting to establish a wealth based class society! Along the same lines, liberals and the standard media are referred to as elite in order to create animosity toward them, when liberals represent the common man and the right is led by the only group that considers itself special.

One of the neatest reversals regards fairness in taxation. The reason behind progressive and inheritance taxes is fairness, but the right considers it unfair for the rich to pay a higher percentage of income than anyone else. For them ability to pay is inconsequential. Languishing incomes for the majority suggests that the Reagan/Bush tax cuts were harmful to the economy, while the wealthy thrived as never before. Their huge gains led to picking up a large share of individual income taxes. Despite an inordinate concentration of wealth, right wingers support an ever lower top tax bracket and elimination of taxes on dividends and capital gains. The complaint against double taxation of dividends disregards that virtually all forms of taxation represent a double or triple levy against the same income. The fairness claim is outrageous when state and payroll taxes are included.

The fairness claim was especially emphasized against the so-called death tax, which is not a death tax at all, but a tax on the transfer of a deceased's wealth to heirs, who did not earn the money. The death tax ploy seeks to gain sympathy for the family of the dead, whose bereavement is usually slight compared to the elation at getting their hands on a big inheritance.

Reversal also helps interpret the news in a misleading manner. According to the right, the UN sided with Saddam and tyranny in Iraq over their preference for liberation and freedom. Therefore, the loathsome UN supporters of despotism should have apologized and come to our rescue. By this line of thinking, it was the UN, rather than the U.S., that was intransigent about going to war. The hateful conduct of Germany, France, and the UN earned our disrespect. This type of reverse reasoning, sold so successfully to the American people by the right wing media, made Bush unworkable for other nations to deal with. Since UN inspectors were blowing up Bush's excuse that Iraq was a threat, it was the U.S. that went back on its word, except that realists knew we were going to invade anyway.

No other reversal better summarizes the destructive nature of arch conservatives than the word treason. Not only is this a Coulter title, it was used by other right wing fanatics, including the President and Vice President, at any mention of getting out of Iraq or criticism of anyone involved. Unilateral foreign policy has proven ill-conceived, but it is not treason. On the other hand, deliberately wrecking government with tax cuts and reckless spending is treason. Killing government is not just the rhetoric of oddballs like Grover Norquist, it was the policy carried forward by the Bush government.

Reversals go on and on, but one more of special incongruity. Christian conservatives have been screaming about the courts rewriting laws through liberal interpretation of the Constitution. At the same time they are the leading force in pressing to pack the courts with far right judicial appointees so laws can be rewritten to suit them.

Reversals tie in with one of the most interesting propaganda tricks: focusing attention on selected words and changing their meaning for the public to the right's advantage. First among these is liberal, by definition and formerly by popular view a word that expressed the heart of democracy. The campaign to change its meaning was launched by Nixon's Vice President, Spiro Agnew, in marrying liberal to negativism, pusillanimous intellectual snobs, unelected elites, and against the values of ordinary Americans. The same associations have been relentlessly applied for almost forty years to the point where Democrats avoid being identified with this once proud word. The effect is to blur the gaping class distinction between the right wing and the public. Bush, a right wing aristocrat with a talent for sounding just plain folks, was a particularly clear example of this effort to distance themselves in the public's mind from who they really were.

Values is another potent word. Nixon originally used it in connection with discrediting war protesters as worthless hippies or effete softies. The values theme was later tied to religion. One of the crazier connections was the so-called war on Christmas, a far-fetched effort at creating the impression liberals were against religion. Faith was turned into a conservative attribute and secular into evil. Association with the word government was another triumph. Confidence in the federal government began to decline as a result of Vietnam and Nixon's Watergate troubles, bolstering the right's anti-government theme.

Reagan's rhetoric was particularly effective and Gingrich regularly identified government as the source of all problems.

Freedom was another word hijacked for use against liberals. Freedom used to be associated with release from oppression until the right turned it into freedom from government regulation. Protections for the rights of citizens became encroachments on freedom. By associating regulation that protected the public with infringement on individual rights, the right was able to assist corporations and bolster their ability to accumulate wealth.

Discrimination was a word captured from civil rights and reversed to provide cover for white resentment about racial preferences. Now they were the ones being persecuted by immoral freedom hating government. Patriotism was used in a similar way to fend off discussion of the debacle in Iraq.

Another way of disguising objectives was to create and popularize myths that obscured the right's true intent. Foremost among these was that government would inevitably mess up anything it undertook, except, of course, military action, which was always brilliant. Another pairs the idea that tax cuts are always beneficial and deficits do not matter. Myth was behind so-called faith based charity, or turning over social services and care of the poor to church based charities. Who could possibly object to that, until you remember that the right thinks public giveaways in any form are bad for the soul. Turning control of charity over to religious organizations was a disguised attempt to reduce social services.

Worried about George W. Bush looking like a weak disinterested president, from the beginning the right built him up as a great man. Bush himself was a creator of myths. When he did not get his way, some new horror was about to descent on the country. The champion Bush myth was that Saddam posed a great and immediate danger to the U.S. The idea was so absurd that the Bush team had to stretch by manufacturing an atomic bomb threat.

Before closing, I want to get beyond falsification and make note of a shrewder form of propaganda, using a February 5, 2004, Wall Street Journal op-ed piece by Richard W. Rahn titled, The Deficit Bugaboo.

The author states, "Tax economists have long known that consumption taxes, for each dollar raised, are far less damaging to the economy than taxes on capital". Here he is claiming that sales taxes, which hit ordinary people hardest, are much preferred to taxes on dividends and capital gains, which are largely paid by the rich. Stating a favorite right wing thesis as fact is a standard trick. It might have some justification in a nation with a shortage of investment capital, but the present day United States suffers from a lack of investment opportunity at home rather than a shortage of capital. This led to investment abroad and in marginally productive speculation. Rahn's argument is part of the right wing effort to eliminate taxes on investment capital that almost exclusively benefit the rich by concocting economic theories.

Implicit in the argument is the contention is that all taxes are harmful, therefore lower taxes are always better and all tax cuts are good, again directly out of the right wing play book. The record shows that the U.S. economy had its fastest growth prior to the Reagan-Bush tax cuts and that the 28% highest bracket level instituted by Reagan did not do wonders for the economy. When it was increased to 39.6%, not only was no harm done, the rate of growth accelerated because of lower interest rates from less government borrowing.

Reagan's unproductive record with tax cuts was confirmed under Bush when his cuts were followed by the slowest economic recovery of the last 100 years and ended in a serious economic bust. The economy turned soft at the time Bush took office not because of an absence of investment capital or excessive taxation, but a normal business cycle decline compounded by over-investment in redundant high technology industries, communications gear, and the internet during a stock market bubble. Although currently low tax rates are helpful in sustaining an economy that has lost its dynamic quality to old age and lost manufacturing, an advanced economy could not operate on no taxes, especially one supporting a large military.

The ideal tax level is unknown. Historical evidence does not indicate that high taxes necessarily inhibit growth. In trying to determine the best level, it is incorrect to assume lower is always better. If anything, impending Social Security and Medicare obligations and the surplus of capital suggest taxes are too low.

The article tries to advance its case by claiming that those who want high taxes on the rich (Democrats) "are calling for higher taxes on productive saving and investment, which would depress investment, productivity and wage growth". In fact, the Bush tax cuts were a monumental bust, as reflected in declining wages and capital investment at an all time low in relationship to cash flow. The times of greatest investment and growth in our economy have been when taxes were much higher than they are today. Willingness to invest is determined by opportunity, not taxes. Lower taxes add to return on investment and therefore should mean greater opportunity, but it is the opportunity itself that is determining. The current problem in the U.S. is a low level of investment opportunity, not a shortage of investment capital.

The right's emphasis on "adding to investment capital" is pointless in an America with a shortage of attractive opportunity and an excess of capital. GE's announcement that its future growth will come largely from emerging areas overseas is a sign of the times. Supporters of the investment theory of no taxes on investment income like to presume that the rich will invest their tax windfall in American industry, but unless there is opportunity they will look elsewhere, and that is exactly what they have done. We were so accustomed to being the land of investment opportunity that the change has been hard to accept. Meanwhile, the Reagan-Bush tax cuts to the investor class ruined our balance sheet and brought on a financial crisis that is broadly impacting living standards.

The op-ed goes on building a false front, stating that "repeated increases and decreases in the tax rate on capital gains have clearly demonstrated that the revenue-maximizing rate is under 20% [since it never went under 20% until 2003 this statement is fabrication]. Higher tax rates, particularly on capital, mis-allocate resources, resulting in lower economic growth. This fact had become so obvious...". Since it is not fact, it cannot become obvious. Although there is logic to the argument that a low capital gain tax rate should encourage investment, there has been no historical correlation. Again, the determining factor is opportunity, not taxes. In practice, the low Reagan-Bush top bracket tax rate led to unethical and economically costly business practices that destroyed much of our industrial base and siphoned off the nation's wealth to benefit a few.

Then Rahn goes completely off the tracks in drawing conclusions from his bogus hypothesis. He claims that supporters of the Rubin (Clinton's Secretary of the Treasury) balanced budget failed to understand that it drained high value private sector capital by running a surplus (the right went with the theory that balanced budgets were bad after the Reagan deficits did not destroy the economy). In fact, during the Rubin surplus period, America was not being drained, it was awash in investment capital. As it wrecks his thesis, the author overlooks that the late 1990s was a period of high capital investment, much of it wasted in unwise speculation. The claim is made that if Clinton had enacted a tax cut for corporations and the highest bracket, plus instituted a no tax policy on dividends, the 2001-2003 recession would have been avoided. This amazing statement ducks the point that the recession was caused by excessive capital investment and a bubble stock market that would have been more extreme with his proposed tax cuts. In line with standard practice for right wing think tanks, the real world and what actually happened are abandoned to support fantasy economics.

Referring back to recessions beginning in 1974, Rahn blames them all on increased taxes on capital, carefully excluding the particularly severe early 1980's recession that took place just after the Reagan tax cuts and the 2001-2003 recession that took place despite the Bush tax cuts. The Reagan and Bush records suggest that big tax cuts cause recessions, though in truth recessions are part of a business cycle unrelated to taxes. John Maynard Keynes tried to alter the severity of the business cycle through tax policy, with some success, but the right rejects Keynesian economics because it also involves eliminating recession fighting tax cuts as the economy recovers in order to have a cushion for the next downturn.

The right claims a historical correlation between tax cuts and higher economic growth. In fact, using several measures, growth has been surprisingly uniform decade to decade, exclusive of the 1930s, until a decided slowing in the present decade despite the Reagan and Bush tax cuts. The reason for the slowdown is maturity of our economy and loss of manufacturing industry.

Richard Rahn is a prominent right wing economist noted for his extreme views on taxation. He holds a comfortable berth at the Cato Institute. This kind of fact twisting with an authoritative tone is a daily affair for think tanks and was actually mild for The Wall Street Journal editorial page. Unlike Fox news, The Journal's editorial page makes no effort at being subtle. Its slam bang partisanship is so unreasonable as to be embarrassing for an otherwise excellent publication.

Since tax cuts are the right's only economic policy, no stone is left unturned to justify them. Tax cuts were first sold as the way to keep liberals from draining the Treasury, then as a supply side way of boosting the economy, and finally as a means of encouraging capital investment. All were rationales that failed to produce an increase in the rate of growth and generated fiscal deficits. If the right followed through on its promises and cut government, that would be one thing, but mad for more arms and pork, government spending accelerated under both Reagan and George W. Bush.

The right mobilized a combination of fear and slogans to develop a climate of opinion supportive of policies that benefited the wealthy. This involved a ceaseless tide of distortion that drowned out thought and reason. That the monotonous unthinking propaganda worked was a sad reflection on the state of the nation. Re-electing George W. Bush after he led us into Iraq with tall tales about a nuclear threat and massive deficits built on tax cuts for the wealthy would have been impossible prior to the wondrous work of the right wing media machine. The sheep were led in ignorance through religious opportunism, obscuring what was going on behind a wall of secrecy, and a false impression of safety from militarism. The consequence was a wrecked economy and overseas wars with no evident way out.

Why did those involved in this effort sell out their honor and betray their country? Some bought into the party line with such fervor as to rationalize deception, refusing to consider that beliefs having to be hidden behind lies and obfuscation must be questionable. People like Cheney, Rove, and DeLay thought anything went in politics and were sufficiently fanatical to believe propaganda was a proper means to a treasured goal. Fame was a factor, being on the winning side too, and the money was great. Hundreds of millions flowing annually through think tanks bought a lot of favorable opinion.

Many aware of engaging in propaganda were media people with a tendency to view truth as what they could make others believe. Being story tellers, they were in the business of creating fantasy. On a professional basis success had its own authenticity. This kind of echo truth grows stronger with time and repetition, until it becomes conviction. The ability to convince makes it so, in the face of common sense, history, and the requisite of lying. This manner of thinking is expressed in the famous quote about the reality based community not being the way the world works any more.

During its triumphant years, right wing media created an America oblivious to how disliked it was around the world and not caring, an America failing to appreciate that its method of fighting terror was creating more terrorists and intensifying worldwide distrust, an America failing to understand that the country was being ruled to benefit a few at cost to the many. The incompetence of George W. Bush, the raw meanness of Dick Cheney, the bumbling of Don Rumsfeld, the power of political serpents like Karl Rove and Tom DeLay, were hidden in jingoistic nationalism and religious quackery.

With sources of genuine information assaulted as biased, the public was left unable to think clearly. Disasters like Iraq were obscured in patriotism. Anyone speaking out in protest was ripped apart. Popularized hit men and women shouted down those who would tell the truth. For many years selfish bunglers were able to set aside all that was just and honorable about the country.

The most tragic consequence of truth manipulation was its effect on politics. By unwaveringly following the party line, Republican politicians were trapped in an ideology built on false foundations. Defending it led to difficulty in telling the truth. A political party saddled with the requirement to misrepresent is inevitably led by the wrong kind of people, those so numbingly wrapped up in the cause that they have neither conscience nor judgment. Their only defense was unity. With Republican Congressmen and Senators you always knew what they were gong to say before they opened their mouths. Getting anything useful done when the controlling party was implacably devoted to aggressive foreign policy and endless tax cuts was not feasible.

12

Right Wing Doctrine: Anti-government

THE NEAR IMPOSSIBLE FEAT OF gaining public support for a program of ever more tax cuts for the rich was accomplished through distracting the middle and lower classes with other issues. Foremost among these was that activist liberal government intruded on individual freedom and inhibited economic growth. The right sold the idea that government was a hopeless bumbler whose efforts for a better society not only interfered with individual rights, they usually went wrong. Government intervention supposedly led to less innovation, reduced efficiency, and added costs, inhibiting broad creation of wealth. Government should get out of the way and let people succeed or fail on their own.

Catchy and instinctively appealing as these thoughts may be, they are also silly. Government has been an important partner in providing opportunity and services that promote growth and make the market work. Although regulation might have become somewhat excessive by the 1970s, the overreach was not extreme. Environmental cleanup regulations did not pay enough attention to cost and as a result the laws were tempered through interaction of corporations and government, yet another example of why our form of capitalism had been so successful. Rather than being content with compromise, in accordance with its insistence on complete victory, the right tried to eliminate all environmental regulation.

While it may be unreasonable, the anti-government line is great propaganda. Government is bureaucratic and wasteful. The table on page 32 listing "other" government spending is evidence of ever more programs, all of which involve a degree of waste. Pork has become a growing scandal.

Thousands of unnecessary projects are funded and worthwhile ones over-funded as favors to assist incumbents in getting re-elected.

The anti-government crusade was an indirect means of de-emphasizing community interest in favor of individual rights. For conservatives individual freedom is more important than majority rule. The argument in favor of the individual was formulated by the nineteenth century English philosopher, Herbert Spencer. A social evolutionist, he believed that governmental interference in the social order hampered man's natural progression. Measures aimed at helping the weak were counterproductive because they inhibited progress. The least talented should be allowed to waste away or the human race would be dragged down and prevented from reaching its full potential. Spencer seemed to offer scientific justification for allowing the individual a free hand. Not only was there a purity of logic to the theme, it added an emotional perfectionism to mere self-interest, allowing followers refuge in thinking they were helping man evolve to a higher status. Supporters can get so worked up about social services that no amount of common decency can offset.

These beliefs, known as Social Darwinism, are at the heart of objection to government sponsored social services. In America the natural selection philosophy was intensified by the race problem. Jobless young black welfare mothers were seen as having no purpose in life other than as breeding factories for ill-begotten badly raised children who ended up robbing for a drug fix. Access to the public trough allowed them to despoil the nation. If welfare was not available and nature allowed its course, far fewer of these low life offspring would be dragging down society. Relief would inevitably create dependency, absorbing more and more of the nation's resources. In propping up the weak, bleeding heart liberals were robbing the nation of its greatness.

The theme is appealing on its own, the problem is that welfare mothers and their failed offspring are extreme cases and Social Darwinism has a negative influence on the broad run of hard working middle and lower income citizens. When allowed to run government, the Social Darwinist elite has always done a poor job because of managing affairs to their own benefit. It was no accident that the economic well being of the middle class suffered after the right wing came to power.

Spencerian beliefs were widely held by well-to-do Americans in the late nineteenth and early twentieth centuries and the courts tended to be sympathetic. The great depression undid rule of the privileged by demonstrating that their direction of public affairs had been flawed. Spencerian thinking faded, but as forty years of progressive democracy developed flaws, in no small part because of mismanagement by the conservative Nixon, it staged a comeback. Spencer's theory became one of the philosophical foundations of reactionary conservativism.

Although the fittest do tend to come out on top in nature, man's status as a superior being is based on altering the circumstances of survival. The fittest do not necessarily come out ahead, for the surest winners are those with the money to perpetuate a favorable status. In a creature so diverse, who is to say which of man's qualities are fittest. Spencer, for instance, and many of his followers, did not think money grubbing American businessmen were the highest form of humanity. Neither did a favorite philosopher of neo-conservatives, Leo Strauss.

Democracy places Social Darwinists in a tough spot, for government services are popular with the majority of voters. This made the new movement's rise to power challenging. The fight was directed along four fronts. The propaganda machine was unleashed in praise of individualism and the failings of liberal government. Second, social services likely to be resented were emphasized, especially those used by African-Americans. Third, effort was directed against all forms of government regulation that limited the freedom of corporations and individuals to earn a business profit. Finally, after the right had come to power and its programs failed to produce promised results, fiscal deficits were encouraged in a longer term strategy of ending social services through squeezing the Treasury. The final strategy amounted to sacrificing the financial security of the nation to the ideology of survival of the fittest, a measure of the moral level on which the right fought.

Harping on freedom provides an appearance of justification for a negative attitude toward government. While individual freedom is a great thing, it often comes into conflict with democracy. In addition, freedom can involve an amoral permissive individualism that leads to anarchy, inequality, and an unjust society. Personal incentives unconstrained by any sense of responsibility leave a system balanced between risk and fraud.

Some of the inordinate individual gains during the last thirty years were justified, but most came at cost to fellow Americans and without commensurate service to the community. Corporations were given freedom to profit from wars, famine, and environmental disaster. Arms races against imagined enemies fed the military-industrial complex and encouraged costly wars that wasted resources. The free market brought a rise in monopoly and the creation of a lobbying structure that influenced government to adopt wasteful policies. The result was domination of the nation's resources by those with a selfish mindset, dysfunctional government, and an economy in serious trouble.

The actions of the new conservatives often seemed confused and scatter-shot. They seemed off in some strange undefinable place until I understood that what they were doing was resisting democracy. The law of the jungle explained their passion, their feeling of divine guidance, their justification for any means of winning, their emotional conviction. The black and white world of the right has no shadings, no exceptions, no compromises. It is a fight to the end for survival of the fittest.

Getting away from philosophy and back to the anti-government position, the appeal lies in its partial truth. Over the years, government became wasteful and overstaffed. Short term worries were met with new agencies that remained after their usefulness passed. Cutting our now massive bureaucracy is certainly a worthy goal, something similar to the restructuring that became so common in industry. A program to reduce staffing by 5% in a year, as many corporations had, would soon reveal additional practical cuts. Due to the bloated nature of government bureaucracy, we could no doubt do 5% cuts for years. In some cases, 5% is too temporizing, major cuts are possible, but restructuring away so many jobs would not be politically feasible, so the process would have to be stretched out. Given the right's alliance with business, where personnel cuts have been the watchword of good management, such an effort might have been expected. Nothing happened. Reagan made a pass at cutting, Bush made none. Bush's team was business oriented to a far greater extent than Reagan's, but it lacked a grand plan for running government agencies in an efficient manner, something voters would surely embrace.

It was Clinton who made an effort at improving efficiency to control spending and balance the budget. The business oriented Bush team might have been expected to further the initiative, but instead used its power to gain favors for wealthy supporters. As with Reagan, reduced government and a balanced budget were sacrificed to tax cuts. The best argument for less government became the right's own inept management, arising from an inability to control greed.

Elimination of entire cabinet departments was formerly a favorite conservative talking point. The Department of Energy was established in overreaction to temporary gas lines in the 1970s. Under Republicans, the Department of Labor seems little more than a statistical service and an effort to thwart the labor movement. The Commerce and Education Departments have often been criticized as useless. All could be reduced in size or combined with other departments.

An anti-government attitude could be useful as the first step toward an efficiency that responded to the nation's needs. Then tax reductions would make sense. Instead, right wing governments became the pawn of big business by focusing on eliminating regulation. The inevitable result, encouraged by low taxes on high incomes, was an explosion in corruption. The anti-government tirade came down to disguise for the pursuit of personal gain.

Less government is the legitimate desire of many citizens, but the emotionally uncompromising anti-government stance of the right is preposterous. Wrecking social services may be attractive to Social Darwinists, but is impractical for a responsible industrial democracy. Government has played a vital role in economic growth. Most advances in commerce - canals, railroads, land distribution, nuclear power, airlines, communications, satellite communications, computers, the internet, biotechnology, medical advances, and education - developed either out of government assistance or directly by government agencies. Private capital usually stepped forward to commercialize only in later development stages. The fact that educational levels are disappointing is a social problem, not the result of the system being government run. Any chance of a sensible energy program, a vital cog in the war on terror and to counter an exhaustion of conventional oil, depends on government action, for left to the free market, an energy shock will not be avoided. The same applies to health care. Our medical system is a lot more expensive than other advanced countries and no more effective because the role of government has been limited. Costs will become overwhelming unless a government system is established.

One of the ideas behind state based social services is providing all a chance at being a winner. Large accumulations of money are antithetical to democracy and to Social Darwinism because they create an automatic position of superiority. Money is used to rig the game. Part of the rig is suppression of opportunity giving social services. Elimination of inheritance taxes would allow the rich to preserve a rigged game for their children, working against natural selection. Spencer recognized that inherited wealth upset natural progression and was in favor of a high inheritance tax.

Since the major concern of the rich is enlarging and preserving their wealth, inheritance taxes are a major issue. One of the reasons for this country's success was being led by men who rose on the basis of merit rather than birth. In the old world, aristocrats originally earned position through ability, but after generations passed and successors retained control regardless of ability, aristocrats dragged down their countries. Notwithstanding a few exceptions, the record of offspring of the super rich is not good. Elimination of inheritance taxes would provide a foundation for creation of an American aristocracy. The far right claims there is absolutely no excuse for the inheritance tax, but the possibility of creating a moneyed aristocracy is more than enough justification. The possibility of another president like George W. Bush is a very present example.

Bush is a perfect example of the consequences of non-fittest aristocratic succession. A man of such limited ability could never have reached the presidency without the status inherited from his father. The right wing, dying for power and desperately searching for someone electable, found Bush attractive, but that was by virtue of his shared belief in aristocracy and willingness to run the country in their behalf. The consequences will be with us for a long time.

The less greedy among the rich recognize the danger in creating an aristocracy and favor the inheritance tax. Among a group of prominent wealthy Americans speaking out against eliminating the tax was Warren Buffett, our foremost common sense businessman. He pointed to the critical role the estate tax plays in promoting economic growth by helping generate a society of success based on merit rather than inheritance. He is fearful that leaders will be created by money rather than competition. "Without the estate tax you in effect will have an aristocracy of wealth, which means you pass down the ability to command the resources of the nation based on heredity rather than merit." This condition was exactly what the right was trying to bring about. Franklin Roosevelt said, "the transmission from generation to generation of vast fortunes by will, inheritance, or gift is not consistent with the ideals and sentiments of the American people". Teddy Roosevelt and Andrew Carnegie were conservatives with strong opinions in favor of the inheritance tax. There is no surer way of undermining our country than elimination of the "death" tax.

The right's original anti-government argument was based on excessive progressive spending and resulting deficits, yet on arriving in power they lost control of spending to a far greater extent than liberals. Fiscal responsibility escaped both Reagan and Bush. Acting out the standard line that private industry could do anything better than government, Reagan unleashed a new form of spending - outsourced contracts as a substitute for internal government work. Under Bush contracting became so pervasive that it led to corruption. A private company will almost always be expensive if political connections insulate it from accountability. The real motive for turning government functions over to private companies had to do with profits for political cronies rather than efficiency.

The two faced position on government had unfortunate consequences. Wall Street was given a free hand to engage in speculation, resulting in the junk bond mess of the 1980s, the high technology initial public offering fiasco of the 1990s, and the recent mortgage bust, to mention only the most prominent. Unnecessary military spending was undertaken because it was profitable to corporate friends, though arms is the most economically wasteful form of government spending. Supposed enemies of Keynesian economics rushed to use an economic slump to justify another cut in income taxes. Above all, the tax code was used to redistribute wealth in a way that was highly beneficial to a few and squeezed the majority. Return on investment was always favored over welfare of the common man. A wide gap developed between the anti-government rhetoric and the right's direction of the federal government.

Business was in an awkward position with regard to government. It recognized government's contribution and wanted all the help it could get. At the same time, it wanted to reduce regulation. Although regulation provides balancing fairness, corporations do not like limitations. As an impersonal legal entity, they can act for their own benefit in a freer way than an individual and have the money to achieve their ends, especially in a right wing government controlled by businessmen. With the right in command, business captured the keys to the regulatory safe.

Anti-government Americans were not paying attention to history. Democracy was not a spontaneous development, it came out of early industrial revolution labor exploitation. Upwardly channeled democracy in the United States lessened exploitation, until it began again during the Reagan years in the form of moving jobs overseas.

One of the manifestations of disrespect for government and turning it to their own ends was poor management. Conservatives directed their attention toward lowering taxes rather than good government. The incongruity of a group that sought power and did not like to govern came out in the concept that since government was useless it should be dismantled rather than improved. If it worked better, taking it down would be more difficult. Under George W. Bush this attitude led to placing government in the hands of reckless irresponsible people so fixed on their own interests as to be incoherent about the nation's interests. They saw power over government as an opportunity for personal financial reward.

The consequence of the right's anti-government stance has been a weaker domestic economy. Successful capitalistic countries, including the United States, have partnerships between government and industry. All of the successes of the post war period, the Scandinavian countries, Germany, Japan, came out of an alliance of government and business. The Chinese economic miracle is a government project.

The anti-government stance contributed to our loss of manufacturing and declining position in the global economy. Other nations regarded their manufacturing as an asset to be protected. In the U.S. a free-wheeling Wall Street was allowed to tear down industry for quick profits.

While the right claimed that government should not play a roll in the market, other countries had no such scruples. A plant in China or India costs a small fraction of what it does here because industrial development, whether in support of domestic or foreign companies, is subsidized. Those subsidies encouraged U.S. companies to move abroad. Instead of defending the greatest industrial machine the world has ever known, our government encouraged its dismantling because business interests profited from the process. Our attitude was that grunt work was unnecessary as long as foreigners would do it for less, when we should have used government to help in remaining on top.

Thinking in the United States, shaped by business interests, is strongly against state planning and in favor of allowing corporations to do as they wish. Manufacturers were encouraged to leave for low cost countries in the interest of maximizing profits. If patriotism was not a business obligation, it should have been Washington's. No one took responsibility for the health of the economy, allowing selfish interests focused on short term profits to take advantage. In the competitive race for a leading position in the globalized worldwide economy, the U.S. committed suicide. China seems headed for the dominant position in manufacturing formerly occupied by the United States, while we became a consuming nation reliant on their willingness to lend us money to buy their goods. If the right had approached our mounting economic vulnerability with the same enthusiasm it applied to military spending, our priorities would have been different.

The record of the right on the anti-government issue is confused. The argument was used as propaganda, especially by Reagan, because its attractive sound lured unsuspecting voters to going along with policies aimed at benefiting the rich. At the same time, a hard core of conservatives conceived the astonishing idea that more spending would destroy government by drowning it in losses. Those so despicable as to think this way must do a terrible job of governing. It showed in fiscal and trade deficits and installing incompetent people in important posts. Rather than reducing, the right turned government into an agency for enhancing its wealth. Power became the overriding principle and power meant more government, not less.

While the right's puffed up anti-government crusade sold big government as bad, it was in the process of using corporate money to overwhelm the elective process. As the right established itself in power, less government was supplanted by using government to shift income upward and roll back the power of popular democracy to constrain corporate elites.

The anti-government position contributed to a decline in the dollar, falling wages, capital flight, and a slower economy, all a reflection of what happens when the state falls into the hands of those who do not believe in government. How can people who do not believe in government govern? When the state falls into the hands of those who think that government's only legitimate function is military, soaring defense budgets, deficits, and unnecessary wars are the result.

13

Bush's Attempt to Sink Social Security

THE SELFISH ATTITUDE OF THE right toward government assistance to the less advantaged is tellingly illustrated by the effort to get rid of Social Security. A program started by the detested Franklin Roosevelt, Social Security is the reactionary's oldest prey. They dislike that it is a government program, a business cost, and provides a reasonably secure old age when workers should be taking care of themselves. Perhaps more offensive is that its success is a reminder of the error of the anti-government position. To understand the argument over Social Security requires awareness of the right's determination to sink the program. The doomsday scenario they presented was aimed at fooling the public into going along. When the facts are weighed against what Bush and other spokesmen said, nothing is more revealing of the ugly meanness of the right wing.

Social Security is not welfare, it is funded by beneficiaries and enforced employer contributions. It happens to be in fairly good shape, except that the trust fund has been spent in the form of deficits run up by right wing presidents. The problem is not future Social Security obligations in excess of contributions, but wasteful spending and deficits that endanger the country's future ability to pay. Even using the right's negative projections, Social Security can be restored to soundness with modest modifications, but no amount of adjustment can offset a Treasury headed for bankruptcy.

Social Security, originally a pay as you go program, was overhauled under Reagan so that it began to generate excess cash flow to build a surplus for future obligations. All of the various retirement funds together reduced the reported deficit in 2008 by $184 billion. Profits have grown impressively since the late

1980s and will continue growing until 2013 or 2014, when the annual gain reaches about $280 billion. Beginning in 2011 the number of people paying in begins to decline relative to the number taking out. In 2014 the excess of contributions over benefit payments begins to decline, and during 2018 may turn negative, though depending on the number of immigrants, cash flow could remain positive longer. The estimated crossover date was extended almost annually until Bush stacked Social Security's Board of Directors so that estimates could be jiggered down. It is true that actuarially Social Security comes up short down the road, but with a few minor adjustments the problem would have been taken care of if acted on ten years ago. With the passage of time, the shortfall grows more acute each year.

Profits are placed in a trust fund and interest earned on the assets. The fund has been growing rapidly and after 2018 will continue to increase from interest earnings exceeding the current net outflow until at least 2028, probably longer as the 2018 cash flow turn will be extended. The accumulated trust fund in 2018 should be about $3.9 trillion, allowing it to earn interest income in "doomsday" year of about $200 billion. By the time the trust fund begins to be drawn down (net outflow exceeds interest earnings), currently estimated at 2028, but probably several years beyond, it will amount to over $5 trillion. Currently the trust fund is $1.844 trillion (other related old age trust funds bring the total to $2.386 trillion).

When the trust fund is exhausted, conservatively estimated at 2042, but more reasonably figured at 2052, and longer with modest adjustments to increase inflow, Social Security would enjoy a large cash flow from those still working, so it would not suddenly close its doors, as its enemies imply.

Employing standard scare tactics, the right contends that when the trust fund runs out, beneficiary payments would immediately be reduced to balance income and outgo, the expected shortfall bringing a 27% reduction that would increase in subsequent years (the estimated shortfall in 2075 is 33%). In practice, payments are unlikely to be reduced for two reasons: 1) the shortfall can be eliminated with a modest addition to revenue, likely now that the right is no longer in control, and 2) the difference would be made up from government funds. There is no reason for Social Security to be the only government program operating at a profit.

Social Security's relative brightness indicates that with a little tinkering it could remain funded for a long time. The marvelous benefits of compounding mean that it should have been shored up years ago and undoubtedly would have been if Gore had been elected. The most sensible adjustments are a slight increase in the withholding rate (0.1% adds up in such a large pool) and levying the tax on earned income above $100,000. Anyone making $1,000,000 has a Social Security tax rate of 0.58% of income, plus $56,000 less cost to the company, compared to 6.2% for lower wage employees. In other words, Social Security is a regressive tax. The original retirement age was based on 65 being normal life expectancy in 1935 and already an extension of the age for receiving full benefits is scheduled. Actual results have consistently proven to be better than Social Security's conservative estimates. For instance, life expectancy, the greatest unknown in projections, has proven to be shorter than estimated as medical advances have not offset bad eating habits.

Other than playing on anti-government emotion, the right's case against Social Security is based on two facts: 1) there is no physically set aside trust fund, as with a corporate pension, the money having been spent as part of government operations in exchange for Treasury bonds held in the trust fund, and 2) despite the good current picture, without changes the program will go cash flow negative in about ten years and the trust fund will eventually be exhausted. A greater threat, rarely mentioned, is in higher than expected inflation that would increase the rate of payout. Chances of high inflation have been vastly increased by the right's reckless fiscal policy and absence of concern about the trade deficit.

The right argues that since the money has been spent and interest earnings are merely a book entry, the trust fund should be considered non-existent. While this position has practical merit, it is in no way the fault of Social Security. The guilty party is right wing administrations intent on deficits run by men who feel no responsibility for carrying out their fiduciary obligations. To the extent Social Security is in trouble, it is because our government has stolen money that should have guaranteed its future. The best argument for privatizing is that this thievery would end and money would be separately set aside for retirement. The right also claims that the Social Security surplus seduces the federal government into excessive spending, a good angle, but not the fault of the program. The case is unconvincing for rightist Republican administrations largely responsible for busted budgets.

Underlying the non-existent trust fund theory is that the real annual fiscal deficit is understated by the amount of the Social Security surplus and the already large deficit will rise as the net cash flow comes down in a few years. The fault here is bad accounting, not Social Security. If government accounted for its annual operations excluding the Social Security surplus, voters would have a clearer picture of the true spending habits of our elected representatives. Present deficits are much larger than Reagan deficits because in Reagan's time Social Security was not yet operating at a positive cash flow. The difference between the reported and the real deficit since 1964 is shown in the data on page 158. In 2008 the real deficit was $573.7 billion, not the $389.4 billion reported. The understatement should be clarified by requiring that the real rather than the Social Security reduced deficit be the official figure.

The so-called crisis in Social Security is a perfect example of the right's anti-social goals and willingness to fool the public to get its way. There is no crisis, just the determination of the right to assert its ideology. On principle the right can't stand Social Security. Bush admitted, "it really is the philosophical argument of the age", though philosophical is a gentle word for screwing the public. The large fund to take care of future obligations is seen as supporting socialism and therefore a cesspool of misdirected money. The right seeks to demolish that fund as quickly as possible.

The beginning of the second term, with its high hopes and glorification of George W. Bush, was the big moment for accomplishing the right's long time goal of sinking Social Security and the fund protecting it. Bush saw his win as a mandate and was determined to use it for this purpose, failing to appreciate that only the most reactionary conservatives were behind him. The urgency he spoke of was not a crisis in Social Security, it was grabbing the moment of political triumph to put one over on the public. Privatization was a means of stepping around the practical solution of adding modestly to revenue to guarantee Social Security's future. Rather than solving difficulties, privatization was the poisonous means of speeding up termination of a remarkably successful program.

With the outlook for Social Security relatively favorable, the right found it necessary to lie and the system offered openings for creation of doubt. Financial calculations for the future are necessarily estimates, allowing right wing think tanks to massage the numbers to devastating conclusions. Alarmist demographic estimates were concocted, along with low income and high outgo forecasts. One of the earliest criticisms was low return on investment, a problem that could be solved through investment in stocks, but the two big bear markets of the present decade put that argument to rest. The new tack was that Social Security awards were too generous and the money was not there to support the system, while privatization provided a prayer of hope that individuals might be able to maintain or increase future payout levels.

According to the right, entitlements are swamping the federal budget. Total federal outlays in 2008 were $2.942 trillion, of which $1.288 trillion, or 44%, related to Social Security and various medical payments. The right has harped on entitlements for so long that the public is unaware that these are bogus numbers. Social Security outflow is more than covered by inflow. Rather than adding to, it reduced the deficit. Medicare outflow is also covered by inflow. When Social Security goes into net outflow in about ten years (if nothing is done to shore it up), money will still be coming in and the appropriate figure in the federal budget would be only the net outflow, not the gross amount of payouts. This is an extreme example of using tricked up data to fool the public (Clinton missed the opportunity to help Social Security by changing the method of reporting).

When right wing ideology is put into practice it always has negative consequences, and so it is with Social Security privatization. The bad side of privatization, never mentioned by Bush or others, was that it would immediately add to the deficit because payments to current beneficiaries would continue while inflow was reduced. Taking about one-third of Social Security into privatization, the President's reduced proposal after opposition was encountered, would have increased the deficit by about $135 billion a year. It would also have eliminated funding for the trust fund, assuring its rapid destruction.

This brings up the hitch with privatization, the gap. Take away current collections and only the trust fund is available to fund current benefits or pay those retiring in the next ten or fifteen years not included in privatization. Partial privatization takes a long term problem and makes it immediate. Full privatization would have created a budget crisis through a jump in the annual deficit of $400 billion. After ten or fifteen years, the gap would be greatly reduced from deaths, so no funding would be required, but getting there is a big hurdle. The gap could be funded through a temporary tax. It could also have been covered by the now lost peace dividend, or the Clinton surplus, but Bush chose arms and tax cuts for the rich over a secure old age for our citizens.

After initially planning for full privatization, reactionaries figured out that this would be too clearly destructive. Running up the numbers on partial privatization, they realized that the goal could be accomplished in a subtle fashion. In only a few years the trust fund would be destroyed, so that only modest privatization was required to achieve their objective.

As resistance to privatization came forth, Bush tried to save the effort by making it voluntary. In that case participation would probably have been low, with correspondingly less strain on the budget, and the privatization brouhaha would not have amounted to much. However, it would have given the destroyers a beachhead. Part of the Bush retreat was initiating privatization in 2009, after he left office. Our Jesus-loving president did not mind being unaccountable as long as the consequences did not occur on his watch.

Privatization was an extremely clever means of destroying Social Security, for it happens to be a great idea. It would allow the accumulation of a substantial individual retirement fund that would be there for retirement, rather than having been spent by government. To illustrate the potential for a much more rewarding retirement system, I used an individual making

$35,000 a year for forty-five years. Under the present 12.4% Social Security tax, half from salary and half paid by the employer, $4,340 a year would be saved, for a total of $195,300. Compounding those funds at 5% provides an increase to $732,000, at 6% to $983,000, and at 7% to $1,331,000. Not only is a nice pot built to live on in retirement, but the funds belong to the retiree and could be passed on. Former Treasury Secretary Paul O'Neil proposed that everyone retire with $1,000,000, a goal that could be achieved through the wonders of compounding with a boost from early seeding by government.

Among major entitlements, there is a real crisis, Medicare. Costs are out of control and the trust fund has many less years of life than Social Security. Medicare not only faces large annual cost increases, costs went up from the new drug benefit, a fiscally irresponsible maneuver aimed at getting Bush re-elected. Bush's so-called Medicare "reform" placed an already troubled program in deeper trouble. Medicare/Medicaid is crying for government attention. With the right wing removed from office, the country finally seems headed for a national health plan.

Health care is an appropriate area for government. Our free market approach created an expensive system that left out many people. With little incentive for cost control, medical assistance was sought on the slightest excuse. New devices were expensive to use and produced only slightly better results. Other nations controlled costs by using simplified systems and price controls, while our multi-private carrier system was immersed in a sea of paperwork. Significant differences in costs within the U.S. indicate widely varying usage, probably due to over-testing and over-doctoring in certain areas. General practitioners were supposed to control patient use of specialists, but once the initial contact was made, specialists could recommend repeated tests and examinations, many of them unnecessary. Hope that private industry in the form of HMOs would limit excessive testing and use of specialists failed when complaints arose about restricting care and insurers attempted to skim the market for patients in good health. Reduction of unnecessary care might be accomplished through a high deductible or some other means of inducing people not to seek the most expensive alternative. This is the area the Obama administration is attacking to cut costs.

Soaring costs as against modest rises in other modern countries is testimony that a government program is probably the only reasonable alternative. The current system of hospital charges, where list prices bear no relationship to what insurers pay, is virtually fraudulent. It leaves the uninsured paying far more than the well off. A government system could also remove or reduce a large corporate cost, making our companies more competitive.

14

Right Wing Doctrine: The Free Market

FROM THE EARLIEST DAYS AMERICANS have been keenly interested in making money. The most successful capitalist society came about through this interest, democracy, and physical advantages, on top of government support that included funding for major projects, an atmosphere of equal opportunity that encouraged entrepreneurship, checked monopoly, and prevented exploitation of labor.

Awe at our accomplishments gave rise to glorifying capitalism as a perfect system, but it has faults. Periodic excesses give rise to the truism that capitalism is its own worst enemy. Allowed to run free, it drifts toward a reduction of democracy and ends in upsetting the economy. Behind capitalism's long term success in America was checks and balances that got the system back on track when it went off in a bad direction.

Capitalism comes in various degrees. The freest form, championed by the right wing, has an idealistic grandeur and a terrible record. At the other end of the spectrum, the Chinese developed a closely government managed capitalism that is performing wonders, though probably only because the Chinese are industrious and naturally capitalistic.

Pure free market capitalism has three major problems. First, it favors a few in a way that undermines democracy and leads to social unrest. Second, it is poorly equipped to deal with the ups and downs of the business cycle. The free marketer's claim that instability is self-correcting is probably true, but a hands off approach to economic trouble is slow to work and believers in laissez faire cannot resist tinkering with the cycle in hopes of reducing its length and severity. Tinkering with the cycle is what active modern economics is all about. Free market champion Milton Friedman was a tamperer, in his case with money supply. The right claimed to hate Keynes, then used recessions as an excuse for added tax cuts. The 2001 slump was seized upon to justify two major tax cuts, though the prevailing tax rates had proven highly beneficial to the economy. Subsequently, they claimed the rebound was entirely due to those cuts, though according to the invisible hand it would have happened anyway. In fact, the economic advance was the mildest in history and its benefits were heavily weighted to the rich.

The third and most important strike against ultra free market capitalism is the greed it unleashes, a greed that leads to major economic blowups. The present economic predicament in the United States and the world is the longer term consequence of Ronald Reagan's re-establishment of free market capitalism. It took twenty-five years to atrophy, but the present point of near-depression was always in the cards.

Free market theory operates on the premise that the market automatically allocates resources and corrects negatives in the most efficient manner. Give business a free hand to maximize growth and everyone will enjoy greater prosperity. Industry should be encouraged in all possible ways because it provides growth to the economy and jobs on which the public depends. Unfortunately, these glorious claims defy human nature. If man was innately publicly spirited, it might work, but when when money is involved and individuals are given freedom to pursue their self-interest, capitalism turns on itself.

The U.S. is both especially competitive and materialistic, a combination that makes its capitalism successful and at the same time requires restraint. The urges providing dynamism also create a drift toward activities that undermine the system. Regulation is an effort to resist these forces and keep the system progressively lubricated. So, why is the right against regulation that makes capitalism work better? The reason is simple, they are the underminers. The free market coterie is not as interested in a truly free market as a market that allows maximum opportunity for individuals to make money, regardless of the method. Their freedom is the market that benefits the individual rather than the nation or the economy as a whole.

On the surface, free market theory is enticing. Without regulation, the minimum wage, overtime pay, taxation, and Social Security, business profits would go up and American industry would be more competitive. Favoritism to corporations produces trickle down, or the public ending up better off from general prosperity despite a disproportionate share going to a few. In theory Adam Smith's sorcerer's hand solves all economic complexities and produces the greatest good for the greatest number. In practice it has never worked that way. The right's passion for the free market results from outcomes that overwhelmingly favor the rich and powerful. Since those outcomes are often detrimental to the majority, democracy demands that the free market be modified in the interest of fairness.

Proof lies in the record. Free market attempts have always come apart, the most recent prior to Reagan in the 1920s. After being brought down by the depression, Franklin Roosevelt shifted to a modified capitalism that gave labor a larger share of the economic pie. As the system unfolded in the postwar years, U.S. capitalism reached a marvelous balance between encouraging entrepreneurship and protecting the public interest. Despite the conservative conviction that a mild element of socialism would inhibit economic progress, the economy boomed. Corporate managers developed an interest in community responsibility and concern for employees. That system began to have problems, not so much for its own failings as outside forces, notably inflation arising from pursuit of an unnecessary war, the rising price of oil, abandonment of the gold standard, and foreign competition eroding the growth and profitability of U.S. industry. The stagflation of the 1970s seemed to discredit the liberal form of capitalism. The malfunctions of post-depression capitalism that came out in the 1970s were also the result of slower growth from shear size and maturity. They were compounded by Nixon's economic mismanagement.

The dislocations probably would have been ironed out as capitalism's self-corrective forces came into play. Carter had already taken the crucial step of clamping down on inflation by supporting Fed Chairman Volcker's tight money policy. But the apparent failure of the system provided just the opening that the new right was looking for. Despite its long record of failure, they pushed for a return to free market capitalism. Reagan terminated a social contract between business, labor, and government that had been responsible for our remarkable postwar prosperity, substituting a system with a proven record of disaster.

The most serious problem facing the economy, weakening of the manufacturing base, was unexpectedly abetted by restoration of the free market. Cutting the top individual tax bracket in half encouraged activities that hastened the industrial decline. No one stood up for American industry as low profitability encouraged a dismantling of domestic manufacturing and movement of capital into speculative investments that were highly profitable to a few, but only secondarily beneficial to the majority. We needed more, not less, interference in the market to arrest the unfavorable trend and prevent an industrial from turning into a financial economy.

If the new system had played out in the normal way, it would have had beneficial results over the short term and been destructive over the long term. It worked out about this way, except that the 1980s economic recovery was about average and problems immediately developed out of de-regulation. Strict rules had proven their merit most clearly in banking. From the beginning of the nation, banking had an atrocious record, including a long series of panics that set back the economy. The panic of 1907 was so serious it overcame longstanding resistance to a national banking system, but supervision was still insufficient to prevent the depression. Roosevelt finally introduced harsh limitations on investments and comprehensive oversight through the Federal Reserve Bank, a formula copied by state controlled banks. The fifty years of calm that followed were a factor in the U.S. becoming the dominant economic power. No sooner did they gain control than the Reagan people began dismembering this structure. Almost immediately the thrift system (savings banks and savings and loan associations) fell into difficulty and by the end of the decade many commercial banks were troubled by bad commercial mortgage loans (bank participation in mortgage loans had previously been limited by regulation). Despite these warnings, the de-regulators forged ahead and the last vestige of serious regulation fell with the restriction on joining commercial and investment banking in 1999. The result is a current banking system that is essentially bankrupt.

The banking collapse was far from the only reason the free market experiment failed. Of greater importance was the Reagan group's obliviousness to changes in American industry. During the 1970s many companies found they were no longer getting a good rate of return on re-investing profits for growth. Looking for help, they called on Wall Street. The bankers had in recent years gained an appetite for the high fees available in mergers and acquisitions. What they saw was not opportunity to help companies, but the big fees available in eliminating them. The result was a substantial increase in mergers and forced takeovers.

A pestilence of industrial destruction developed at a time industry needed government support to resist the import threat. Tariffs would have draw negative reaction, but domestic industry could have been encouraged by incentives for capital investment, much lower corporate taxes, penalties for outsourcing, and establishment of an efficient national health system to offset a major expense. While Reagan did reduce corporate taxes, the cuts were insufficient and too broadly based in not being directed at manufacturing. The Reagan cuts went to wealthy individuals, with the effect of encouraging the activities that harmed domestic industry.

American business had emphasized growth. As the focus shifted to transactions that yielded an immediate profit, power shifted away from growth corporations to Wall Street. Funding moved from the ongoing growth of industrial companies to company trading. Slow growth companies, a mounting list as the economy matured, became poker chips in a trading game that generated immense profits from downsizing the industrial base. The process of de-industrialization is discussed in more detail in the following chapter.

The every man for himself culture of Wall Street fit perfectly with the right wing. It became the way business was done. Unions were out, corporate chieftains were in. The corporate legal structure, necessary to large scale enterprise, became a breeding ground of questionable behavior by providing an umbrella of protection from responsibility for anti-social acts. Freed from regulation, having difficulty achieving growth goals, and encouraged by Wall Street, management lost its sense of responsibility and the corporate structure became a means of personal aggrandizement. Separation of ownership from management led to managers stealing from owners in the form of excessive salaries and option awards, selling the company for an immediate bonanza, and actions that give a short term boost to the stock, but were negative for the long term health of the company.

Roosevelt had appreciated the temptations of the securities business and how they could harm the economy. He famously made Joseph Kennedy first head of the Securities and Exchange Commission under the theory it took a great trader to understand the devious ways of Wall Street. The securities industry had sufficient control over money to influence the economy far beyond its small size. The extreme focus on profits often led to an absence of morals and lack of judgment about what was good for the economy.

While the job of the Securities and Exchange Commission was later described as protecting the public, its original purpose was to forestall the securities industry from doing things that harmed the public and the economy. As Wall Street came to exercise greater control over the economy and its political power grew, the SEC found it had to stay on the good side of the industry it was supposed to be regulating. Regulation was tempered and representatives from the industry came to dominate the commission. The head of the SEC being an executive appointment, a free market president could render the agency ineffective. Brokerage companies began to run wild and the major firms did as they wanted, while keeping up appearances through much touted self-regulation. Wall Street's tentacles extended to dominating the Treasury Department, the SEC, and the economy. Never was this more apparent than at the end of the Bush administration, when Hank Paulson, Secretary of the Treasury and former head of Goldman Sachs, directed massive funding to save the big banks and brokers under the theory their status determined the entire economy.

Into the cauldron of reduced banking and Wall Street regulation, Reagan threw the gasoline that ignited motivation to do the wrong thing, a cut in the top income tax bracket from 70% to 50% to 28%. Misbehavior immediately surged. By the mid-1980s Wall Street was directing investment at stock manipulation rather than support of companies that lifted the economy. The process of tearing apart companies was immensely profitable and led directly to income disparity in the form of wealthy individuals making fortunes destroying jobs. The trade deficit, the fiscal deficit, wasteful defense spending and soaring medical costs do not exist for those solely concerned with putting more money in their own pockets. That they do not care about national problems is testimony to the terrible power of greed.

As free market theory came to be exercised it took a more extreme tone. The right was never satisfied, it always wanted more tax cuts and less regulation. They began to claim that rules and regulations aimed at protecting capitalism by making it more equitable were a drag on the economy. The theme was developed that if a government activity was not covered in the Constitution, it was not legal. Among the illegal regulations and activities were:

- minimum wage and maximum hour laws
- zoning
- all environmental laws
- Federal Communications Commission
- Environmental Protection Agency
- Occupational Safety & Hazards Administration
- Social Security
- Medicare
- Securities and Exchange Commission
- Federal Reserve Bank

By this line of thinking, anarchy is no reason to restrict precious freedom. No matter the long history of corporate despoiling of the environmental, any effort at cure is illegal. From management's point of view, workers can never be taken advantage of, for how can the gift of a job be exploitive? Without regulation, individual liberty would flourish, at least their own liberty, the only one they care about. They want us to forget that over the centuries business has exploited labor when given the opportunity, diminishing individual freedom until there is some form of revolt. Overlooked in the self-centered claims of individual rights is that we live in a democracy and in a democracy the common good calls for limits on those who would use their money and power to take advantage of others. The right's never ending cry of unconstitutional is one of its phonier habits.

It took about twenty years for the new direction to be manifested in a weakened economy. The 2001 recession was a Wall Street induced occurrence. High technology, on which the Street had lavished so much hype and capital, blew up. It turned out not to be the hoped for savior of the aging U.S. economy. The economy slowed permanently, despite massive stimulus from another round of tax cuts and uncontrolled government spending.

Signs of what was to come appeared during the Reagan years. First was a crisis in the thrift industry. Savings banks and saving and loan associations had been closely regulated to pursue the special purpose of funding home ownership. The business became strained when high interest rates reduced the value of its main asset, long term mortgage loans, and deposit loss to higher yielding alternatives. The Federal Home Loan Bank system made loans to offset deposit withdrawals, allowing the industry to survive until the interest rate storm blew over, but the Reagan people saw the troubles as a free market opportunity.

The old regulations restricting thrifts to home lending were thrown out and they were encouraged to sell securities to the public, while using grotesque accounting rules to cover up the difficulties. Mergers brought billions of assets under control of unscrupulous operators funding personal real estate projects and taking large up front fees for unworthy developments. Thrifts were encouraged to hedge their fixed rate risk in the option market, only to show a knack for playing the market the wrong way (interest rates turned down almost simultaneously with being granted the authority). They were also allowed to buy low grade high yield junk bonds, with disastrous results when that market went into a tailspin. The simplicity of the business meant relatively limited management skill that often was not up to the new competitive challenges and made mistakes. Regulators were pressured by operators in cahoots with officials from the Treasury Department not to enforce the remaining rules. Much of the industry was soon in a mess.

The affair happened out in the open so that those familiar with finance and banking were aware of the impending debacle. One who did not know, or perhaps care, was Donald Regan, Secretary of the Treasury and former head of Merrill Lynch. Merrill and other leading brokers were cleaning up helping illicit operators attract deposits and arrange deals. The blow up cost the Federal Deposit Insurance Corporation almost $200 billion. If interest rates had not declined significantly, raising the value of a massive accumulation of foreclosed properties, losses would have topped a trillion dollars.

Like most of Reagan's free market initiatives, the thrift debacle had dire consequences. An entire industry devoted to home mortgages moved on to other investments and mortgages became part of national financialization run by Wall Street. A home mortgage became part of a package bartered around the world rather than a personalized local loan. The brokered mortgage market was driven by volume generating commissions rather than credit quality. In 2007 the de-personalized procedure led to old fashioned runs on banks and a national mortgage crisis that shook the financial markets to their roots and brought on a severe recession.

A variation on misfortune swamped an attempt to deregulate the public utility industry, operated on a compromise of local monopoly in exchange for regulation of rates. When the market was opened up in the name of free market competition, utility companies ran off on a diversification binge. Wall Street investment bankers descended like vultures, talking gullible managers into a series of the most consistently unsuccessful acquisitions ever made. Many of the companies were almost ruined, only to be bailed out by selling new stock, diluting existing stockholders, and going back where they started in traditional operations. The round trip benefited only Wall Street deal makers taking down big merger and underwriting fees. This time the financial loser was public stock and bond holders rather than the federal government. Another loser was the public in higher utility rates.

Privatization was also directed at the federal government. A process of outsourcing government jobs was begun under a theory of greater efficiency, improved performance, and lower cost. The outcome was higher costs and an orgy of marginal projects awarded on the basis of political influence, reflected in the defense and "other" categories of government spending. Although civil servant rolls declined about 15% (largely as a result of Al Gore's work on efficiency in government), the number of people engaged in government work expanded and the outsiders were paid more. The greatly increased "other" category of government spending under George W. Bush (see table on page 158), despite reduced activity at government regulatory agencies, is explained by contracting to outsiders. An army that no longer fed itself, or in many instances drove trucks or performed other routine functions, could be downsized and a higher percentage of troops engaged directly in combat-ready functions, which was all to the good, but the cost was high. The military is an example of a pattern that prevailed throughout government.

Privatization of government services created a divergence of interests: profits took precedence over the public good. Putting public activities into private hands had an inevitable result - corruption. Deflection of the resources of government to private hands led to influence peddling, bribery, buying and selling public office. Once on the government list, outsiders invented more projects to keep the money flowing, using influence to close the contracts. Business interests took over portions of government. The vast increase in Washington lobbyists was directly related to this new form of pork. The hoped for efficiencies did not result, rather costs went up. The downside was not only cost. In case after case the Bush II government was unable to perform tasks, the result of a combination of corruption and ineptitude. The small government right ended up with a larger disorganized monster.

Reagan style capitalism did have a bright side. Wealth creation was extraordinary and thanks to outsourcing, the inflation expected from a money oriented economy was avoided. The wealth class expanded so much that despite a tax rate cut in half, the percentage of total personal income taxes coming out of the top bracket increased greatly because there were many more of them and some had huge incomes. Annual income millionaires spend a great deal of money and add considerably to the nation's fund of invested capital. Major new companies might be scarce and likely to be operations such as gambling casinos, but thousands and thousands of small businesses to service the expanded wealthy class were formed as an outlet for their capital and as a source of jobs.

The stimulated stock market accompanying free market capitalism opened up opportunity for entrepreneurs, with electronic high technology the prime beneficiary. On the other hand, too much stock market activity was speculation that did little to build the economic base. The drift to speculation rather than investment is best illustrated by venture capital. The traditionally aim of venture capitalists was creation of significant companies with long term futures. Venture capital flourished in the 1980s, but as high technology industry matured and opportunity diminished, venture capital began looking for quick gains in dressing companies up for initial public offerings and pushing brokers to foist these marginal investments off on the public. The internet brought an orgy of quick hitting in the IPO market. Like the rest of Wall Street, venture capital organizations had been converted from a source of entrepreneurial capital to supporting short term traders.

Let's credit the right with a remarkable job in selling free market capitalism. In the liberal days of Democratic rule, corporations had been painted as villains. The right convinced the public that corporations, if not the worker's friend, were their savior in providing jobs. An atmosphere was created in which business got credit for all that was good in the economy, justifying support for corporations and for an anti-government attitude. Corporations were turned loose to do as they pleased with no responsibility to the public. They promptly began weeding out less profitable portions of their business and shifting resources overseas, with no regard for the domestic economy.

Laissez faire economics is an extremely attractive concept and it could work if corporate executives recognized that their position involves a fiduciary duty to their employees and to the nation rather than an opportunity to become extremely rich. When the right disconnected corporations from any social obligation and tax cuts provided management with an incentive to misbehave, laissez faire became an excuse for the pursuit of personal gain. The fruits were fake accounting, stock manipulation, unacceptable rewards to the heads of public corporations, bribery, and most importantly, the downsizing of American industry, leaving the U.S. economy facing a difficult future. As it works in practice, free market ideology is nothing more than an elaborate mask of sound bites aimed at hiding the grim reality of class power. Disguise takes the form of think tanks and supporting university economics departments spreading the word about the magic of the invisible hand. Language was developed that hid the intent of empowering the few by presenting free market capitalism as a plan to better mankind. In America the wealth grab was far advanced by late in the term of George W. Bush, with the disparity between the rich and the rest having reached pre-depression levels. A severe recession and a new New Deal were on the way. The free market form of capitalism had once again destroyed itself in speculation.

15

Wall Street Versus the Economy

THE NEW EXERCISE IN FREE market capitalism took the traditional path of labor exploitation. Reagan's breaking of the air traffic controllers union in 1981 signaled to big business that it no longer had a responsibility to workers. Government support for unions was officially withdrawn and they were regularly attacked. Exploitation took a new form, outsourcing jobs to low labor cost countries.

NAFTA, passed under Clinton, was a further step toward abandonment of the social contract. A crucial boost to the trend toward giving up domestic industry in favor of cheap foreign labor, NAFTA put the stamp of approval on outsourcing to low cost countries. It had the unpleasant side effect of accelerating illegal immigration, as poor Mexicans assumed the trade alliance meant a political joining and sought to escape Mexico's centuries-old peasant suppression. If NAFTA was about cheap labor, Mexico remained dirt poor, perhaps poorer than it had been from displacement of farmers by imported U.S. subsidized agricultural products.

Supporters claimed NAFTA would create jobs here, but that was never plausible. It had no political cost to the right because of being passed through the efforts of Bill Clinton. The NAFTA effort carried through to establishment of the World Trade Organization and China's entry. The thought behind WTO was expanding American corporate power on a worldwide basis. The goal was opening up sources of cheap labor without regard to the effect on American workers. China won the free trade competition because it employed state planning rather than free market capitalism.

At the end of World War II the U.S. had about 60% of world manufacturing capacity. Although imports began to gain a foothold, we remained by far the largest manufacturer entering the 1980s. In a growing worldwide economy manufacturing should have continued to grow at a good rate. Instead, it fell into decline.

Part of the economic misery that allowed the right to gain command under Reagan came from manufacturing lost to foreign competition. By the late 1970s, Japanese inroads into our automobile market had become substantial enough to cause alarm. Reagan reacted by subjecting automobile imports to quotas. Japanese manufacturers responded by building plants here and German companies followed. Other than automobiles, however, Reagan showed no concern as the trade deficit grew from nothing to $151 billion in 1987. Since the price of oil declined substantially during this period, the increase in non-oil imports was greater. Other opportunities to induce foreign companies to manufacture in the U.S. were available, but free marketers opposed any form of state planning.

Beyond automobiles, a wide swath of American industry was having difficulty attracting funds to modernize because of a slow growth status. The situation was aggravated by the long stock market doldrums. Many companies were left with greater immediate value in liquidation, or merger and downsizing, than as independent entities. They attracted a new style of vulture capitalist seeking profit in liquidating companies.

The vulture capitalist was born out of the Reagan tax cuts. At the 70% pre-Reagan top bracket (it had been 90% until 1962), financial piracy was not attractive because taxes took too much out of a trade. Since long term capital gains were the only way of accumulating wealth, emphasis was on long term growth. As the top bracket fell from 70% to 28%, investors could think in terms of immediate reward. A poor company could pump out many millions in salary, bonus, and transaction fees while its assets were being sold off. If the tax cuts had been directed where they were needed, at manufacturing, many of these companies would have survived. Penalties for sending jobs abroad could have been imposed and nationalism appealed to, but none of this was possible for right wing ideologues focused on individualism, especially when some of them were making awesome amounts of money off the process of destruction.

With regulation eased and taxes reduced, corporate raiders went on an orgy of company destruction. Capital was diverted from building companies to supporting asset shufflers, who often ended up dismantling their targets. Fascinated by big jumps in takeover stocks and unprecedented fees advising on acquisitions, Wall Street jumped in to support corporate raiders. Investment bankers brokered sale of thousands of companies to competitors who could afford to pay a premium price through assimilating and dismantling, thanks to the abandonment of anti-trust regulation. Importers sometimes found a vacuum created by speculators breaking up companies for personal gain, with the assistance of Wall Street investment bankers.

At the moment in history when the nation needed to react to the downtrend in domestic industry, those in command did not believe in government action and the high profits available reinforced the decline. With the perception of history, we can see that the Reagan years marked the beginning in the decline of United States industry and it did not happen by accident, it was self-inflicted.

In the late 1960s, regulation of the securities brokerage business was still significant. Major changes occurred during the 1970s as a result of a back office crisis and the severe 1973-74 bear market. The outcome was a far more centralized industry with more aggressive sales practices. Rather than accepting regulation, Wall Street was able to compromise its overseers and the SEC's actions became more cosmetic than proactive. The agency began to take Wall Street's perspective.

Probably the best illustration was the man who ran the SEC throughout the Clinton years, Arthur Levitt. A former Wall Streeter who meant well, among his strong points was pushing for better accounting and specifically getting stock options counted as an operating expense. The effort was crushed by the growing power of big business and Wall Street in Congress (it finally passed in the aftermath of Enron). Despite this and other noble efforts, Levitt completely missed the dreadful practices in initial public offerings and broker research later turned up after the Enron scandal by New York State Attorney General Eliot Spitzer. The SEC had put low grade IPO bucket shops out of business, only to allow major firms to adopt their practice of rigging markets through control of trading and promotional research support. When the Sarbanes-Oxley Act passed in 2002 in reaction to this and other problems, the new law was endlessly assaulted by The Wall Street Journal and other right wing organs, and barely enforced. As Wall Street's role in the economic collapse of 2008 became recognized, the new President appointed as head of the SEC a tepid veteran regulator whose previous job had been head of the industry's smoke screening self-regulatory organization. The SEC directed its attention to peripheral problems rather than Wall Street's role in bringing down the economy.

A more subtle, but in the end more significant, change began to bedevil the brokerage industry in the Reagan years. Their operating status changed from partnerships or wholly owned corporations to publicly held companies. The reason for the restriction on selling stock to the public was sound – as organizations owned by their operating "partners", self-interest dictated relatively responsible management, important in an industry full of temptation and playing a vital role in the economy. There had been concern that compensation was so high that not enough would be left to properly reward outside investors, but the real problem turned out to be accelerated speculative activity with access to public funds. Brokerage did not require a great deal of capital and typically operated with ten to one leverage ratios. Greatly expanding their capital base not only allowed greatly expanded activity at ten to one, but the leverage rations were tripled.

Partnerships or wholly owned corporations had meant management paying for mistakes. As public companies, the public paid the price for over-speculation that brought massive bonuses to active management during the good years. The set up of heads brokers win, tails public shareholders lose encouraged ever more risk taking and ever more aggressive intrusion on the corporate finance front. In organizations devoted solely to making money, questionable practices became normal. Profits were especially high in industry destroying merger/takeovers, poor quality over-hyped initial public offerings, and ethically questionable in house trading. The latter became a principle source of profits. Big brokerage companies became oversized hedge funds, with a special advantage in the insider knowledge coming out of their brokerage, underwriting and merger activities.

The industry also became more centralized in a few large companies. Brokers kept getting themselves in trouble and falling by the wayside. The handful of survivors achieved such great political power that they could not be regulated. They invented new forms of speculation in options and other derivative instruments that were not regulated. It was not hard to see they were headed for catastrophe.

Among their deviant activities was the high tech stock market bubble of the late 1990s and mortgage financing crisis of 2007-8. Deal making in high fee marginal transactions often left a residue of toxic waste on the balance sheet. The mortgage crisis that began in 2007 would never have happened if regulation thrown out by Reagan had remained in place. These regulations had not been installed out of socialistic leanings, but in reaction to prior failings of the free market.

The astonishing profitability in company destruction attracted capital. After raiders fell into disgrace following blow up of the junk bond market in the late 1980s, Wall Street refashioned the takeover game under the more respectable title of private equity capital. In private equity investors include management, brokerage companies, and institutional investors, all out for a rapid payoff from squeezing cash out of perfectly good companies. Public companies were privatized with mostly debt, followed by stripping out assets to pay quick dividends to the investors and reduce debt. The ability to take out cash was what counted, not growth. In the 1980s the axe mostly fell on marginal companies, but by 2000 slower economic growth made larger and better companies creators of excess cash flow and therefore ripe for the treatment.

The takeover phenomenon derived from slowing growth and the generation of cash flow for which there was limited reinvestment return. By devoting cash flow to paying off the loans used for their purchase, a pot of gold was left for those organizing the transactions. Having put up little money, it was a neat trick for the investors, but further trimmed U.S. industry. The few instantly rich raiders of the 1980s became larger organizations eager to tear down American industry. Creative entrepreneurs faded away in favor of instant wealth from one time transactions.

Private equity was attractive to corporate management, which could cash in options and termination rewards, then turn around and continue with a free slice of ownership. Some private equity organizations provided real talent to assist the company, but the rush of new entrants included many with little management value. The goal was turning a company over for profit, the faster the better. Under these conditions, there was no incentive to finance long term growth projects. Private equity became the ultimate reflection of the preeminence of finance over operations.

Not all takeover activity was destructive. A few leading leveraged buyout firms did wonderful work resuscitating tired companies, but the successes were so heavily leveraged that operations had to emphasize debt repayment rather than growth. The end product might be a better company and capital had been directed in a more productive manner, but the improving process involved cutting personnel and weeding out less profitable operations. The big winners were not producers of goods, but financial types making bogus claims of modernizing and redirecting capital to more productive areas. Many industries were reduced to no benefit other than excitement in the stock market and astounding wealth for those putting together and financing the deals. The capital released from closing less productive companies was not recycled to higher return forms of production that benefited the overall economy, it went into Wall Street speculation.

The takeover binge that began in the 1980s had no higher purpose or economic benefit than the creation of money. The stock market became obsessed with takeovers, leveraged buy outs, and asset sales. Trading soared and investing for the long term became old fashioned. Companies were lost that could have survived if money that went into the pockets of the super greedy had been used for improvements.

Companies became less living enterprises than pieces of paper traded ever more actively on Wall Street. Without quite realizing what was going on, our economy was converted from a great industrial giant to paper shuffling financialization. Great new industrial companies, other than a few in electronic high technology, developed less frequently. Swapping companies for a commission or trading profit came to dominate the corporate scene. Many industrial companies making up the heart of middle class employment were broken up, closed, or the jobs outsourced. Company trading produced great wealth for a few, who continued to fuel the economy and create jobs, but the nature of the new work was different. It tended to involve personal services and real estate rather than manufacturing. The jobs paid less and were less stable, often lacking such added benefits such as medical care and pensions.

A hidden cost was a changed approach toward the achievement of business success. A get rich quick attitude replaced company building as the leading element in American capitalism. Growth oriented investors found an outlet in high technology companies and specialty retailers thriving on an increasingly consumer oriented economy, but the broad range of older industry attracted little interest other than profits coming out of financial transactions, many of which ended up eliminating companies in whole or in part.

Raiders had a deadly influence on corporate management. Attention was diverted from what was good for the company to lifting stock prices and management looking out for itself. Maximizing shareholder value in order to raise the stock price and hold off raiders often led to abandoning growth except by merger, shucking off rather than revitalizing slower growth divisions, and financial manipulation.

The process of impersonalizing industry and turning companies into trading vehicles converted emphasis from internal growth that lifted the economy to individual wealth. The system was dominated by financial wheeler-dealers out for a fast payoff and those taking commissions from assisting transactions, rather than by creators of new business and manufacturing growth. The new multi-millionaires and billionaires did not build companies, they traded companies. Million dollar and up annual earners became routine in the brokerage industry. The markets were set up to provide the greediest, most unscrupulous, individuals the opportunity to become extraordinarily rich. The result was an economy losing ground industrially and generating a lot of concentrated personal wealth. Other countries would have thrown the plunders in jail for activities we honored.

Aside from de-personalizing business and an absence of concern for employees and communities, capital invested in the new ways was less productive for the economy and tended to become centralized in the few taking advantage of the change. Profit in company swapping often came out of lost jobs. Capital invested overseas did nothing for the domestic economy, except indirectly in what the rich spent. Although financialization and a growing wealth class did create a lot of jobs as the economy became service and consumer oriented, the work was not as satisfying and did not pay as much.

The tone of investing in the 1980s was different. Big price jumps from takeover stocks attracted attention and the stock market became a game of rumors and fads for quick hits. Much of the advance was based on financial maneuvering rather than nurturing enterprises that provided growth to the economy. We were becoming a nation of financial manipulators rather than great manufacturers. The foundation was laid for a massive shift of wealth to a few able to profit from the change and away from the large majority of Americans.

The market crash in the fall of 1987 along with collapse of the junk bond market ended the raider period. It was followed by the option phase. Corporate executives had been encouraged by their insecure position to look out for themselves. Management began to think about getting its rewards more rapidly and the way to accomplish that was through stock options combined with financial manipulation that would hopefully boost the stock price. At numerous corporations, management stole from stockholders and kicked out employees, with no sense of fair play, in a mad dash to become rich.

The original purpose of stock options was as incentive for long term growth, that often involved short term sacrifice of earnings. Options were not granted annually as a regular part of compensation, but periodically based on results. Unexercised options were a small percentage of outstanding shares, making them only slightly dilutive to existing stockholders.

As management pushed its board of directors for more compensation, the dilutive effect of options was overlooked and executives could capture effective control of companies as a free ride at no risk to themselves. As it happened, a large portion of the stock was held in institutional portfolios with rapid turnover whose managers focused on short term price increases. As long as the stock went up, they did not care if management was stealing ownership. Option grants were encouraged by not counting as compensation cost in the same manner as salary and bonus. Directors, whose theoretical duty was to represent existing shareholders, were bought off by cutting them in on generous option grants. They were also induced to comply with whatever management asked for in compensation by higher fees and inclusion in company pension plans. Before long, exercised and unexercised options commonly represented 20-25% of outstanding shares, a change from zero to at most 4-5% prior to Reagan.

Through the combination of options and a strong stock market, management could become extremely wealthy when the stock, if not necessarily the company, performed well. Such incentives encouraged management to make decisions that boosted the stock price over the short term and were harmful to the company over the long term. Growth strategies that worked against near term profits might be avoided. In the 2003-2007 economic recovery profit margins hit record levels, but capital investment was at a record low relative to cash flow and much of any spending went overseas. Profitable non-prosperity paid off for management and stockholders, but not for the economy.

It was safer to squeeze growth out of maximizing profitability and gains in earnings per share through treasury stock purchases than to invest in long term growth. Management rewards were now so large as to encourage playing safe. Incentives to sell a company were strong in order to cash in options at a premium price, often accompanied by exit bonuses for management to encourage the transaction. Management of the combined company needed to justify a high price by selling off assets and getting rid of employees. Thousands of perfectly good companies that would have been able to carry on profitably were terminated so management could become rich.

The need to boost the stock price led management of many companies to devoting much of their time to manipulating Wall Street analysts. Sometimes this took the form of unwise ventures in fields popular with analysts for a quick lift to the stock price. Get rich quick capitalism included a plague-like spread of financial maneuvering and accounting gimmicks that produced a short term boost in stock prices, but were destructive to the long term health of companies. Acquisitions were frequently aimed at taking profits out of asset reshuffling and manipulative accounting to generate a short term increase in reported profits. While a certain amount of financial finagling had always taken place, beginning in the Reagan years it became commonplace among publicly held companies. If stock boosting gambles failed, employment contracts, themselves a relatively new device, guaranteed a bonanza exit. Management fired for poor performance often walked out with huge payoffs from exit bonuses they themselves had arranged. American corporations lost their focus on growth and became devoted to making their executives extravagantly rich.

Accounting became a primary means of stock manipulation. Among the many gimmicks, the worst and most widely used was restructuring. Past mistakes could be wiped out and future reported earnings increases virtually assured through a single large charge off that erased past mistakes and set up reserves for future contingencies. Bad accounting destroyed companies by papering over troubles until they could not be saved. Restated earnings, an indication of cheating on the original figures, were especially common in companies with high management compensation. The practices were so common that executives on the way to prison could justifiably say that everybody does it.

Both from leveraged buyouts and excessive management salaries and options, industry changed. Emphasis was no longer on internal growth, but instant wealth through financial transactions. This was also reflected in treasury stock purchases, a way of bootstrapping a stock up instead of investing for growth. It was a reflection of diminished opportunity and excess capital in the system.

The effect on the job market was dramatic. For instance, when I started as a banker in 1957 there were a couple of thousand executive positions in numerous banks and savings and loan associations in my home city. Today, not a a single bank remains, other than a few tiny ones, and only a handful of significant banking positions are still available. Management cashed in option grants made large by their own pressure on boards of directors, urged on by investment bankers seeking the juicy fees that go with company extermination. Why should that particular bank president be entitled to cash in selling an institution built by his many predecessors? Bank management had been regarded as a semi-public trust responsible to the local community. Now selling out was negative for the community in that money formerly nurturing local commerce escaped into the national pool financing Wall Street activities. Other than playing to the God of profitability, much of which came from job elimination, the benefit of this kind of merger is hard to find.

With all of this activity being guided by Wall Street, it became the center of American business. The consequences of a Wall Street centered economy showed up in the corporate scandals of the early 2000s, the political scandals of the Bush administration, a higher level of de-industrialization, and a trade deficit. Rather than a fountain of entrepreneurship that had helped build American industry, Wall Street more or less took over the economy and placed its funding behind get rich quick schemes. The heart of industrial America was funneled through Wall Street, where it was torn apart because it was profitable to do so.

These changes had consequences in accordance with free market experiments of the past: awe-inspiring rewards for a few while middle and lower class incomes stagnated and later declined. Clinton's balance budgeting economic policy extended the good times, until living standards began to decline under Bush. A democracy will put up with income disparity, but not when incomes of the large majority decline. Besides, such a trend is an indication of underlying troubles in the economy.

The U.S. had become dependent on outside suppliers and was saddled with a high trade deficit. In pursuit of greater profits, American corporations sent their manufacturing to low labor cost countries, with the result that trickle down dried up. As corporate profits reached record highs from earnings overseas, the American people did not share in the gains. Excessive

Wall Street speculation in the mortgage market blew up a system that had become unsustainable.

Surprisingly, the immediate reward economy led to a decline in exactly what the free market claimed to encourage, entrepreneurship. Responsibility for this loss was shared among maturity of American industry, control of most industries by large companies, and the phenomenal rewards in bloodsucker professions such as lawyer, financial manager, and financial sales, drawing off the most creative people. Another factor was urgency to get rich quickly by selling out as soon as possible rather than developing new enterprises. America began to dry up as the land of entrepreneurship.

The change was seen in the market for initial public offerings. In the lengthy 1969-1974 break in stock prices, a backlog built up of flourishing high technology and specialty retail companies anxious to raise growth capital. As stocks recovered, a flood of initial public offerings came forth. Although the flow did not let up in the 1980s and 1990s, it began to be dominated by non-earning high technology companies with questionable prospects through a marketing process relying on hype. The severe 2000-2002 stock market decline generated only a modest backlog of new prospects. Most new publicly traded companies were spin offs and privatized former public companies coming back to the market. Foreign company offerings were the conspicuous new element. A large fund of venture capital raised in the boom years was never invested. Financial wheeling and dealing drew most of the capital flow. The concern about New York City losing its place as financial capital of the world reflected growth centers moving elsewhere.

Rather than creating new businesses, the most talented people were attracted to the rapid rewards available as brokers, traders, and financial managers. Payoffs from these activities are open ended, that is to say not subject to the plodding disciplines of productive organizations that take time to build. Men using mathematical computer based derivative systems went on to make over $1 billion in a single year. It might be immensely clever, but there is something wrong with an economy where such things can happen with so little benefit to the rest of society.

What was unfolding was a different attitude toward the pursuit of wealth. The road to a high state of success used to be the creation of new companies and new industries. Now the most talented people went into financial service areas, where life was more fun and more immediately profitable. Many new super rich were created and a lot more qualified by past standards of wealth, but a large number of them reached an exalted financial status through questionable activities and in companies that later collapsed.

Such were America's strengths that the mad dash of would be billionaires to destroy U.S. companies has so far been survived remarkably well. The depth of the U.S. economy and the ability to create something positive and new out of company wreckage was such that we got by. The wealth class greatly expanded and they spent so much money as to have a significant influence on the economy. The economic rebound that began in 2003 was wealth based rather than the kind of broad industrial growth that marked past expansions.

While the fruits of free market capitalism may have been restricted to a relatively small group, the group was not as small as often imagined. There are believed to be over 9,000,000 millionaires in the U.S., which on a family basis makes up about 8% of the population. If being a millionaire is not what it used to be, the number with financial assets over $5 million is estimated at 1,500,000, over $10,000,000 more than 500,000, and over $25 million about 100,000. Prior to the stock market crash, Forbes Magazine said there were 1,125 billionaires, almost 500 from the U.S., worth $44 trillion as a group, against none when Reagan was elected. About 5,000 corporate managers are paid over $2,000,000 in annual salary, bonus, and option awards. Those with household income over $500,000 are estimated to number 1,700,000 and over $1,000,000 at 400,000. It used to take a lifetime to build a fortune, most often by growing some form of business. Now wealth is coming at a relatively young age out of finance or liquidity events.

The over $50 million clique has a significant influence on the economy. This is not old money with spending controlled by trust funds and a generous, but not king-like, life style. The nouveau riche spend. If an estimate that the richest one half of 1% spend $650 billion a year is correct, the over $50 million group would easily top $1 trillion. Private jet ownership exploded, builders of huge yachts were backlogged, multi-large home ownership with big staffs became normal, multi-million dollar annual water bills not uncommon. A new profession was created similar to old Europe: valets, butlers, ladies in waiting, house managers, financial managers, with large staffs of servers, landscapers, and maintainers. A study reports that 20% of households account for 70% of consumption, implying that the 1% at the top could account for somewhere over 10%. Considering that income of the large majority has been reduced since 2000, economic growth coming out of the 2000-2003 slump was powerfully oriented to spending by the rich. The economy was staggering until passage of the extraordinarily beneficial to the rich tax cut of 2003, with its steep reduction in taxes on dividends and capital gains.

Although conspicuous consumers may create disgust as well as envy, many of the nouveau riche appear to feel an obligation to society. They tend to be closer to George Soros than Richard Mellon Scaife. Their charitable giving is huge, some of it directed at worldwide humanitarian efforts rather than building monuments to themselves at their alma maters. They have become a force in politics counter to the corporate and established wealth supporters of the right wing. Many of the new rich are embarrassed by the selfishness of conservatives and by Bush's incompetence. Democratic presidential candidates suddenly struck gold, out-raising Republicans for the first time in 2008.

We will not go back to the pre-Reagan 70% top tax bracket, for the rich have become too important to the economy. Obama planned to go immediately back to Clinton's top bracket tax rate of 39.6% and eliminate the favorable rate on dividends, only to defer in view of the recession. Clinton surpluses were entirely based on the huge tax payments coming out of the stock market bubble at the end of the century. The task of a Democratic president will be finding a top bracket level that pays for universal health care, safeguards Social Security, and eliminates deficits. The wealth class has become sufficiently large that these goals may be reached at the Clinton tax rates, but a somewhat higher rate would be preferable if it halted the growing share of the nation's wealth going to the top and controlled the degree of anti-social activities emanating from Wall Street.

The overall effect of the new reign of free market capitalism was distressing: declining incomes, college education too expensive for more and more Americans, limiting the springboard for the next generation, higher economic status no longer guaranteed for those with a college education, layoffs that undermined family foundation and led to rising school dropout rates. Education levels declined and the right cheered when Bush set upon science, inhibiting progress and making us a laughing stock abroad.

At the moment in history when the nation needed to arrest the downtrend in domestic industry, those in command did not believe in such action and laissez faire capitalism reinforced the decline. De-regulation of Wall Street and creation of multiple trading vehicles led to the massive company fraud revealed in 2001 and 2002, followed by the mortgage meltdown of 2007-8, and economic crisis. Looking back, we can see that the Reagan years marked the beginning of what may turn out to be a long term decline in the United States economy.

16

The Effect of Lost Manufacturing

FINANCIALIZATION OF AMERICAN BUSINESS PUT the brakes on an already troubled industrial machine. Caught up in the euphoria of its political triumph and devoted to laissez faire, the Reagan team paid no attention as the key to economic power, manufacturing, began to decline. The process was nothing like the Russians lifting every piece of machinery they could find in eastern Europe and hauling it back to the motherland, rather the erosion was gradual. With a right measuring success in terms of corporate profits without regard to where the profits came from, the decline was ignored. Growing military power also tended to obscure declining economic power.

Although labor intensive manufacturing was going to be lost regardless, plenty of areas remained that could have been revitalized if the attitude had been preserving and building industry as a national treasure. Flush with stock profits, business interests were not concerned that the basis of U.S. economic power was being undermined. That was the job of the leadership, except that free marketers were in command and they thought all would be fine as long as they did nothing. Nothing that is except lower taxes, when it was the low level of taxes that spurred the destruction.

Although there were early signs of trouble in a rising trade deficit, the pending squeeze on the middle and lower classes was easy to overlook as the economy boomed in the 1990s. Above average pay in growing high technology industries seemed to offset losses in older forms of manufacturing. The exciting initial public offering market and instant wealth for those involved seemed to indicate a new age of prosperity, when the chaotic nature of that market, with its gross overpricing and runaway promotion, should have been a warning.

Reality set in during the recession of 2000-2003, when factory closings and down-sizings accelerated and were particularly severe in high technology. A weak presidency distracted in foolish wars did nothing as incomes among a broad spectrum of American families declined. Weakness of the subsequent recovery should have been alarming, especially after a high degree of Keynesian pump priming. As the economy recovered, the gains went mostly to the well off, while about 75% of households barely staged a comeback, their income levels remaining below 2000. A right wing president did not care.

Other than automobiles, loss of basic industry attracted little attention throughout the period of conservative leadership. Industrial decline, subtle at first, was becoming clearer by the Clinton years, but high productivity numbers led to complacency about the trend. Productivity growth was astounding.

	Employment	Manufacturing Profits
1960	15.4 million	$ 23.8 billion
1970	17.8	27.5
1980	18.7	78.3
1990	17.7	113.1
2000	17.3	166.3
2007	14.0	296.0

However, the gain in profit per employee does not reflect productivity as much as outsourced product and parts, in addition to profits from foreign subsidiaries. The manufacturing category includes many companies engaged in assembling mostly foreign made parts. While economists cheered gains in productivity, in large part they reflected business lost overseas. Harping on productivity gains became a feel good excuse for doing nothing.

If less expensive products could be imported, were we not better off as long as workers could find alternative jobs? On the surface, the loss was in alternative jobs not paying as well, but equally important was a rising trade deficit. Countries with a trade deficit are more or less forced to correct the imbalance. If not, their currency will decline, inflation will grow, and the standard of living will fall. An import discrepancy is self-correcting as a declining currency lowers relative costs, boosting exports through competitive pricing. The self-correcting process can be seen in a mix of modest trade surpluses and deficits all over the world (though there is a growing trend to deficits in Europe and surpluses in East Asia). A financial crisis brought about by a major decline in the value of their currency allowed many countries to recover. The philosophy of not helping foreign countries in economic straights derives from the self-correcting free market.

The United States was different. As the trade deficit rose, self-correction did not take place for two reasons: 1) since the dollar was the world's reserve currency, foreign exporters were willing to hold excess U.S. currency as a reserve asset; 2) exports became so important that many countries supported the dollar to protect their market. The Japanese kept their currency from rising relative to the dollar by driving down the exchange value of the yen through low interest rates and buying dollars. The Chinese did the same. Since the usual declining currency consequence of a trade deficit did not occur, there was no pressure to defend manufacturing. Those undermining our industrial base could proceed without clear cut damage to the economy.

The relaxed attitude was furthered by our own corporations being responsible for much of the import imbalance through outsourcing production or building plants in low cost countries. Since our manufacturing companies were not under siege, as would have been the case if imports had come from foreign companies, we were indifferent to a situation that would normally have been alarming. Outsourcing worked for American corporations. Profits soared from 2003 through 2007 at the same time as the trade deficit raced from $421 billion to $764 billion (up from under $100 billion in 1995) and working class incomes declined. Although the influence is hidden over the short term, the trade deficit has a real cost. Capitalism's mysterious self-corrective process will eventually work against the United States economy.

Since exporters are motivated to support the dollar to protect their own economies, the right claims there is no reason to lose our special advantage, but the advantage has merely papered over and delayed the consequences. Gradual decline in the dollar and strong economies abroad began to boost exports and the trade deficit declined modestly in 2007, and again in 2008 due to the recession. It will again in 2009 with the decline in consumption and much lower oil prices, but it is doubtful the long term trend has been reversed. Fifteen or twenty years ago the trade deficit could have been solved relatively easily, now free market policy has placed us so far out on a limb that getting back to earth will require a crisis.

Why would we, the world's leading country, gamble our future by becoming dependent on imports? Partly it was the imagined benefits of the free market, more practically we were counting on high technology. Old fashioned heavy manufacturing did not matter if it could be replaced by high technology industries with faster growth. America was far ahead in high technology and first mover advantage was expected to leave newcomers unable to catch up. It was a bad guess, as the Japanese had demonstrated years before in home electronics. Rapid change and modest fixed asset requirements made high technology easier to relocate overseas than traditional manufacturing. It also happened that Far Eastern women were particularly talented at the labor side of high technology.

Another reason for neglect was lack of concern for the working class. Although blue collar workers had little opportunity in advanced industries, the typically anti-labor attitude was that they would just have to catch up. Many of them had been hoodwinked by race into voting with the right, robbing themselves of an advocate for protecting their jobs.

During the 1990s the economy was beguiling. The trade deficit declined from the Reagan years and investors were getting rich in the bubble stock market. They took no notice as we drifted toward second rate manufacturing status. There was a lack of concern with the status of the middle class.

If not the wonder of previous high tech innovations such as railroads and automobiles, electronic high technology was a great growth field. Early warnings that it might not provide as much stimulus as hoped to the economy could be seen in most of the newly popular high technology companies not being sound. Me too-ism was a hallmark of the field due to the availability of financial support for almost any company. Although similar overbuilding had been seen in railroads and automobiles, it happened faster in high technology.

As brokers discovered that their promotional talent allowed them to sell non-earning companies to the public, niche growth areas were flooded with cheap capital, their competitive environment undermined. Trillions went into unsound companies, including many that were little better than flimflams. Names like Goldman Sachs and Morgan Stanley at the bottom of the cover page of prospectuses gave stock offerings legitimacy and acceptance for undeserving companies. Promotional follow up research lifted stocks that had come to market at already ridiculous prices. If the massive flow of money to the internet helped its rapid development, much of the funding was eaten up in losses. The net gain to the economy was difficult to see and buyers of the stocks suffered big losses. The internet vastly accelerated the exodus of business by extending outsourcing to services.

Another reason for neglecting loss of industry was the comfort of an indulgent life. Economists say more savings and less consumption are needed to restore economic health, but neither is likely to happen voluntarily. As long as they were raking in so many chips, the right did not care if the underpinnings of the economy were weakening. Excessive credit creation got out of control, bringing on a depression-like recession.

We still do a lot of manufacturing so that the extent of the decline, other than in jobs, is not easy to measure. Look at the following indexes of industrial production:

| | Metal | | Computers/ | Motor |
	Primary	Fabricated	Electronics	Vehicles
1974	145.3	75.3	1.4	43.4
1980	115.3	78.2	3.8	38.6
1990	96.2	80.7	11.9	55.5
2000	110.3	111.2	101.8	99.5
2007	110.3	112	183.4	92.2

Primary metal is the only category with a decline, but it is probably the best indicator of purely American durable goods manufacturing given that fabricated metal includes a growing component of imported parts. The growth area, computer and electronics, now has a major import component, probably well more than half. Motor vehicles are strong because of foreign company plants in the U.S. Even there, imported parts are making a significant contribution.

A category not shown separately is defense. Employment in defense industries is believed to represent about 15% of the manufacturing total. The only part of our manufacturing base defended by the Bush government was steel, an industry that staged a remarkable comeback in recent years. The right had a fit over Bush's temporary steel tariffs, but a little bit went a long way and steel was our strongest industry during the recent economic expansion.

These are durable categories and many nondurable are also declining. Plastics is considered nondurable and it continued to grow until peaking in 1999. Nondurable includes many categories that will remain domestic, but it too is suffering. Old standbys like paper are down and chemical is flat.

The recession of 2000-2003 was marked by a major move to outsourcing. The breakout of corporate profits in the following economic expansion was attributable to overseas earnings, as domestic profit growth fell below normal rates. More than half of IBM and GE's non-financial sales are now foreign and that is where their capital investment is going. Both were buying large quantities of their own stock, until the economy turned down.

For the purpose of evaluating the right wing, the question is, how much of this grim picture results from free market capitalism and halving the top income tax bracket? Although no exact measure is possible, the attitude of anything for a profit and to hell with the national interest had a lot to do with the present economic setback. The new group coming in following the right's disgrace has had to use extreme measures to find a way out of a jam that has been building for thirty years.

Although the dollar staged a big comeback as it was sought for liquidity during the worldwide financial crisis, the ongoing trade deficit means more trouble ahead. The massive quantity of dollars being shipped abroad accelerated with the financial rescue effort, the stimulus package, and the huge impending deficits. The dollar is in danger of being swamped by excessive supply, making it increasingly likely that the U.S. will pay the price in a lower standard of living. Pressures are already upon us in lower real incomes. The crisis based strength of the dollar adds to dammed up pressure that is likely to end in a run on the currency.

Evidence of the dollar's fate can be seen in export nations not buying U.S. assets or investing here to soak up surplus dollars, as the Japanese did twenty years ago. Despite pressure to buy U.S. assets with the huge supply of surplus dollars abroad, surprisingly little has been invested. Much is made of a few small deals, but there is a general understanding that our economy is not a good place for long term investment. Right wing economists like to say investment is pouring into the country, but it is merely surplus foreign dollars trying to protect their own markets or participate in our consumer market rather than productive investment. The preferred home for excess dollars is the safest refuge, U.S. Treasury bonds.

The mystery about our deteriorating economic condition is the absence of action to counter a trend that must end badly. In its peculiar self-justifying way, the right concocted the idea that the trade deficit was a sign of healthy consumer demand and economic strength. Rather than recognizing that a trade deficit can only lead to misfortune, the right made certain it would get worse by loading on a large fiscal deficit to soak up the excess dollars created by the import imbalance.

So far the most serious consequence of lost manufacturing has been reflected in declining incomes. On an individual basis, median income is believed to have peeked during the rise in inflation that began in 1973. With Reagan's arrival, unions were undermined and manufacturing began to decline. Individual incomes remained fairly flat during good economic times until 2000, when they declined again. From 1973 through 2008 median individual income is believed to have fallen about 15% despite longer hours and many holding two jobs.

The more widely available household figures reflect better results, boosted by growth in the number of two or more worker families.

Mean Household Income
Inflation adjusted (000)

	lowest 20%	21-40%	41-60	61-80	high 20%	top 5%
1970	$9,492	$25,713	$41,405	$58,365	$103,325	$158,593
1980	10,663	25,699	42,407	62,476	111,395	166,466
1990	11,020	27,728	45,800	69,052	134,006	213,390
2000	12,229	30,535	50,850	79,048	171,297	303,898
2007	11,551	29,442	49,968	79,111	167,971	287,191

Increase from

1970-80	12%	0%	2%	7%	8%	5%
1980-90	3	8	8	11	20	28
1990-00	11	10	11	14	28	42
2000-07	-6	-4	-2	0	-2	-5
1970-07	22	15	21	36	63	81
1990-07	5	6	9	15	25	35

The figures indicate growth in all categories until 2000. Since these are gross income figures, after the Reagan tax cuts the gains at the top were far greater than indicated here, but acceptable as long as the lower ranges also increased. 2000 was the peak year. Although all categories declined through 2004, just as the gains were smaller at the lower end on the upside, the losses were greater on the downside. Less income for the lower ranges was serious because they have less flexibility to adjust. The income squeeze since 2000 explains why the public did not think much of the Bush economic expansion.

The figures demonstrate mounting income disparity. After Reagan's election, gains went up steeply as income rose. In absolute terms, the gain in the lowest 20% from 1980 to 2007 was $888, while for the top 5% it was $120,725. The low 20% declined for five straight years beginning in 1999 and all groups fell from 2000 to 2007. In addition, the number of workers covered by company paid health insurance declined. Those choosing to remain insured suffered a severe hit to their spendable income as health insurance cost soared.

Many observers believe that inflation adjustment has been understated since hedonistic pricing, or odd weighting and allowance for improvements, began in the 1990s. With considerable discretion in the final computation, there is suspicion that the official figure has been politicized to the downside, with the added advantage of limiting growth in Social Security and other forms of inflation adjusted government payment. If so, the affect would be particularly telling for the bottom categories.

The 2000-2007 span was the first since the 1930s that household income declined for a full cycle, and it did so over all ranges (the highest category is skewered by the stock market payoffs in 2000 from cashing in on the high tech bubble). Incomes normally decline in recessions, then recover to new highs.

These figures do not reflect the giant gains for the top 1% and more so for the top one tenth of 1%. Free market capitalism is working as it always has: large gains for a few at the top and stagnation or decline for the majority. The great uplifting American economy has ceased to uplift for over half the population. There is still a good bit of movement up the income scale from initial employment, but that appears to be diminishing with the number going to college flattening and less opportunity for graduates.

More serious than the disparity is that income gains at the top have come from financial activities that were directly responsible for the declining incomes of the majority. Nations have experienced pain when those at the top received an unusually large share of total income and the situation in this country has become historically extreme.

The positive side is that a median income level of almost $50,000 reflects a prosperous country. In addition, the Bush tax cuts turned the income declines into slight gains for all except the lowest group. At $30,000 a well organized family can own a home, two cars, a television, and a personal computer, all items that have gone down in price. Most consumers are deprived only relative to those with two or three multi-million dollar homes with garages full of cars and a private jet. There is a squeeze, however, in items such as health insurance and the cost of college.

Favoritism to corporations and the rich was reflected in a major breakout of corporate earnings after 2002 exceeding any past level as a percentage of sales and return on investment, at the same time as employment growth was modest and incomes declined. Employment increased at only an average of 1.3% annually compared to a normal 3-4%. America remained the land of opportunity for a few at the top and for poor immigrants, but economic advancement became rarer.

Maintaining manufacturing would have been relatively easy, getting it back requires time and a painful adjustment. As a start the impulses that created the destruction should be reversed: hands off government policy that gave plunderers a free hand, the unsavory influence of corporate power over government, and the Reagan/Bush tax cuts to the highest bracket. Entrepreneurs and company builders should become wealthy, bloodsuckers should be restrained. The deserving get their payoff over many years in capital gains, the bloodsuckers get it quickly. CEO pay is not the free market at work, it reflects management control over the board of directors. By sharply increasing taxes on income over $1 million, eight digit corporate salaries and nine digit hedge fund manager and private equity partners would be curbed.

In 2008 the top tax bracket rate was 35% on income over $357,700. There is no reason to stop progression at this level. If the tax rate went up a modest 1% for each income increase of $200,000 over $1,000,000, a 50% rate would be reached at annual income of $4 million and the old pre-Reagan 70% at $8 million. I would keep going to 80%. CEOs taking annual compensation of $25 million, not an uncommon amount, would then pay almost $18 million in taxes. At that level they would think twice about being so generous with themselves, compensation should return to sensible amounts, and encouragement to destructive management decisions would be lessened. Gross corporate salaries, exit bonuses, option cash ins, insane sports hero earnings, over $100 million a year awards for hedge fund and private equity owners, would be rare if government got most of the money. A 20% long term capital gain tax rate, perhaps graded down for holding over five years, would then become meaningful and talented individuals might direct their efforts to building rather than tearing down. The financial system could return to long term growth oriented investment, to the benefit of the economy.

The trade deficit could also be attacked through tax rates. A zero tax rate on domestic manufactured products and a low cost single payer medical system that reduces a major business cost, plus penalties on added outsourcing, are the most apparent. The largest item in the trade deficit is oil. A major program of alternatives and encouraging development of domestic oil to eliminate imports should be a government priority.

17

Globalization

As the U.S. economy matured and the limits of size slowed opportunity for growth at home, corporations began to generate more capital than they could profitably employ.   One of the results was more mergers and acquisitions. Another response was looking abroad.   Foreign companies were bought to gain entry to new markets and overseas factories were established, as the largest companies had done years before.   Looking at business on a worldwide basis, American companies began to think about free trade.   Our companies thought of themselves as the best, so why not expand into worldwide markets.

This trend was reinforced by the Cold War concept of spreading democracy and the post Cold War position of sole superpower.   Americans were confident.   In a worldwide market, their companies had to be the winners.   Lower labor costs was an attraction to overseas expansion, but only a secondary consideration, as it was assumed that high productivity high paying jobs at home would increase from expanded worldwide markets. High labor content industry relocated to low labor cost countries would spread industrialization and generate added customers for advanced American made products.   Government assistance was enlisted, the position of trade representative became a cabinet post, and the new thrust became known as globalization.

Conceptually globalization is difficult to argue against.   Economists had long favored free trade.   Each nation would make what it could produce most advantageously and the world would be a low cost mutually supportive trading paradise.   Industry displaced at home would be on the lowest end of the productivity scale and capital coming out would be put to use at higher return. Economists and businessmen proclaiming free trade as America's gift to the world understood there was nothing altruistic about globalization. They saw greater profits for U.S. companies and as national policy it was conceived as furthering American dominance.

On the surface, outsourcing appears advantageous because goods are available at lower prices, often impressively lower, a boon to consumers. It also holds down inflation, allowing greater monetary stimulus to maintain growth, though recent data indicates that the crossover point from declining to rising prices on imports from China has been reached.

Transnational corporations benefiting from both sides of transactions were globalization's particular beneficiaries. Concentrated on profits, they had no interest in considering negative influences on the domestic economy. Like all developed capitalist nations, the United States had built its economy by protecting domestic markets and using government to support homegrown industry. Now in a state of supreme confidence, American corporations were willing to give up protection in exchange for opening up new markets. They were disregarding serious negatives.

1) Lack of consideration of the working class. One of the right's most distinctive characteristics is its disdain for labor. Unions are the enemy, to be attacked at any opportunity. Globalization allowed unions to be broken by sending work abroad. Displaced workers were not equipped for the higher paying service tasks substituted for industrial jobs, but the attitude of the right was tough luck. Blue collar workers would just have to upgrade their skills or be content with less income. Workers were not fellow Americans, they were a cost. If this attitude might be costly at the voting booth, the right had ameliorated the damage by appealing to race.

2) Failure to anticipate how rapidly foreign competition would produce the products and services we planned to sell abroad. Confidence about supremacy in high technology was at the heart of enthusiasm for globalization. Technology based industry would make up for losses in older industry. First mover advantage was seen as creating a lead that foreign rivals would not be able to overcome. That vision proved false. Innovative products quickly became commodities that could be produced more cheaply abroad. Perhaps the greatest upset to America's high technology future was internet connectivity, as it allowed a shift of knowledge based services to cheap foreign sources. Service jobs began to move out, including areas of presumed dominance, such as computer programming and software design. Technology companies, eager to take advantage of lower costs in India, Russia, and China, focused their capital spending abroad. Attracted by greater profitability in lower labor costs, corporations raced to destroy not just metal bending industry, but high technology as well.

3) Although our overall education levels are acceptable, at the high end they are not exceptional, so that our leading position in high technology products and services was due to an early start rather than an ongoing ability to maintain that advantage. Not only are many college students underemployed, the number with advanced degrees is falling short of other countries. The probable reason is less opportunity that leaves less incentive to improve education levels. Many business school graduates now become stock brokers, work that provides a rare opportunity to earn high income, but does not require a high level of education or contribute much to the economy.

4) Intensified worldwide competition forced domestic companies with no desire to move production abroad to do so anyway, hastening the decline in domestic manufacturing. So much industry has already moved, and the trend remains strong, that the battle is probably lost until there is a major readjustment. The likely outcome is a period of high inflation until the dollar is sufficiently adjusted in relationship to world currencies that the U.S. can compete. For Americans that means a reduction in their standard of living. A trend to lower real income has already begun, a harbinger what is on the way.

5) Other nations did not throw themselves into globalization with self-sacrificing enthusiasm. Honoring our corporations like no other nation took the form of allowing them a free hand, rather than recognizing how important they were to our economic health. Other countries made an effort to protect their manufacturing and will continue to do so. We have an opposite policy, chasing trade deals that send American industry and jobs abroad. The right defines national interest in terms of advancing the profits of multi-national corporations rather than health of the domestic economy. More than half of the non-oil trade deficit is reflected in production our own companies moved elsewhere. The policy works for companies and investors, if not for the nation.

According to the right, free trade is the new formula for growth, but competition seized the opening in giving away our advantages. Other nations laugh at laissez faire theory that leads to weak competition lacking a long term view and support from their government. Japan and Europe worked hard to keep manufacturing at home by identifying their strongest products and protecting their position. We look down on Europe and Japan because our growth has been faster, failing to note its dramatic slowing in recent years. Others have no desire for the kind of deficit based consumer borrowing that places our future on a dangerous footing. The U.S. consumer market is the one being exploited and that gives us advantages if we are willing to use them. Our industry should be seen as a national treasure, rather than an opportunity for the greedy to become extravagantly rich sending business overseas.

The Chinese are accomplishing the fastest economic growth in history on the backs of the American consumer. They are our major competitor, the odds on choice for world leadership during the first half, perhaps the first quarter, of the twenty-first century. The right gets steamed up about the threat they represent militarily, but the real war is economic. Merely by increasing their defense budget by 5-10%, in terms of our spending a tiny few billion dollars, China can induce us to spend four, five, or ten times as much. They may succeed where Reagan failed in bankrupting their chief rival.

Militarists viewing China as the ultimate target forget that it is already in position to deal us a deadly blow without firing a shot. Another ten years of growing trade imbalance and their internal market should be sufficiently large to absorb loss of U.S. customers, so that the dollar could be squeezed without serious consequences to their own economy. The steep drop in Chinese imports during the present recession has the effect of preparing them for the future. Resting on laissez faire theory, the U.S. forfeited the economic advantage. Those who would use arms to assert American power handed the future to our most likely rival.

6) Globalization worked because the United States carries large trade and fiscal deficits. The worldwide economy became dependent on U.S. households spending more than they earned, but we can not go on consuming our way out of economic slumps. As America cuts back, globalization is likely to unhinge. The day of reckoning is all the more likely as the immense quantity of dollars sloshing around the world translates into inflation. A healthy growing economy comes from productive capital investment, but in our current competitive position those investments are not going to be made.

7) Capital coming out of downsized and closed domestic industry was redirected in ways that were only marginally beneficial to the domestic economy. The theory of comparative advantage, the basis for enthusiasm about free trade, claims that losses from industry given up to foreign goods are more than made up by redirection of capital from low to higher return investment. The record of the last twenty years, however, demonstrates that the theory is not necessarily true for a mature economy. Rather than re-investing in ways that lifted the overall economy, most of the funds went into Wall Street speculation that benefited a few at the top of the income scale. The returns were higher, but the benefits narrowly directed and this was reflected in growing income disparity. The new condition allowed a few speculators to make incomes of previously unknown size, while the average American had to deal with a squeeze. The right wing and many economists claim that in the aggregate there is no evidence supporting the claim that globalization is not benefiting Americans. That maybe be true in the aggregate numbers that reflect the huge increase in wealth by a few at the top, but for the majority

of Americans globalization has worked against their interests. As a result, a growing number of economists are changing their minds about free trade.

Specific promises of free trade have not been fulfilled. Mexico did not thrive after NAFTA and become a customer for advanced goods. Instead, Mexicans seemed to feel the trade agreement was an invitation to enter the United States. Displaced American workers found jobs, but at lower pay.

Many observers of the business scene recognized that the economic slump of 2000-2003 was different from cyclical recessions of the past. It was not based on overproduction and excessive inventory, the traditional source, or excessive speculation in real estate as in 1990, but on a stock market bubble that generated over-investment in high technology goods and services. As high technology fled overseas and all forms of outsourcing increased, the right wing government of George W. Bush failed to recognize what was happening. Rather than reacting, they used the slump as an excuse for two more tax cuts, with the benefits going largely to those engaged in the activities that were weakening the economy. Eight more years passed of fading U.S. industry, while deficits piled up from the cuts and unnecessary wars. Not surprisingly, the economic structure broke down.

Controlling outsourcing would not have taken a lot of effort. Some industry would have been lost, but much could have been saved if national policy had been directed at preserving domestic manufacturing. Many outsourcing decisions were based on small margins that could have been offset with appeals to patriotism, by tax policy, reducing costs through a national health plan, government subsidies such as are used by other countries, or other similar means. The distinguishing feature is government activism directed at the goal of preserving and building American manufacturing and services. The right is unalterably opposed to such action. While selling the nation's industry down the drain, it was vigorously propagandizing the anti-government line.

Our economic well being cannot be sustained in the face of a $700 billion trade deficit. A favorable exchange rate against the Euro and strong economies abroad stimulated exports and the trade deficit came down slightly in 2007, but it is still far too high and American companies go on planning more moves overseas.

Globalization and outsourcing will end up harming the wealthy as the inflation that goes with a trade deficit, combined with the shortage of higher paying jobs, squeezes the overall economy and depresses the stock market. Outsourcing corporations are probably only temporary winners, for in time direct foreign competition will become more significant.

The U.S. likes to consider itself the engine of the world's economy, and it is, but not for the right reasons. We need for forget these kinds of conceits and recognize that our industrial decline must be arrested. Instead, the Bush people told others they should run their economies in the same delusional way we did. The trade deficit and absence of savings was blamed on "excessive" savings elsewhere, as if those with an excess of exports over imports and an inclination to save rather than spend were not managing their economy properly. For the first time, importing was claimed to be more favorable than exporting. By viewing ourselves as exceptions to the laws of economics and paying no attention to a strained financial condition and fading domestic industry, we were living in a dangerous state of denial.

The tax cuts, together with increases in military spending and no effort to control other costs, add up to foolish economic policy. Guided by right wing theory, the U.S. made all the classic economy ruining moves under the belief we were too powerful for them to pertain to us. Virtually every country that propelled itself to the leading position among nations fell from excessive military spending and waging wars as an excuse for increasing it further. Specifically, the Roman Empire fell from three principle causes: 1) a decline in moral values, most importantly reflected in an inability to govern itself in a civil and publicly spirited manner (similar to the poisonous political atmosphere created by the overbearing right wing), 2) an over-extended military stretched thin from excessively broad commitments, and 3) fiscal irresponsibility.

The first two Roman failings are clearly evident in the U.S. The third can be seen in lower taxes to gain favor with voters and fatten the rich, while neglecting deficits and printing money to make up the shortage. Another destructive device is to beguile the public with false information so they will not recognize declining conditions. Rather than taking steps to meet our challenges, economic difficulties arising from implementation of right wing policy were used as excuses for more tax cuts. When crackpot theorists with selfish motivations are in control, misfortune is at hand.

Nothing would be more strengthening for Americans and bring about a break from self-absorption than a sweeping national project that put excess investment capital to use in this country. The project should benefit the domestic economy and provide new forms of investment opportunity and jobs. It should counter terrorism, while putting Americans in the mood for sacrifice. That project is ending dependence on imported oil through a ten year program to reduce usage by at least 50%. It could be done through the following:

- Get gas guzzlers off the street with subsidies to the poor to buy hybrids and other experimental cars, while imposing tax penalties on buyers of SUVs and other heavy automobiles.

- A major increase in minimum automobile mileage to at least forty miles per gallon.
- Save our floundering automobile companies by making them the outlet for subsidized projects to develop better hybrids and super light vehicles using advanced materials.
- Increase the federal gasoline tax by at least 50 cents a gallon, better yet by $1, to discourage usage, encourage alternative programs relative to automobiles, and provide funding. Better yet, use a high guaranteed minimum price, with government getting anything over the world price, so that assured high prices encourage development of alternatives.
- Programs to support biomass fuels, coal conversion and oil shale development, along with a necessary parallel project to counter air pollution.
- Encourage greater usage of natural gas, now in surplus from new domestic discoveries.
- Encourage nuclear power plants in the form of sites, standardized design to reduce costs and simplify safety standards.
- Strive to maintain and hopefully increase domestic oil production by opening up offshore reserves, the Arctic National Wildlife Refuge, and National Petroleum Reserve. Objections to such drilling could be overcome as part of a national emergency effort at self-sufficiency. Development of domestic reserves could be supported through the absence of taxes (exploration and development companies do not pay much income tax anyway as long as they actively pursue added reserves), price guarantees, or tariffs on imports that have the effect of subsidizing price. Secondary recovery projects would also be more vigorously pursued with guaranteed pricing. If usage can be halved, added reserves might allow self-sufficiency (though, of course, only temporarily).
- Other forms of conservation, such as more energy efficient appliances and building insulation.
- Government funding of research into more exotic forms of energy.

Part of the aim is countering terrorism by removing dependence on Middle East oil, permitting a benevolent foreign policy and no troops in the area, assuaging hatred of the United States. We must get out of Iraq and Afghanistan, both are dead ends. The only reason for staying is access to oil, so eliminate that need. In addition to allowing major cuts in military spending, a substantial portion of the trade deficit would be eliminated.

America would be leading as it should, by example rather than force, re-establishing its influence on the rest of the world.

Greatly reduced U.S. demand would lower the cost of oil, giving other countries an economic advantage that could be offset in part by eliminating the threat to world peace from the coming shortage of oil. Higher cost energy can be offset in cutting pork and the military, raising tax rates on the highest bracket, and a gasoline tax.

18

Adding Up the Score

To the right's way of thinking, the economy of 2003-2007 could not have been better. Corporate profits doubled the previous peak and profit margins reached the highest ever level. Wall Street had discovered that the securitized mortgage market generated a flood of fees when conducted in high volume. Below the surface, all was not well. Economic growth was slow, with GDP and job gains the lowest for any advance since the 1930s. The strong profit numbers came from outsourcing and therefore benefited stockholders rather than the domestic economy. Private equity capital transactions picked up because American companies were not reinvesting in growth and became cash cows that appeared able to support large amounts of debt. The strongest area of the economy was luxury goods and real estate in exclusive areas.

Both the good and the bad are explained by the influence on the economy of the right wing revolution. Corporate profits came from less regulation and moving operations overseas. Lower top bracket taxes unleashed a feeding frenzy for the rich, while the large majority barely saw an increase in income from recession lows. The mortgage boom was fueled by over-valuation, over-lending, and high fees.

The trends that played out so unfavorably in the first decade of the twenty-first century had their origin in the ascendancy of Ronald Reagan. The right remained in essential control until the election of Barack Obama in 2008, with modest limitations during the Clinton years. Contrary to conservative promises, growth slowed and became dependent on encouraging consumers to spend beyond their means, assisted by fiscal deficits. The figures on the following page indicate the problem. The real deficit (excluding the Social

Federal Finances (billions of $)

	Federal Deficit		off budget		Overhead	Price	Trade
	Inc. SS	Ex-SS	surplus	Defense	& Pork	Index	Balance
1964	-5.9	-6.5	0.6	54.8	22.6	1.3	6.0
1965	-1.4	-1.6	0.2	50.6	25.0	1.6	4.7
1966	-3.7	-3.1	-0.6	58.1	28.5	2.9	2.9
1967	-8.6	-12.7	4.0	71.4	32.1	3.1	2.6
1968	-25.2	-27.7	2.8	81.9	35.1	4.2	0.2
1969	3.2	-0.5	3.7	82.5	32.6	5.5	0.1
1970	-2.8	-8.7	5.9	81.7	37.2	5.7	2.3
1971	-23.0	-26.1	3.0	78.9	40.0	4.4	-1.3
1972	-23.4	-26.1	2.7	79.2	47.3	3.2	-5.4
1973	-14.9	-15.2	0.3	76.7	52.8	6.2	1.9
1974	-6.1	-7.2	1.1	79.3	52.9	11.0	-4.3
1975	-53.2	-54.1	0.9	85.5	74.8	9.1	12.4
1976	-73.7	-69.4	-4.3	89.6	82.7	5.8	-6.1
1977	-53.7	-49.9	-3.7	97.2	93.0	6.5	-27.2
1978	-59.2	-55.4	-3.8	104.5	114.7	7.6	-29.8
1979	-40.7	-39.6	-1.1	116.3	120.2	11.3	-24.6
1980	-73.8	-73.1	-0.7	134.0	131.3	13.5	-19.4
1981	-79.0	-73.9	-5.1	157.5	133.0	10.3	-16.2
1982	-128.0	-120.6	-7.4	185.3	125.0	6.2	-24.2
1983	-207.8	-207.7	-0.1	209.9	121.8	3.2	-57.8
1984	-185.4	-185.3	-0.1	227.4	117.9	4.3	-109.1
1985	-212.3	-221.5	9.2	252.7	131.0	3.6	-121.9
1986	-221.2	-237.9	16.7	273.4	141.4	1.9	-138.5
1987	-149.7	-168.4	18.6	282.0	125.3	3.6	-151.7
1988	-155.2	-192.3	37.1	290.4	138.7	4.1	-114.6
1989	-152.5	-205.4	52.8	303.6	158.2	4.8	-93.1
1990	-221.2	-277.7	56.6	299.3	202.6	5.4	-80.9
1991	-269.3	-321.5	52.2	273.3	223.7	4.2	-31.2
1992	-290.4	-340.4	50.1	298.4	172.2	3.0	-39.2
1993	-255.1	-300.4	45.3	291.1	158.0	3.0	-70.3
1994	-203.3	-258.9	55.7	281.6	171.7	2.6	-98.5
1995	-164.0	-226.4	62.4	272.1	160.3	2.8	-96.4
1996	-107.5	-174.1	66.6	265.2	167.3	3.0	-104.1
1997	-22.0	-103.3	81.4	270.5	157.5	2.3	-107.9
1998	69.2	-30.0	99.2	268.5	188.8	1.6	-164.6
1999	125.5	1.9	123.7	274.8	218.1	2.2	-263.3
2000	236.2	86.3	149.8	294.4	239.8	3.4	-377.6
2001	128.2	-32.5	160.7	304.8	243.3	2.8	-362.8
2002	-157.8	-317.5	159.7	348.5	273.2	1.6	-421.1
2003	-377.6	-538.4	160.8	404.8	302.5	1.9	-494.9
2004	-412.7	-568.0	155.2	455.8	311.3	3.3	-611.3
2005	-318.3	-493.6	175.3	495.3	339.9	3.4	-716.7
2006	-248.2	-434.5	186.3	521.8	393.8	2.5	-764.0
2007	162.0	-343.5	181.5	552.6	318.1	4.1	-700.3
2008	454.8	639.0	184.2	624.1	355.7	1.2	-700.0

Security surplus) topped $100 billion for the first time only after Reagan was elected, subsequently reaching a high of $340 billion in 1992. After being steadily reduced and brought to surplus under Clinton, the deficit burst to a high of $568 billion in 2004. Although it fell to "only" $343 billion in 2007, another sharp jumped occurred in 2008 and the deficit will go over $1 trillion in 2009.

Three reasons are behind the increase: 1) insufficient taxation, 2) excessive defense spending, 3) a significant increase in other government expenses.

One of the traditional hallmarks of conservatism was a balanced budget. Despite the talk of less government, the figures reveal the fiscal indulgence of the present form of reactionary conservatism. Tax cuts always took precedence and maintaining itself in power required vast spending on the military and on pork. When they came fully into power for the second time with George W. Bush, financial discipline was completely lost. The budgetary shortfall involved a lot more than the war on terror, a puny affair compared to Vietnam and in any event discretionary. The bona fide deficit in 2008 (excluding the Social Security surplus) almost doubled the post-Reagan peak. Overhead and pork increased from $157 billion in 1997 to $394 billion in 2006.

The trade deficit, never as high as $200 billion prior to 1999, soared to $764 billion in 2006. Imports, less than $50 billion in 1971, went over $1.9 trillion in 2007. Except for growing exports, a meaningful portion arms related, the trade deficit would have been worse. The reported federal deficit declined in 2007 to $162 billion ($343 billion without entitlement surpluses), as strong profits raised corporate tax collections and incomes at the highest level, but this was under peak economic conditions when something close to breakeven is the normal expectation.

Russia was less a threat in 1981 than in 1964, yet defense spending soared from $55 billion to over $300 billion under Reagan. On an inflation adjusted basis, defense spending in 1964, when the Cold War was in full bloom and Vietnam was gearing up, was $337 billion compared to over $600 billion in 2008. Considering the international tension of the 1960s, when Russia was a threat, the intercontinental ballistic missile race was on, and we were engaged in a bigger war than Iraq, the increase in defense spending was inexcusable.

Aside from defense, the other area of excessive spending is grouped under the heading overhead and pork. A steady climb in this category was under way when Reagan arrived as the champion of less government. It was here that the anti-government position was supposed to pay off. Reagan stopped the increase and reduced the total, but as we have seen, only temporarily and by far less than needed to control the deficit. The effort to bring down the deficit under Bush I and Clinton led to a meaningful reduction between 1991 and 1997, though the numbers were still high in relationship to the past.

Wasteful spending had become habit. The Clinton surplus led to a breakdown of restraint beginning in 1998 and the pick up under Bush II was appalling. The figures since 1984 suggest one paramount fact, the failure of the right to deliver on its promise of less government.

Loss of control over spending resulted from members of Congress buying re-election through bestowing gifts on their home districts. Pork, or spending attached to otherwise concerned bills, larded most of what came out of Congress. Each year's budgetary starting point was last year's fat filled level and effort was directed at keeping the increase to some low sounding percentage of that already bloated amount. The process was worse than shown in the overhead category, for defense was the biggest offender. Warships were built just to keep shipyards working in the states of influential senators, scores of unnecessary bases were maintained, and exotic projects of little practicality were supported. Controlling the budget requires strong leadership, something the right always lacked.

In order to blame entitlements rather than military and pork spending for deficits, annual government spending is presented in a manner that is essentially fictitious. Entitlements are included as standard outlays, though they are separately funded and operate at a surplus. A more realistic picture is as follows:

Federal Outlays	2008	
Total Outlays	$2,979 billion	
Medicare	391	
Social Security	617	
Net Outlays	1,971	
Defense	624	32%
Other	1,347	68

The figure for defense does not include $85 billion for veterans benefits, an amount that rose greatly as a result of Bush wars.

The data suggests the opportunity for hundreds of billions in cuts with a modest degree of discipline, particularly in defense. Pulling back defense by $100 billion in the 1990s would have provided ample funds for supporting domestic industry, allowing dependence on imports to be avoided. The Russian economy moved ahead strongly once it was freed of the military burden. China, our most likely challenger, staked its future on the economy rather than arms. They were happy to have us forfeit the economic war by spending on military paraphernalia that was never likely to be used. While the right fussed about its growing defense spending, China was getting into position to pressure our economy and achieve worldwide supremacy without firing a shot.

The war on terror is not World War III. The defining challenge of our generation is a deeply troubled economy, not Muslim jihad. Moslem terrorists are not intent on the destruction of western civilization, nor are they a totalitarian military power out to conquer the world. Lacking the least semblance of unity and organization, there is no chance of a mighty oil financed caliphate defeating the Christian west. Moslems are more intent on killing one another than killing Americans. Their ranks include crazy fanatics, but the violent leaders do not have much of a following. That makes them tough to get at, but limits their ability to strike. We must concentrate on eliminating the extremists and engaging internationally, not run around threatening anyone getting in our way.

The military spending "requirements" bandied about by The Wall Street Journal editorial page and other right wing publications are outrageous. They claim that at a minimum we should be spending 6% of GDP on defense, with the implication that 10% is fine and easily affordable. That would have amounted to $865 billion in 2008, almost 200% of the present non-war budget, when spending is already more than the rest of the world combined and ten times the Chinese. We spent well more than 10% of GDP during World War II and 9% in 1962, but the latter figure is accounted for by the nuclear build up associated with intercontinental ballistic missiles. These unavoidable costs were paid for by much higher tax rates. In trying to justify high spending, the only excuse the right can find is that 6% was Reagan's average.

Relating defense spending to past levels of GDP overlooks that our economy is now a massive consumer spending machine with defense requirements that bear no relationship to the past. 6% of GDP would make defense 40% of government spending, excluding self-funding entitlements. If the Soviet Union spent about 15% of GDP on defense, that was related to a stripped down dying economy. The spendthrift Pentagon would have trouble spending $865 billion without a war. As it is, the Pentagon is complaining about too many politically oriented make work projects.

How conservatives can make such proposals and at the same time push for tax cuts reflects the utter illogic of their position. The right wing program adds up to fiscally irresponsible militarism unbefitting of the great democracy. For Russia after centuries of Czarist rule and post World War I wrecked Germany and Italy, plunging off in an ultra conservative direction was understandable, but why would the U.S. want to emulate them?

The answer to that puzzling question is that the goal of the right was to reverse progressivism and democracy in favor of an old world class society of haves and have nots. If they did not go so far as the fascism of Hitler and Mussolini, they hoped for a kind of totalitarian capitalism. That goal could be realized only by suppressing the democratic principles on which this country was built. Buckley and Goldwater were patriots, but the movement they got under way evolved into an alliance of callous plutocracy and a jungle liberty that took form not in the Elysian Fields of freedom, but in a hellish movement of the antis: anti-civil rights, anti-foreign, anti-public education, anti-gay, anti-minority, anti-liberal, anti-government, and anti-tax.

19

Religion

THE MOST UNEXPECTED RIGHT WING feat was attracting politically oriented religious elements. Focus on money and absence of concern for the common man would seem to place the religious out of reach, but the right was conscious of the need for just this kind of help. In trying to attract religious support, the strategy was to package their program in simplistic moralistic terms that would appeal to religiously inclined Americans sufficiently to induce them to relinquish their critical facilities. The opening was found in thriving fundamentalist and evangelical forms of Christianity. The breakthrough occasion was the 1973 Supreme Court decision legalizing abortion.

The right's lack of interest in Christian virtue probably contributed to the deftness of its moves. They drove beyond abortion to seize the moral high ground, at the same time obscuring from the religiously inclined that they were the party of wealth, godless big corporations, and militarists. A group doing its best to suppress social services for the less well off, pursuing profit as life's ultimate goal, and asserting American hegemony with unprovoked war, staked out the territory and defended it by tagging liberals as responsible for abortion, absence of prayer in schools, and the general secularization of society.

Those aligned with Enron, Halliburton, fake accounting, option stealing, silly IPOs, and the whole crazy spectrum of Wall Street bilge, had no business claiming the moral high ground, but that is exactly what they did. Liberals were not on the side of Christianity and right wing money grubbers were. Democrats, clinging to separation of church and state, let them get away with it by not defending the territory that was their birthright. Only the exaggerated self-righteousness of George W. Bush and an avalanche of favoritism to the wealthy drove them to finally fighting back.

Since the intense self-interest of the right goes against Christian principle, assumption of the religious mantle by those supporting the haves and casting the have nots adrift was a phenomenal feat. It was accomplished by attracting prominent right wing religious spokesmen, particularly those with a keen interest in money and power as reflected in leading profitable organizations. These religious leaders had a compulsive self-righteousness that left them blind to doubt, their narcissistic self regard requiring no explanation or justification. They manipulated the flock, expecting conformity while teaching intolerance.

Neither Reagan nor father Bush was particularly religious, though Carter had taught them the importance of the religion vote. Reagan bought in on abortion, Bush senior was silent. Young Bush was different. After his religious awakening in 1986, he became his father's point man with religious groups in the 1988 campaign, groups that were to become an important element in his own rise. He talked the lingo with an evangelical tone, regularly referring to Christ as his inspiration. As a result, religious sects voted overwhelmingly for him in 2000 and 2004 and bear considerable responsibility for his disastrous presidency. Bush so thoroughly captured religiously oriented voters that neither of his opponents for the presidency dared to point out that his religion was fuzzy, aristocratic, and not particularly Christian.

While I have suggested that the right simply went after these voters and Democrats did not, there was more to it than that. Although religiously oriented groups represented a significant portion of the original settlers, religion had not been an important factor in politics. As growing numbers flocked to the more emotive forms of Christianity in reaction to insecurity, materialism, and preoccupation with sex, an opportunity was created. Evangelical Christians increased greatly in number, while other forms of Christianity declined. While extreme fundamentalist views attracted the most attention, the majority of the religious element was more properly identified as evangelical. They are more tolerant, cheerier, and open to social action to improve human welfare. For them the Iraq War and rising wealth gap were eye openers and the Republican hold over them slipped in 2008.

Religious groups attracted to right wing politics often do not follow traditional Christianity. They emphasize worldly social matters such as abortion, pornography, and gay marriage, whereas the Bible is focused on compassion, tolerance, helping the poor, and generosity toward the afflicted. Non-evangelical Christianity is less about performing rituals as the price of a ticket to heaven than living an honorable life.

The political opportunity for the right arose from evangelical Christianity being less about traditional Christian values and more about man as a sinner. Mystical beliefs such as an apocalyptic Armageddon and a violent end of the world during a second coming created the kind of fearful atmosphere the right knew how to exploit. Dramatic forms of religion are attractive to those in despair, as their persecutions are sanctified and hope is gained of release from their fears. When the world ends, only Christians delivering themselves to Christ in ways defined by fundamentalist churches will go to heaven. Normal Christians, Muslims, Hindus, Jews, or other faiths need not apply.

Evangelical groups seeing man as an imperfect sinner find it easy to embrace doubt about government. Liberal hopes for improving mankind through governmental services are seen as false, for only the church can provide succor. Thinking this way can create an atmosphere where hostility can be built to ideas such as world order based on secular morality and global peacekeeping institutions such as the UN. Dealing in absolutes leads to thinking that any cooperation with oppressive governments is immoral. The harshest view of the Kremlin was easily sold. Likewise with terrorists. As a result, evangelicals were easy marks for the right's militarism.

The best known of the religious leaders were Jerry Falwell and Pat Robertson, televangelists who turned religion into a financial bonanza. They had something in common with the right, admiration for wealth. Both were wooed by Paul Weyrich, one of the godfathers of the right wing, a great organizer and idea man. He admired hardball methods and taught them how to politicize religion by tying together such themes as abortion, anti-gay, and civil rights.

In 1979 Falwell and Weyrich started the Moral Majority, devoted to the union of Christianity and right wing doctrine. Falwell became a leading television spokesman for the right, skillfully couching the ideology in religion. Corrupted by financial and political success, he became a kind of cartoon character for the right wing religious movement. His extreme partisanship was expressed in a scurrilous and mostly fictitious book on Bill Clinton.

Pat Robertson was more effective politically. In 1989 he began working with Ralph Reed, a forceful political organizer and right wing fanatic. They started the Christian Coalition, devoted to infiltrating the political system at the grass roots and tying religion to conservatism. Both Falwell and Robertson treated liberals as the anti-Christ. All the troubles of the world were caused by the evil Clinton. George W. Bush, on the other hand, was the messiah.

The right was Machiavellian with regard to religion, using its emotional impact to attract voters in order to get by with policies lacking in Christianity. Voting based on abortion and gays, with little reference to economics or foreign relations, or assistance to the less fortunate, was bound to provide an opening for opportunists. At the height of the right's power, one hundred and thirty members of the House of Representatives claimed to be born again Christians. Without speculating on how many were political opportunists, the number speaks to the effectiveness of the religious line in the political field. Many genuinely religious people never seemed to understand they were being used. They overlooked that Christ was unquestionably a liberal, the polar opposite of a right winger.

The unscrupulous among those identifying with religion regularly referred to their religious virtue, at the same time following a straight right wing party line notable for its absence of Christian values. Religious hypocrites among preachers could be spotted by behavior that was uncompromising, threatening, and dictatorial. These doubtful characters tended to be outspoken against homosexuality and gay marriage, as well as liberalism.

As the politicized religious movement worked out for George W. Bush, its drawbacks for a president stood out. Bush's tying his star to it was an early warning that he would be a hapless president. Separation of church and state is central to our government and one of the wisest moves of the founders. Bush was high in the polls for a long time because too many people cared more about keeping gays from marrying than preventing wars and making the economy a play toy for the rich.

Religion directed Bush into many of his worst mistakes, notably an obsession with making policy in terms of what he perceived as good and evil. The absence of an intelligent approach to terrorism and study of potential problems in Iraq was in part the result of blind moral certainty that our use of military power was somehow divinely inspired. They could not recognize behaving similarly to unprincipled aggressors of the past. The warmongers, Cheney, Rumsfeld, and Wolfowitz, were able to take advantage of a Bush thinking of himself as a crusader. Religion also sustained him in not making corrections as disasters piled up. If he had taken religion out of the equation and looked at Iraq from a practical perspective, he might have been rescued from making such a grievous misstep. Or, if he had been genuinely Christian, Iraq would never have been invaded.

What the right does, as distinguished from what it says, demonstrates a lack of interest in both loving Christianity and the high principles of those who started the nation. For the right, religion is about winning votes, not responding to the wishes of its religious following. Bush, their great hope, was so overwhelmed with larger considerations that he failed to deliver for them. The faith based charity effort was used for voter recruitment by staging local rallies in key areas of swing states. Abortion was exploited, the problem never dealt with. The right accomplished another exploitation of poor and middle class whites through preaching anti-liberalism and anti-government side by side with religion.

Although the leadership had no interest in religion except as a political tool, President Bush claimed to be a born again devotee. His actions as chief executive, however, bring the genuineness into question. The original attempt to picture him as a compassionate conservative was drawn from his father, his own much advertised compassion was hard to find.

The teachings of Jesus were never apparent in what Bush did. His looseness with the truth, emphasis on tax breaks for the rich, threatening foreigners, preemptive wars, encouraging torture, and enthusiastically embracing the death penalty, were the direct opposite of Christian principles. Where was Christianity in lack of concern for the poor or lies about the environment? Those who play to the interests of big corporations fail the test of Christianity. When asked if he slept well amidst the chaos brought to Iraq and to his country as a consequence of preemptive invasion, Bush said yes, that it did not bother him in the least. Based on what we saw of him, this could be braggadocio, but that it might be true was all the more shocking.

If Bush was our divinely anointed leader, then God had dictated the sapping of our financial strength, perhaps with the goal of making us humble, and our loss of international prestige, perhaps as a prelude to becoming a more thoughtful peacemaker. Did God dictate that we invade other countries at will, kill innocent civilians in uncounted numbers, and brutalize prisoners? The evidence suggests that Bush worshiped some pagan idol, perhaps the god of arrogant pride, not the Christian God.

Although Bush appeared unaware that success of the right wing movement was dependent on bigotry, as a politically focused man, it would have been hard for him not to be. He worked closely with Lee Atwater on his father's 1988 campaign and Atwater is known to have had a comprehensive understanding of the subject.

His actions told the real story, that Bush's religion had little to do with Christian theology. His faith was something he used as a crutch to deliver himself from alcoholism. The utilitarian purpose may have led to interpreting the Bible in terms of thoughts that appealed to him personally, rather than those representative of Christian thinking. This selective approach was evident in use of Biblical quotes out of context or inserting Biblical words into political statements that did not fit. Another habit was to replace references to God or Jesus with the word America to play on the idea we were the chosen nation.

Another suggestion about Bush's religion was that instead of using the Bible, he relied on selected interpretative works. One of these has been identified as Oswald Chambers, "My Utmost for His Highest". Chambers claims that absolute surrender to God results in divine inspiration. For a man like Bush who resisted thinking things through, the idea that inspiration was superior to thoughtful consideration had the strongest appeal. His hunches were inspired, a thought further reinforced by Chambers idea that reflection actually gets in the way of divine inspiration.

Chambers goes on to say that troubles along the way do not indicate that the inspiration was wrong. Thus, true believers should never doubt regardless of contrary evidence. This helps explain Bush's never change/never in doubt mode that plagued his presidency. That he could carry through so blithely on Iraq with the blood of thousands of Americans on his hands and placing the nation in an awkward position is partly explained by these abnormal religious beliefs. While his religion may seem phony to many, those claiming it is genuine may have a point. The truth about Bush's religion probably lies in a combination of Machiavellian politician, disinterest in genuine Christian doctrine, a snobbish perspective, and the need to protect his conscience.

Bush's blatant favoritism to the rich and the Iraq disaster left the Christian right becalmed. As Iraq unfolded and vulgar displays of wealth opened eyes to favoritism to the rich, the religious following began to notice that the anti-government crusade was phony and the right had done almost nothing for them. Evangelicals renewed their interest in the teachings of Jesus and took a less negative attitude.

As businessmen took control of American politics, their own moral code was going down the drain. Corporate management was enriching itself through false accounting, stock promotion, and the elimination of whole industries, in addition to gaining payoffs from Washington at the expense of the financial health of the country. Although in command of the high ground, the right's moral position was weak on all issues with the exception of abortion, which they cared nothing about other than its political impact.

On increasingly shaky ground with regard to religion, the economic collapse may have ended the attachment of many religious elements to the right. The gross unfairness of right wing economic policy stood out when it ended in catastrophe. Liberals began to grasp that common decency was their issue and that in a moral world of truth, they held all the cards. Peace and social justice were moral values on a higher level than abortion and gay marriage. Liberals finally learned how to gain support from erosion of middle and lower class incomes. Helping the poor began to be reinstated as the highest Christian value. Despoiling the environment to serve the interests of the right's corporate contributors was a sin. A foreign policy that made enemies instead of friends, an exaggerated terrorist threat that shielded immoral aggression and mistreatment of prisoners, over 4,000 American lives wasted and many more terribly scarred in a mistaken venue, and God knows how many Iraqis, were moral issues reflecting badly on the right wing. The message finally got out. Basic Christian values made a comeback.

20

Right Wing Foreign Policy: Marketing Fear

TRIUMPHANT EUPHORIA AT THE END of World War II soon gave way to dread about the U.S.S.R. A combination of factors intensified that fear. Osama bin Laden and Saddam Hussein were saints compared to Joseph Stalin, who assassinated anyone hinted at being a rival and put to death an estimated 20 million of his own people. Returning prisoners of war were sent to Siberia for not having fought to death. Unlike Saddam and Osama bin Laden's weak forces, Stalin commanded the most powerful army in the world. World II was an allied victory, but Russia's contribution far exceeded the others. While a few boastful American generals spoke of taking them on, wiser heads wanted no part of such an engagement.

Because of the Soviet Union's great sacrifices, the western allies were accommodating to Stalin as the war drew to a close. At conferences late in the war the leaders agreed that the Eastern European countries overrun while defeating Hitler would remain in the Russian sphere of influence. Although they did not annex the territory, harsh communist rule was imposed and the beginning of the Cold War was expressed in Churchill's famous Iron Curtain speech only ten months after the war's end.

At first the menace was offset by our sole possession of the atomic bomb, but in 1949, years ahead of expectation, the Russians had the bomb and shortly thereafter a bomber thought to be capable of reaching the United States. They were less than a year behind in testing a hydrogen bomb. In 1949 China fell to the communists. Although Mao was at odds with Stalin and the Kremlin provided little help in the civil war, Americans thought of communist countries as monolithic. Addition of the world's most populous country to the communist camp was alarming.

In 1950 the Korean War began. Thanks to the common sense of China, the Soviets, and Truman's resistance to reactionary Republican efforts to start World War III, Korea ended up demonstrating the futility of full scale conventional warfare. Although the Russians never participated in Korea, the U.S. persisted in believing they were behind both it and later Vietnam. Nuclear intercontinental ballistic missiles soon added to the pressure by casting the shadow of mutual destruction.

Russia's centuries old desire for an outlet to the Mediterranean Sea was reflected in communist efforts to take over Greece and Turkey after the war. This was Great Britain's sphere of influence and in 1947 they balked at the cost of holding off Greek communists. When the U.S. stepped in, the Russians stepped back, as they had earlier in seeking a naval base near the Bosporus and withdrawing from Iran. Other than maintaining control over the Iron Curtain countries, they did not pursue conquest. Official American policy since adoption of NSC-68, however, remained that the Soviets were out to conquer the world.

Magnifying war fears was the political threat of communism, a doctrine that had spread rapidly during the depression. France had a communist premier in the 1930s and after the war the Reds almost won elections in France and Italy. Communism aimed at the foundation of western life. Enforced equality was terrifying to capitalists. Religion was also a target. For those who lived through this period, the fuss about terrorists after 9/11 seemed ridiculously overblown.

U.S. Cold War strategy was consistently marred by imagining the worst. NSC-68 made a doomsday attitude toward the Soviet Union official policy. This stance intensified their suspicion of our intentions. In reality, the Soviets had internal problems and the international communist movement was never purely Russian. Communism was to prove an impractical utopian dream. As practiced in the Soviet Union it was a bust. Nevertheless, the Kremlin remained devoted to the doctrine and we associated that devotion with a desire for military conquest. Never mind that the difference between annexation and satellite status signified caution on their part. If until Reagan the Soviet Union spent more than we did on arms, that reflected fear of western attack, which our own actions encouraged, and the fact that internally they were a partial police state.

Although Truman moved to hold off the Russians militarily, he wisely emphasized resisting communism through rebuilding economies. The Marshall Plan was the most successful of all anti-Soviet moves. Eisenhower continued to stress the economic angle, while concentrating militarily on deployment of nuclear weapons. During these years of maximum threat, presidents recognized that nuclear bombs made war unlikely.

The enemy's looming presence in Eastern Europe was threatening, but they never attempted to expand and satellites began breaking away as early as 1948 in the case of Yugoslavia. China was never under Russian sway. Stalin's military thinking, going all the way back to the 1939 pact with Hitler over Poland, had always been based on building a buffer against the west rather than territorial expansion. He saw himself surrounded by capitalist nations eager to wipe him out. Stalin was naturally paranoid about Germany, imagining our turning a rebuilt Germany back upon him. The NATO build up that began 1949 was defensive in our terms, but to Stalin and his successors it was an offensive threat.

Stalin's death in 1953 might have been an occasion to reduce tensions and his successor, Malenkov, did make an effort. Recognizing that the Soviet Union's substantial defense spending would have been better directed toward the domestic economy, Malenkov and his successors probed for diplomatic openings for mutually downsized armaments. By this time, however, Americans were convinced of the Kremlin's evil nature and NSC-68 was official policy. Until Nixon the overtures were refused.

This is not to say the Russians were innocent bystanders. The Berlin Blockade of 1948, a reaction to setting up the West German nation, was nerve racking. Stalin could have kept North Korea's Kim Il Sung from invading South Korea. Nikita Khrushchev was a loose cannon who sent missiles into Cuba. Still, as the years passed, the U.S. was the more aggressive party. This was probably a wise course, as our economy could absorb its defense burden more easily than the Russians. Through much of the Cold War we were spending only about 5% of GDP on defense, while the smaller Soviet economy was absorbing costs believed to be on the order of 15%. Giving them no rest helped with the destruction of their economy.

An official policy of always thinking the worst of the Soviets opened up opportunity for extremists. The John Birch Society saw any exchange with the Russians as a form of treason, as if communism was a communicable disease. Any thought of negotiation was equated with the dreadful memory of pre-World War II, appeasement. As the threat worsened with introduction of nuclear intercontinental ballistic missiles, the newly organized right wing made an extremist view of the Soviet Union its principle means of building support.

A distinction was never made between the political effort to spread communism and military conquest, though in many cases communists were supporting popular uprisings against oppressive rulers backed by the U.S. A socialist rebellion anywhere in the world was seen as a form of Russian invasion. Fearmongers sold the idea that compromise with the Kremlin was impossible and that a war for domination of the world was unavoidable. We now know they were wrong, but with the public attuned to thinking the worst, the purveyors of doom found an audience.

Following the frantically reactive Truman years, relative calm prevailed under Eisenhower. History has rendered Truman a near-great president and Eisenhower a mediocrity, but the former's reputation is based on responding to mistakes and the latter's to a judicious approach to problems that produced a dull orderliness. Eisenhower recognized that military confrontation was unlikely because of the futility of land warfare in the nuclear age. Despite being a general, he believed in the American non-military tradition and the containment concept of resisting communism through advancing capitalism. Eisenhower was the only president who thoroughly understood that containment was less a military than an economic concept. Believing that capitalism would triumph, he reduced defense spending following the Korean War and balanced the budget, with defense concentrated on nuclear.

Eisenhower, and all of his successors until Reagan, recognized that a large defense budget was bad economics and the threat was probably overdone (Reagan agreed on that point). On the other hand, the public always reacted to the menace position. Kissinger was particularly effective blaming the Soviets when he messed up a Middle East negotiation or failed to settle Vietnam. It was always good politics to take the dimmest view of the Kremlin's intentions. All Cold War presidents recognized that nuclear arsenals made war with the Soviet Union unlikely, but only Eisenhower was strong enough politically to operate on that assumption. The war gang in Congress had a big following and a large segment of the public fell for the idea that ultimately war was unavoidable.

Still, the course chosen by all presidents until Reagan was restrained defense spending, except during the Vietnam folly. When Reagan tripled defense spending, no use of the arms was anticipated, rather it was a deliberate attempt to create an arms race as a strategy for pushing the Soviets over the cliff economically.

Disturbing developments overtook Eisenhower's later years. Cuba went communist, reviving the political threat. The orbiting Russian satellite Sputnik was a shock to the American scientific community, followed by a military threat in the form of intercontinental ballistic missiles. In the late Eisenhower years the voices of doom marshaled a more fearful view of the Russian menace and the missile gap became a familiar refrain.

Kennedy used the missile gap as a major talking point in his run for the presidency. His Secretary of Defense, Robert McNamara, was a curious type who wanted to know the size of the gap so as to make a measured response. Using just initiated spy satellites, he found that there was no gap. Contrary to expectation, the Russians had not moved aggressively to take advantage of their space lead. They had a handful of ICBMs before the U.S., but the nuclear missile race of the 1960s was led by the United States. We remained in the lead in number of ICBM sites during the 1960s and had far more launch capability from the air and sea. The missile gap, the nuclear bomb gap, and other forms of military gap came up again and again over the years with militant groups and their political followers, but they were never true. By the early 1960s spy satellites permitted presidents to keep a sharp eye on Soviet capability.

Nuclear intercontinental ballistic missiles intensified fears, especially as a race developed into dumbfounding excess. Both sides deployed enough nuclear weapons to destroy the world many times over. When the Cold War periodically heated up, stress was high. One trembles to think what would have happened if the trigger happy couple of George W. Bush and Dick Cheney had been confronted by the Cuban missile crisis. That affair led to the first compromise by the U.S., removal of missiles from Turkey, a deal hidden from the public for fear of an outcry from the war crowd. It led to disarmament talks, culminating in a ban on above ground nuclear testing (an effort begun by Eisenhower). It was a beginning, though hawks in Congress and the military were able to hold off further progress for nine more years.

One of the ideas cooked up by the war crowd to keep the public riled up was a staged nuclear war and survivability. Protracted nuclear war was based on the idea of a first stage aimed at ICBM launch pads. After a pause to assess the damage, the side with the most remaining attack capability would be free to threaten cities and presumably the loser would surrender. Since these were in ground concrete silos, chances of a precise hit were slim, though the U.S. worked hard on accuracy and frightened the Soviets that they had succeeded. The concept led to an abundance of silos. The Russians built over 2000 on the theory that accuracy could not knock out more than half.

Cities were to be defended with intercept missiles capable of exploding a nuclear bomb close enough to set off an incoming missile. Equipment was installed until the public called a halt when presented with the thought of multiple exploding nuclear bombs overhead. The impracticality of ICBM defense led to the Anti-Ballistic Missile Treaty of 1972. While the Treaty was later vilified as a policy of mutually assured destruction, it was actually based on the impracticality of defending against a multi-missile attack.

With a Kremlin anxious to cut defense spending, Nixon reached agreement limiting the number of ICBM pads, though by then both sides had so many that further expansion would have been ridiculous. SALT I was a five year freeze on land and submarine based ICBM launchers, with the Russians allowed 2,400 compared to 1,700 for the U.S., the disparity based on our far greater deliverability by air, sea and short range. Brezhnev later agreed to parity as part of negotiations for a more advanced SALT II and talks continued under Presidents Ford and Carter.

How either side could have felt a fraction of the number of nuclear bombs in place (many in the silos were hydrogen) was sane policy remains a mystery. U.S. strategy was utter destruction of Russia and China to the extent of making the planet unlivable. Despite the right claiming that nuclear holocaust was inevitable, initiating war was so foolish it never happened. Periodic warnings of a missile gap drove escalation. According to the warmongers, first Russia was surpassing us in bombers, then in missiles, then in nuclear submarines. The conviction they were on the verge of wiping us out was shaped by our own plan to wipe them out. Fear remained at high pitch, exactly where the right wanted in order to build its political power. If not a direct political strategy, they chose to believe because it was politically advantageous to do so.

Years of exaggeration of the communist threat was not inordinately costly until the decision to go into Vietnam. Both Johnson and Nixon seem to have recognized the futility of Vietnam, but were unwilling to acknowledge defeat both for personal reasons and from fear of the effect it might have elsewhere on relative Soviet influence. Both were guilty of pressuring intelligence agencies to provide information that supported their position on the war.

Putting aside the alarmists, pressure was easing and ending the Cold War was a possibility during the 1970s, a prospect frightening for the right's political ambitions. How much the conservative movement's resistance to any form of accommodation represented ideological conviction and how much was political gamesmanship cannot be measured. For Ronald Reagan, who became their political leader, it was largely political, for he recognized Soviet weakness. As we have seen, the goal was to gain the presidency and cut taxes, the rest was political noise. Worried about their hold on voters ebbing with the Cold War, the right began to kindle fear more actively. They struck back against détente, assisted by Brezhnev's tough talk about winning the Cold War and backing rebels in Africa and the Americas.

An organization know as the Committee on the Present Danger became the front line for resisting further accords with the Kremlin. It relentlessly puffed the Soviet menace and pushed for larger defense budgets. Far-fetched notions were concocted, such as America was growing weak because of a lax society and the commies were getting stronger, so fight now or die. The organization was full of prominent industrialists, retired military men, and defense intellectuals, led by the icon of doomsday scenarios, the author of NSC-68, Paul Nitze. Over thirty of its members became part of the Reagan team, including Richard Allen (National Security Advisor), William Casey (CIA head), Jeane Kirkpatrick (UN Representative), George Schultz

(Secretary of State), and leading neo-conservatives. In 1979 Ronald Reagan became a member of the executive committee.

An early triumph for the Committee on the Present Danger was establishing a shadow intelligence group known as Team B. Given access to CIA files by the then head, George Bush, it quickly developed into a propaganda effort aimed at refuting the official view of Soviet military strength and inciting trouble to upset détente. The CIA was already overstating Soviet military spending and economic growth, now Team B created a more far out view. Semi-official status gave credibility to the wild speculations of the right wing defense lobby. Extreme scenarios unsupported or refuted by intelligence were legitimized. The Soviet threat was made to look greater despite thirty years of relative calm at the moment the two sides were beginning to speak more openly to one another. Capitalism had slain communism in the developed world and the Soviet Union was listing economically, but according to the warmongers things were getting worse and we were about to lose the struggle.

The voices of doom made inroads on policy prior to Reagan. Ford's Secretary of Defense, James Schlesinger, was so outspoken as to embarrass the President and he was replaced by White House chief of staff, Don Rumsfeld. The man who later became identified with the Iraq disaster played a role in the militarization of the United States that was to unfold under Reagan. Backed by the gathering force of extremist views about the Soviets, which he shared, Rumsfeld was able to launch major new weapons projects. While Carter ran on reducing the defense budget, the new programs begun by Rumsfeld locked Carter in to defense spending that for the first time exceeded $100 billion.

Peculiarly, of the two major Rumsfeld backed programs, the M-l tank and the B-l bomber, neither met expectations. The B-l had been an on again off again project for years when it was finally built by Reagan at the exact time cruise missiles made it obsolete. Large subsequent expenditures have been made in an effort to find some use for the plane. The B-l's only excuse is that it fit Reagan's plan for bankrupting Russia through an arms race. The much praised M-l tank was built to overcome Russia's long standing superiority in large tanks just as the enemy disappeared as a threat. Oversized for modern conditions, the advanced turbine engine had limited mileage and was prone to blowing up under the difficult conditions normal to a battlefield.

The extreme militarists gained the upper hand during the Carter years, leading to the election of Ronald Reagan. Carter was determined to push ahead with détente, but his relationship with the Kremlin was soured by a self-righteous attitude and pushing on human rights. That subject had been brought up in the Helsinki Accords of 1975, but face to face Brezhnev considered it a personal affront. Upheaval in Africa that led to some communist governments helped increase tensions. Carter was pounded as weak and a threat to the nation's security. The argument gained force with the hostage taking at the American embassy in Iran. Carter obsessed over the hostages, huffing and puffing about swift retaliation and losing support by looking weak. Release of the hostages on the day he left the White House revealed that a more judicious approach would have ended the crisis earlier.

The decisive incident in breaking detente was Soviet invasion of Afghanistan. In 1978 a communist style government took over there and the leaders immediately began fighting among themselves. After repeated requests, the Soviets sent troops in December, 1979. For the first time they had invaded a foreign country unrelated to World War II conquests. Extremists immediately overreacted, screaming about a march to the Indian Ocean. The Committee on the Present Danger was ecstatic.

Afghanistan was always a phony issue. The Carter administration did its best to trick the Kremlin into Afghanistan, from the beginning seeing it as their Vietnam. The Russians went in reluctantly by invitation, planned to stay only briefly, and usually had only about 100,000 troops in the country. In fact, it worked out as a carbon copy of Vietnam, but a firestorm was set off that led to withdrawal of the U.S. Ambassador from Moscow, abandonment of SALT II, trade restrictions, and boycotting the 1980 Olympics. This silly affair helped the increasingly strident right sell the idea that containment was losing the Cold War and built support for a more vigorous military effort, when in fact it was another example of Soviet weakness. It added to the stress, however, boosting the right's Red baiting presidential candidate, Ronald Reagan.

Here we were thirty-four years after the start of the Cold War, with signs of its winding down, electing a president whose primary appeal was belligerence against the Soviets. Continued exposure to a threat that never materializes usually diminishes its hold, but the warmongers had worked long and hard to maintain their effectiveness. Reagan took the victory as a mandate for a military build up that served no purpose as related to the Soviet Union.

The U.S. won the Cold War exactly as the founder of containment, George Kennan, had expected, on the economics. Rather than a crafty enemy determined to rule the world, the Russians were bumbling oafs struggling to support an unworkable economic system. By Reagan's time the U.S.S.R. was dying of it own ineptitude, but the fearful imaginings of Americans, stimulated by those aligned with Reagan, managed to prevent recognition of what was happening right before their eyes. The end of the forty year Cold War was approaching and the alarmists still could not get it through their heads that the battle was economic rather than military. They were to repeat this oversight in the later so-called war on terror.

Reagan was in an odd position, tough-talking the Kremlin because he knew it was weak and at the same time selling an arms build up by picturing them as an imminent threat. It was somewhat like Bush II's later approach to Iraq, except that Reagan had no intention of acting on the talk. Because he was one of the few who recognized Soviet weakness, Reagan often appeared confused and was accused of acting the Hollywood cowboy, then turned out to have good judgment.

On the other hand, his judgment was lacking in the realm of economics. The strategy of bankrupting the Soviets was costly in terms of the deficit, lost opportunity to support a domestic economy beginning to suffer from foreign competition, and an excessive military force that produced delusions of grandeur, eventually leading to Iraq.

Whether the end of the Cold War is considered to be Gorbachev's commitment to a reduced military and withdrawal from the satellite countries in 1988 or fall of the Berlin Wall in 1989 or break up of the Soviet Union in 1991, the change vastly altered our military requirements. The grossly excessive nuclear arsenals neither side had any serious intention of using were not the only example of military excess. The recent non-nuclear Reagan build up was responsible for a deficit at a time the economy was beginning to experience problems from lost manufacturing.

Although the arms race strategy for destroying the Soviet economy was the primary reason behind Reagan's big increase in defense spending, other factors were beginning to shape military planning. The idea of aggressively spreading democracy was developing out of the humanitarian aspect of the Cold War. The theme of a U.S. led effort to democratize the world went back to Woodrow Wilson at the end of World War I and Roosevelt's late World War II pronouncements. Not only did right wing militarists embrace the idea, they were joined by evangelicals. The direction was further advanced with the idea of moral obligation. In 1992 these ideas crystalized in unilateralism, or expansion of U.S. influence abroad by military means.

The grandiose new ideas meant that as to military spending, the Cold War might as well never have ended. Although the defense budget was cut, it remained at levels far higher than had prevailed during all except the last years of the Cold War. Deployment of armed forces all over the world continued. The spirit of triumph coming out of the end of the Cold War and the Kuwait walk over led to an attitude that America did not have to choose between military and domestic spending, it could have both.

In chapter 6 I noted the factors that led to only a modest cut in defense spending at the end of the Cold War and continuation of our vast worldwide military commitments. If the increased Reagan defense spending had not taken place and planning been determined on the basis of defense needs and sound economic management, the Soviets would have lost the Cold War anyway, fiscal discipline would have been maintained, and the economy directed in a more productive manner. The military-industrial complex would never have taken hold. Most importantly, the American approach to its position of world supremacy would have been based less on military and more on the kind of soft power reflective of our democratic tradition. As it was, the powerful military coming out of the build up had a profound influence on foreign policy. Our diplomatic failings in the Middle East were long standing, now we added a military component. All of the engagements undertaken in the thirty years between Vietnam and Iraq could have been successfully completed with a smaller military.

Ominously for the future, military extremist neo-conservatives had gained a foothold in the Reagan government. While among the most outspoken and uncompromising anti-communists, their devotion to the military went beyond the Soviet threat. When the Cold War ended, they were prepared. Backed by the growing influence of right wing media, they managed to establish the perception that the world had become less safe and launched a search for new enemies. Into the idea vacuum of what to do next with our overlarge armed services, neo-conservatives launched the doctrine of unilateralism, or employing military power to coerce the rest of the world under the guise of furthering democracy. The proposal amounted to throwing out the principles of the founders in the one practice that most threatened democracy, militarism.

As hard as selling such an immoral policy to the public might be, the right and the neo-conservatives were old hands at such tasks. Having for decades hyped the Soviet threat as a central part in their rise to power, with barely a pause for breath they brought forth the same old alarmism. Minor disturbances were pictured as life threatening. Gas was poured on brush fires. Saddam was a recurring theme, his weapons of mass destruction cited so often that, despite a lack of evidence, they convinced themselves of their existence. Americans responded. Clinton's light employment of the military for humanitarian purposes advanced acceptance of the need for involvement all over the world.

The right operates at two contradictory poles: taxes are always too high, defense spending always too low. The Wall Street Journal editorial page preaches the gospel of inadequate defense spending on a daily basis. The recurring theme is relating current to past levels as a percentage of GDP, without ever addressing what the hell for or how much more productively the money could be spent. The trade off between an expensive military without much to do and other aspirations of Americans is never considered. Social Security, Medicare, a national health plan, maintaining the infrastructure, helping the poor, and above all balancing the budget and running a sound economy that does not burden future generations, are not of interest to the right. For them the only legitimate function of government is the armed forces, their sole aim in life lower taxes. Stripped of the flowery language, this is a plan for a militarily totalitarian government.

Similarly to Romans looking for an excuse to end the Republic, the right wing sought to own government by making it more military. Their excuse arrived on September 11, 2001, in the spectacular terrorist strike. Now they were in position to turn the federal government into a servant of the rich by whipping up panic over a few thousand tent dwelling nomads. Their aim was to dominate the world. Terrorism, minor as it might be in the overall scheme, served as a front.

The military build up connected with the war on terror saw the same kind of exaggerated emotional oversell used during the Cold War. The threat was again set forth in lurid worst case scenarios and this time they had a single big happening to focus attention on. Rather than recognizing that 9/11 was an extreme incident unlikely to be duplicated, or that avoiding a repetition was not a military matter, the idea was put forth that the next attack, about to happen at any moment, would have to top the last. The propaganda was a culmination of decades of using foreign threat to build a political following. They saw the opportunity to keep Americans so frightened that they could dominate the political scene for decades.

A propaganda machine had been built that could fool Americans into not seeing news realistically. That machine was all the more effective when the White House joined the chorus. The degree of danger was far less than during the Cold War, military action was a secondary factor in meeting the problem, the pathetically weak enemy was unworthy of the term war, but the ghastly fear of sudden attack created political opportunity in those spectacularly falling towers. The strategy was brilliant from a political point of view, but devastating to intelligent conduct of an effort against terrorism.

The overblown silliness worked for a while. In time of war, opposition is restrained and criticism can be treated as disloyal, allowing the right to sell its nonsense more effectively. Bush won a second term despite numerous examples of ineptitude and the worst foreign policy blunder in American history. The exaggeration inevitably led to mistakes. Bully boy talk drove away allies and led to intensified efforts by North Korea and Iran to develop nuclear weapons.

The U.S. had frequently dealt with terrorism, hitting back on some occasions and on others removing troops from positions that were not worth the exposure. The only time terrorism became politically serious was Carter's obsession with the embassy hostages in Tehran in 1979, an incident brought about by his own poor judgment in harboring the deposed Shah. Overstating the terrorist threat for political advantage led to the wrong counter moves. The right was on the road to self-destruction.

Partly as a result of over-hype, the White House never understood that this was a ghost-like rather than a fixed enemy and that terrorism was a political tactic more than a physical target. Since terrorism was insignificant compared to the real goal of world dominance, the Bush team never bothered to figure out a practical approach to the problem. World domination could not be quickly achieved, so they declared what sounded like a state of perpetual war. When al Qaeda was routed in Afghanistan without deploying a single division, they quickly moved to the prime target, the Middle East, where Saddam provided an ideal excuse for entry.

Thinking about conquest of the Middle East, which did require military power, the Bush team missed the point that tiny groups of terrorists require a different approach. Dealing effectively with terrorism involves hard to reach factions spread throughout the world, so that international effort is mandatory. Intelligence is cardinal, yet not only was no effort made to strengthen the CIA, it was politicized, leading to the loss of disgusted veteran agents.

What had been started by Reagan and completed by George W. Bush, with help from his father and Clinton in failing to size the military to post Cold War conditions, was sacrifice of the American economy to military glory. As a new age of international competition based on economic power began, the United States was saddled with an expensive military that rendered it less competitive. Wasted money was not the only problem, military power made for complacency about defending economic power. The steady upward drift of trade deficits accompanied by fiscal deficits and a trillion dollars thrown away in Iraq placed our economy in a weakened condition from which it became vulnerable to a devastating economic setback.

21

Rise of the Neo-Conservatives

THE RIGHT'S AGGRESSIVE STANCE AGAINST the Soviet Union attracted another group that became known as neo-conservatives. They began as radical Trotskyists, a form of communism that not only did not support the Soviet Union, it was violently opposed. For them Roosevelt liberalism and World War II were capitalist plots, until the holocaust won them over. The original neo-conservatives were Jewish and as Israel became a nation they were devoted to its interests.

The Trotsky past is instructive to understanding the neo-conservative mindset. Trotsky, a leading Bolshevik who lost out to Stalin, remained a socialist. Neo-conservatives shared his anti-Soviet fervor and an apocalyptical view of the world. As they drifted away from socialism, their dark view of society took form in the vision of a highly unstable world. Out of this ominous view developed the theory that the only hope for stability was a world forcefully dominated by the United States.

Neo-conservatives were extremists, ideologues rather than planners. It was not their nature to measure cost or willingness of Americans to make the sacrifices necessary to give world dominance a chance of success. With the U.S. in possession of the large majority of modern military weapons, and other major powers reducing their commitment, supremacy through arms seemed a practical goal. That military conquest went against American ideals did not interest them in the least.

Similarly to the right wing, neo-conservatives were a small elite group trying to take over national policy. They brought special qualities to advancing their point of view. First, they were convinced of being the smartest people on earth and anyone objecting was simply not up to their intellectual level. Second, they thrived on intellectual conflict. Absolute conviction included willingness to twist facts and do whatever was required to win. Typically of ideologues, financial and practical limitations meant nothing to them.

Unilateralism, or control of the world through exercise of military power, was a neo-conservative plan. When put into practice under George W. Bush, it turned out that, despite their purported intellectual prowess, neo-conservatives had never thought through the difficulties. It was more concept than actual plan. Anyone equipped with common sense, awareness of history, and the elements that made America great, should have recognized that unilateralism was foolish. To neo-conservatives, however, those inhibited by practicalities were short sighted and lacked the intellectual capacity to face up to the fact that aggressive unilateralism was the only solution. Of such certainty the worst mistakes are born.

Many of these characteristics were close to the right wing, the major difference being the sharp contrast between socialist and free market philosophy. Although neo-conservatives were suspicious of liberalism, they instinctively leaned to the Democratic Party, all the more so for Truman's recognition of Israel and willingness to fight in Korea, plus later in Vietnam. It was Vietnam protest that led to disenchantment with Democrats. The moderate Republican party of detente was also unattractive, until they became caught up in the new right wing's strong anti-Soviet position and push for a military build up. They also recognized kinsmen in the "practical" right wing approach to politics. The ends always justified the means, lying was sometimes necessary. They, too, believed that a society had to be run by an elite and fooling the masses was a necessary part of ruling. Once in the Reagan vortex, forcefulness and intellect carried them to the dream of influencing national policy.

Neo-conservatives with a heritage of scholarship and political pamphleteering took immediately to right wing think tanks. Before long they had virtually taken over the American Enterprise Institute and become prominent at the Heritage Foundation, strengthening ties to the right. The conservative reputation as a fountain of new thinking drew in no small part from neo-conservatives.

Protesting against Carter, harping on the softness of Americans leading to loss of the Cold War, wild imaginings about Soviet intentions in Afghanistan, the election of their new hero, Ronald Reagan, marked the arrival of neo-conservatives as a force in American politics. They achieved several significant, if not yet major, positions in the administration, but the glory soon faded. By 1983 Reagan was committing the unpardonable sin, talking to the Russians. As talks proceeded and progress was at hand, their crusading internationalism led to taking up the idea that the U.S. had a moral obligation to spread democracy.

Reconciling traditional neo-conservative Marxism with capitalism might have been a problem, but after dropping socialism, they found right wing enthusiasm for individual freedom attractive. While the free market was an anathema to Marxists, they were lured by the concept that freedom and the free market were synonymous. The worldwide crusade for freedom became a crusade for capitalism. As they began to think about assertion of U.S. military power to spread freedom and developed the concept of unilateralism, free market capitalism became one of the tools for dominating the world.

Suddenly becoming politically influential was a factor in converting Marxists to free market capitalists. Power was a heady tonic for a group so obscure it had been overlooked during the McCarthy witch hunt of the early 1950s. Although their positions on the Reagan team tended to be in State or Defense, they found it useful to voice the party line on economics as well. When right wing economics began to produce the favoritism to the rich and exploitation of workers that Marx deplored, not a peep of protest was heard, in part because economics never much interested them. As former communist revolutionaries, they had to have recognized that free market economics was propaganda for the masses, but that was an acceptable price to pay for influence over U.S. foreign policy.

Like the right, neo-conservatives distrusted democracy, feeling that the masses must be led by the intellectually superior. Although the right felt superiority was reflected in ability to make money, neo-conservatives believed in the intellect. They felt more strongly than conservatives that man cannot be left to his own desires, he requires strong leadership. A leader was justified in lying, indeed lying is required to keep the public in hand and enemies misinformed.

With the U.S.S.R. break up, suddenly they were without a reason for existence. Claiming to have personally won the Cold War was hardly convincing. Bush I had no interest in them and he called Israel to task for unwillingness to deal with the Palestinians. The taste of power had been heady, how were they to maintain position and protect beloved Israel? A new cause was needed.

The opportunity to launch a new crusade was found in efforts of the military to preserve itself after the end of the Cold War. Colin Powell, Chairman of the Joint Chiefs of Staff, led the counterattack to limit reduction of the military. Recognizing that cuts could not be avoided, he developed a rationale for reduction that left sufficient force to maintain the overseas bases and defend against two simultaneous major threats. President Bush saw the need to cut and Powell's proposal, which amounted to about a one-third reduction, carried the day.

Not so with Secretary of Defense Dick Cheney. He was dead set against any reduction, particularly as the Kuwait War had demonstrated the new high technology capability. Whether or not Cheney was directly involved in development of the unilateral concept, his undersecretary for planning was the prominent neo-conservative, Paul Wolfowitz. Encouraged by the strong spirit of military pride coming out of the Kuwait engagement, Wolfowitz and his group of in house neo-conservatives came up with the plan for worldwide dominance in the name of democracy.

Unilateralism was a plan from hell. It reflected the kind of animal exuberance the victor might feel after a fierce battle, though the Soviet Union had never been met in battle and the Kuwait encounter involved an opponent that turned out to be pathetic (remember, though, it was widely believed that the battle hardened Iraqis would put up a good fight). It is indicative of the extended state of American confidence that a suggestion for world supremacy through military power was not immediately rejected for its Roman-Napoleonic-Hitler-like quality. While ostensibly spreading democracy, stripped of the sound-bite idealism it was a plan for ruling the world by taking advantage of our military superiority. Unilateralism was about as far from American tradition as you could get. Practically speaking, exercise of the doctrine would require a substantial increase in the military, the ultimate desire of neo-conservatives.

That a policy of military aggression was not immediately repudiated by President Bush may be attributable to its seeming so preposterous as not to be taken seriously. The President failed to see its dangers and probably encouraged aggressive thinking by speaking out for a new world order. Both Bush I and Clinton accepted the idea of American hegemony in the form of a mission to guard the world. As already noted, Bush missed the opportunity for a comprehensive review of post Cold War military requirements that left out the biased opinion of the generals and how the military fit within sound economic policy.

The fact that Dick Cheney was unilateralism's quiet champion was to have fateful consequences nine years later. Well thought of after a long Washington tenure, some of those who knew Cheney saw a changed man when he became vice president. The difference derived from moving from practical doer to diehard unilateralist. Cheney had always been a rabid right winger, with strong views on the need for forceful leadership.

With Cheney back in a leadership position, unilateralism was going to have its day. Remarkably, neither Cheney nor neo-conservatives had thought through what a monumental and expensive undertaking unilateralism would be. The oversight was serious, for when all its ramifications were considered, unilateralism was the work of madmen. Not only was it internally un-American and externally destructive of the relationships built up around the world over eighty years, it was impractical without a large increase in manpower and the arms budget. To have any chance of success, world dominance through military means would require immense sacrifice and change the nature of the country.

In its seductive quality, unilateralism was like free market capitalism. It floated around for ten years as an intriguing idea, boosted in its most idealistic terms by neo-conservatives and their supporters. They never sat down and asked, does the United States want to be involved in world conquest? If this is to be the policy, what are its requirements? Certainly a manpower force of 1.4 million, or 2 million at the time of the original proposal, was far from adequate. It was a concept developed by intellectuals with no understanding of the military or of economics. When formally adopted by George W. Bush in 2002, the administration was in such a state of overconfidence that no analysis of the requirements was undertaken.

These oversights might be considered surprising, but not for neo-conservatives, who were always fiscally blind. They failed to understand that under the best of circumstances the financial requirements were huge and our waning industrial power meant that we were incapable of supporting the extensive arms required. Dependence on imports and foreign funding left us dangerously exposed to possible enemies. Unlike Eisenhower, neo-conservatives had no conception of the connection between military and economic power.

They also chose to ignore that, while military muscle flexing had popular appeal, Americans had no desire to sacrifice for unnecessary wars. That was reflected in failure of the Bush II government to ask any sacrifice of Americans when launching forth on the unilateral path. The war on terror was useful as propaganda in establishing unilateralism, but they never considered the requirements of fulfilling such a commitment or the immense financial burden. To neo-conservatives pushing for America to fulfill its destiny, anything was justified, the details could be worked out later.

In the drift toward unilateralism under Clinton and its adoption under George W. Bush, our leaders were overlooking what made the U.S. different. Unlike prior world leaders, we had reached the top through economic power and moral leadership rather than military action. Neo-conservatives were oblivious to the worldwide contest unfolding in the economic sphere. If all that energy had been focused on building America's economic power, something positive might have resulted. A desire of most nations to join the globalizing market was fostering democracy without coercion, even in a deviant form in China.

The rest of the world recognized that nuclear weapons made war dead as an operative strategy for anything other than small encounters. Neoconservatives saw nuclear weapons differently. If they could be used without fear of retaliation through an anti-missile system, then control of the world could be achieved. The pathetic anti-missile system deployed by Bush hardly seemed worth the fuss, but it was a beginning. Ultimately they aimed at control of space, from which a controlling anti-missile system could be launched.

While the announcement of unilateralism in 1992 was greeted with surprise and disgust in liberal circles, its dramatic premise was captivating. The goals were laid down in subtle terms of peacekeeping, limiting violence, and encouraging the spread of democratic forms of government. The combination of attack and idealism appealed to many Americans. Originally targeted at Russia and China, out of recent memory still seen as the major threats, it was big power, big war oriented, though there were no such enemies. The concept also grew that we would not necessarily have to fight, that merely by maintaining overwhelming military strength others would not dare to challenge. In this way, military power would be a form of diplomacy. More, not less, military spending was necessary now that the Soviet Union was gone, not to fight battles, but to preserve world order.

There was a familiarity to unilateralism in the longstanding policy of offering other countries protection in exchange for giving up their military aspirations. The model was Germany and Japan, whose armed forces had been kept well below their economic power under protective cover of the U.S. Other nations might become like them, anti-military and dependent on the U.S. for defense. However, the love your enemy approach had been abandoned. Russia was an obvious target for the treatment, but the chance to make it an ally was passed up. Just the opposite, as the U.S. sponsored a threatening expansion of NATO into former Soviet satellites and generally treated the Kremlin with contempt. Continuation of NATO as an ongoing peacekeeping organization was a good idea, but pushing it toward Russia, including a proposal to add Ukraine, was destabilizing.

Clinton also failed to follow through on earlier plans for mutual reduction of nuclear arsenals, probably out of consideration that in the growing spirit of militarism, Congress would not go along. After originally neglecting foreign policy, Clinton worked out a sensible compromise - a trimmed, but still large, military that extended our lead as others cut back. Clinton sidestepped the UN with go it alone moves, while maintaining friendly relations around the world. If his foreign policy was successful, restraint was deplored by neo-conservatives, who could not wait to get on with what they considered to be America's destiny. Clinton's actions represented a partial embrace of unilateralism that ended up encouraging a military approach. Sticking our nose into other people's business was coming to be seen as duty for the sole super-power and the military as the best means of accomplishing foreign policy objectives. Clinton's reign of caution advanced the unilateral cause and positive reaction to his relatively safe interventions established in American minds that unilateralism was sound policy.

Neo-conservatives used the calm Clinton years to build acceptance for unilateralism. It was given the right wing treatment - disguised in flowery language that made it acceptable among the public. They played to nationalism, expounding on American destiny to save the world from evil and the mighty power of high technology arms for quick surgical victory. Their leader became Bill Kristol, son of the long time neo-conservative warhorse, Irving Kristol. Bill had served as Chief of Staff for Vice President Dan Quayle, a foolish figure to most, but a hero to the right. Kristol used the typical methods of persuasion through focus groups and political magazines. He founded the Weekly Standard in 1997, an anti-Clinton and anti-Saddam newspaper, rabid supporter of Israel, and above all a source for spreading the poison of unilateralism. A standard neo-conservative publication, overstated and extraordinarily partisan, its widespread acceptance was a sign of the times. Unilateralism was far more popular among Americans than reason or history would have allowed.

Right wing think tanks unleashed a flood of propaganda, with the American Enterprise Institute a virtual unilateral advertising agency. Fox news was established, with Kristol and a group of extremist sidekicks near daily participants in the channel's discussion panels. In 1997 Kristol founded the Project for the New American Century, a group of unilateralists, including Dick Cheney and Don Rumsfeld, formed to spread the idea of global mastery, punishing Saddam Hussein, supporting Israel, proclaiming defense spending inadequate, and that Clinton was ruining the U.S. position in the world.

Cold War style propaganda found new life. Americans were pursuing pleasure rather than taking on the duties and responsibilities of great power. Diplomacy was bad, military action was the manly way to get things done. The absence of crisis was frustrating, for it did not fit their view of a chaotic world requiring American dominance.

In their frustration, they reached out for trouble. Aided by the masters of illusion at the think tanks, trouble spots around the world were blown out of proportion. Rather than being warned by interventionist disasters like Vietnam, Lebanon, and Somalia, unilateralists claimed the fault was not going in with greater force. Clinton's reaction to trouble spots abroad with quick minimalist military strikes amounted to bypassing the opportunity for glory. The U.S. should seize these tiny outbreaks to shape the world. The loudest drum beating was about the neo-conservative target for moving into the Middle East, Iraq.

The hype about a less safe world after the end of the Cold War was not born out by events. The first five years of the post war era saw calm brought to the troubled Balkans. The apparently hopeless problems in the Holy Land moved from peace between Egypt and Israel in 1979, including restoration of Sinai to Egypt, to discussions between Israel and all of its Arab neighbors, to concessions to the PLO and territorial divisions. The Middle East was far from settled, but except for a vast increase in terrorism, it would have been.

With the U.S.S.R. gone, neo-conservative focus shifted to the Middle East, where Israel was seen as the fortress of the west in a sea of mortal enemies and oil required a permanent U.S. presence. The Kuwait War arrived as a dream come true. Saddam's continued presence played into their hands. Neo-conservatives managed to force through legislation in 1998 stating that regime change in Iraq was nation policy. Clinton signed the inane bill, then ignored it.

Infatuation with Iraq related both to oil and as an entry for military action in the region. Saddam was merely an excuse. The Persian Gulf oil basin is a small area, only eight hundred miles from the northern Iraq fields to the southern in Saudi Arabia. Everyone wanted that oil, all the more when growing demand and ebbing supply tightened the market. Neo-conservatives saw conflict over oil as inevitable and the most militarily powerful country would win, assuring mastery of the world well into the century.

Absorbed with launching their protectorate of Middle East oil through weak Iraq, neo-conservatives committed a fateful mistake. Overconfident about force, they disregarded conditions that might limit the ability of an invader to control the country. Obsession with putting the grand design into action made immediate problems seem unimportant, leading to carelessness about details. To them such a powerful nation could not possibly stumble in a backward country.

With the election of George W. Bush, Vice President Dick Cheney took command of foreign affairs. He installed Wolfowitz in the number two spot at the Defense Department and brought in his old buddy Don Rumsfeld to head the department. While Rumsfeld was not an idealistic right winger, he was thoroughly militaristic. Other neo-conservatives were installed all over the administration and following 9/11 Bush quickly fell in line. With the President on board, the policy of world domination was restated and strengthened, including embrace of preemptive invasion and use of nuclear weapons. Principles that had stood throughout the nation's history were thrown out without a thought they were exercising man's worst instincts. Nothing better expressed the incompetence of the Bush team than that they jumped head first into an irrational policy that went against what the country had stood for.

Probably because it was merely a front, they overlooked that terrorism was perfectly adapted to resisting large armies and tended to get worse until grievances were addressed. Invasion imposed the added burden of cleaning up a messy aftermath and the responsibility of nation building. Reaction to invasion in the form of nationalism, hatred, and use of terrorism, were among the many details overlooked.

After being dressed up in years of enabling propaganda, unilateralism was fully exposed in the President's June, 2002, commencement address at the U.S. Military Academy and in a National Security Policy statement the following September. In the speech Bush specifically noted a break with the past and taking the battle to the enemy with preemptive military action. The policy statement was less direct, couching its preventive military theme in words such as values, making the world safer, human dignity, alliances, globalization, and creating democracy, but the direction was clearly on global dominance rather than serving as international peace keeper. Offense was the approach rather than defense. Terrorism was the excuse, not the target.

Neo-conservatives might be intellectuals, but the Trotskyist past and the policy of unilateralism suggests they were fanatics lacking common sense. There was something strange about a group swinging from international socialism to the conservative political establishment, with all its accompanying temptations. By ingratiating themselves with the religious right and accepting free market capitalism, they had politicized away their integrity. The rise to influence and power brought a softening in their idealism, but the old rigid crusading Trotskyist myopia was sustained. Everything was crystal clear, including how to deal with the opaque Middle East, where favoritism to Israel clouded their judgment.

Despite the disgrace when unilateralism was put into effect, they have no intention of adjusting. On they go as if nothing had happened, admitting not a single mistake, willing to stay in Iraq after the oil runs out to protect Israel, their focus redirected to stirring up trouble with Iran. They appear almost as often on Fox news and the Weekly Standard is almost as popular as ever. The nationalist and exceptionalist cards continue to be played as if Iraq was a triumph.

22

The Origins of Unilateralism

To COMPREHEND HOW A POLICY so diametrically opposed to our tradition and ideals, so disastrous for other nations that had attempted it, gained a following in the U.S. requires an understanding of the background. After becoming a leading military power during the Civil War and World War I, the U.S. had stepped back. It had after World War II as well until Korea, but after that war and again after Vietnam the draft had ended and the nuclear deterrent remained our principal defense. Still, for the first time the Cold War created the requirement for a larger standing army. Forty years with an active force made going back harder. If the build up during the Reagan years had not occurred, the choice would have been easier. As it was, with the military-industrial complex lobbying hard, the decision was to continue at a high level.

That did not mean using the military aggressively, as neo-conservatives proposed. After all, diplomacy and containment had just triumphed. War had been avoided and hundreds of millions of lives saved, a success interrupted only by two errors on our part: invasion of North Korea and misreading a Vietnamese fight for independence as an effort to expand international communism. The grossly excessive inventory of atomic and hydrogen bombs held by the U.S.S.R. and the U.S. was being reduced. Peacekeeping was a relatively minor job that involved internal strife more often than war between nations.

But neo-conservatives were serious about their proposal and they had a lot more going for them than was generally understood. The humanitarian and democratization themes aroused as part of resisting the Soviet Union

190

remained popular. America had a tradition of military interference in obscure countries of the Western Hemisphere. It was easy to believe right wing propaganda that Reagan's military had brought down the mighty force that crushed Hitler's Germany. In the minds of the military and its supporters, the shame of Vietnam had been reversed in Kuwait. A four day victory that cost barely over one hundred American lives brought forth an astonishing puffery about our military might.

This confidence was not soundly based. We had not beaten the Russians on the field of battle and the hubristic attitude was strongest among those who had never fought in war and discounted its horrors and dangers. We might be the mechanical masters of the battlefield, but the messed up aftermath of Kuwait demonstrated that we were still neophytes at the art of war as an extension of politics. There was little appreciation that the end of the Cold War found the U.S. in an awkward position: overwhelming military power relative to the rest of the world, but insufficient to do what neo-conservatives wanted and too expensive to be affordable.

Since unilateralism is a vague term, let me define it through expanding on the thinking and intentions of its supporters. At best it is a grand ideal: leading the world through creating a community of like-minded democratic nations, thereby eliminating conflict and keeping the world at peace. Our leadership of this blissful state was possible as a result of being different from other nations past and present in that our motives were pure and our governing system a model for others. However abhorrent military methods might be, our moral purpose made them legitimate. We would be acting on behalf of human rights bearing the gift of freedom. These noble aims would overcome human nature and national pride. This wondrous condition was made possible by our unchallenged military strength.

We had an obligation to use this power to noble ends. Since our motives were pure and we saw ourselves as Santa Claus arriving on the roof top, those we had bombed would welcome us as saviors. Actions against other nations, however much chaos may have resulted, were acceptable as they were for the good of the people. Military action, economic sanctions, and other coercive means, were approved in the name of human rights and introducing democracy. Overwhelming power would make any engagement short and modern weapons would make the conflict relatively painless.

The argument had two principle problems. First, with a few minor exceptions, the world was already at peace. In a way, war had become obsolete. Other countries were attempting to build their economy, not their military. The sole country that had repeatedly used its military aggressively, Israel, was moving in a peaceful direction.

Second, the plan was less about preserving peace than using peacekeeping as an excuse for interfering in the affairs of potential rivals. In other words, unilateralism's justifications were phony, they were an excuse for exercising power. It says something about neo-conservative thinking that they could dismiss the moral shortcomings of a policy of world military dominance on the basis of high minded intent. Those capable of such rationalization are not worthy of trust.

Not only was moralism and idealism a front for aggression, unilateralism was a bad idea on any basis. History has shown again and again that when a nation allows religion or some other apparently high or low minded purpose to guide its foreign policy without regard for pragmatic limitations, incomprehensible mistakes are made. The "obligation" to stick our nose in other country's business amounted to searching for trouble. A nation's foreign policy should first of all guard its self-interest. As the leader of the world economically, militarily, and morally, the priority was settings a good example. Instead, neo-conservatives sought to do exactly the opposite and dominate in the manner of Rome, Napoleon's France, and Hitler's Germany. Only Rome did not come to a quick end once it went off in that direction. Fortunately, we were not in the position of Napoleon and Hitler on invading Russia. We could extract ourselves from Iraq without serious damage and move on to sensible policy.

Underlying public acceptance of unilateralism was the concept of American exceptionalism. Exceptionalism is the belief that because of the high principles on which we were founded and our historical evolution, the United States is on a higher level than other nations. Because we offer a unique brand of opportunity and hope, we are not bound by conventional standards of conduct. America is always good, its judgment is not to be questioned. Our strength is so exceptional, our democracy so successful, our guidance so benign, that we are the promised land, "the last best hope of mankind". That was Lincoln's quote and he meant it in a different way from those who believe in exceptionalism. We do possess the opportunity for greater international achievement than any nation in history, but unilateralism is a direct threat to realizing that potential. The qualities that made us exceptional are the opposite of those employed in the exercise of unilateralism.

Confidence and national pride are necessary to leadership, but carried to extremes they are dangerous. Thinking you can do no wrong leads to the worst mistakes. In the case of Iraq it led to overestimating our military capability and not planning properly. Original mistakes were compounded by unwillingness to accept error and adjust. When free market capitalism began destroying our industrial base, rather than reacting the profits were celebrated. Rot in the economy became clear during the presidency of George W. Bush, yet policies that furthered the downward drift were pursued.

Exceptionalism had the effect of countering our highest and best values. International law did not apply to the U.S. or our own law to the president. The traditional champion of law over force, of the Geneva Convention, and of the UN, set aside its traditions and adopted the methods of vile conquerors of the past. Regard for the law is a foundation of democracy, yet unilateralists dismissed it as irrelevant for such a militarily powerful nation. Only a small additional step took them to circumventing the law domestically when it got in the way.

The shortcomings of applying exceptionalism to a military context were demonstrated in Iraq. Overconfident that military power could solve any problem, the political difficulties were disregarded. Cost was deliberately neglected. Here we were, a country whose economy was showing signs of age, forging ahead with military plans that would threaten an already troubled situation. The obligation to reconstruct an invaded nation and oversee a democratic form of government was assumed to be easily solved, though forcible westernization of Arab countries had always failed. Assuming that making our victims part of the globalized free market would quickly solve their economic problems, freeing us from further obligation, was fantasy. In practice, the attempt to immediately open Iraq to the free market proved counter productive. Even the oil resource failed them.

The idea that Americans could act in ways that would be improper for others played out in many unfortunate practices. The U.S. began to de-personalize aerial bombing late in World War II when it got away from "precision" to carpet bombing Japanese cities with incendiaries. The atomic bomb was reconciled with an estimated loss of one million American lives in an invasion of Japan. Although bombing in Vietnam was subject to some restriction, the general loss of civilian life in both North and South Vietnam marked a new era for America. The so-called precise accuracy of bombing in the first Iraq venture had the effect of removing all restraint. Claiming we hit exact targets, the U.S. began raining bombs on civilians in the Kosovo War of 1999 (2 1/2 months of persistent bombing) and Afghanistan was hit hard in the first month despite an absence of military targets. The effort at precise targeting still left many civilian casualties, but the attitude was to care only about American losses. Safely ensconced high in the sky or launching missiles from far away, home team non-casualty exceptionalist war carried a rationalization serving an absence of conscience.

Exceptionalism produced an extreme form of nationalism not dissimilar to how Romans, or the Napoleonic French, or Hitler's Germans, thought of themselves. Exceptionalism was paired with patriotism to produce an irrational form of nationalism. My country always right is not patriotism, it is an invitation to misguided foreign policy. In dealing with the UN during the run up to Iraq, Bush treated other nations as if they should gratefully follow our lead, when our actions went against the primary function of the UN, peace and prevention of preemptive military acts. The tragedy of unilateralism lies in its break with the ideals that made America exceptional.

Great military force has always been a drug that compromises enlightened principle, and so it was for the United States in thinking of itself as entirely noble and the standard bearer for democracy. The only difference between aerial bombardment as a method of killing the innocent and what we saw as terrorism was the imperial idea that anything was acceptable for the all powerful. For others these killings raised questions about the nobility of our intentions. Iraq provided the entire Moslem world a rallying cry against the United States far more pointed than the meager rantings of Osama bin Laden.

In going about the business of international relations, Americans had formerly bargained from strength due to the high regard they had earned. This advantage probably led to not developing diplomatic talent. An essential in negotiation is the ability to see yourself as others do and the other side's point of view. Compromise is useful when it ends in cooperation. Arrogance and self-righteousness are sure ways of flunking diplomacy. Demanding trust in our generosity and assuming we will always be correct is not diplomacy. Self-righteous, arrogant, our way or no way "diplomacy" forfeits the high regard with which we sometimes maneuvered the world to follow our lead. Probably no American in high position ever had less diplomatic talent than Dick Cheney, who directed our foreign policy for most of the last eight years.

Were our leaders so unwise as to believe use of force in Iraq would produce friends and followers? Although the ever-clueless George W. Bush, fed a diet of idealistic pabulum by Cheney and other neo-conservatives, probably did believe, the others surely did not. They saw a goal that could be accomplished by arms - control over the oil rich terrorist prone Middle East. So confident were they of our military prowess that the practicalities were missed. Right wing ideologues were brilliant at political planning, their specialty, but always fell down on implementation of national policy because they had the heart of a Napoleon or Hitler rather than of Abraham Lincoln or Franklin Roosevelt. Neo-conservatives were crusaders believing themselves enfranchised by history to sponsor killing because it served what they saw as a noble end. In this regard, they were no different from terrorists, except they operated on a much larger scale.

Conviction that benevolent intentions justified military aggression was supported by a theory that national sovereignty did not automatically accrue to a country, rather it had to be earned. Authoritarian nations may be invaded in the name of their suffering people. Use of the term sovereignty in connection with establishing the puppet Iraq government was hypocritical and typical of the inconsistency and false propaganda of the right wing.

The final ingredient in Americanizing the world, by force of arms when necessary, was the miracle of freedom. Bush's second inaugural speech about freedom and democracy as the solution to all problems was not mere political grandiloquence, it was an excuse for the failure in Iraq. He was saying, our intentions were good, so we deserve to be forgiven. The assumption that all people want freedom and democracy regardless of their traditions overlooks that they may not be capable of governing effectively in a democratic manner and therefore are likely to slip back into authoritarian rule. Success with a democratic form of government has not come easily and was usually achieved only after a period of upheaval, but for unilateralists the dream of freedom overwhelmed practical considerations, perhaps because it was more an excuse for attack than a genuine belief.

Underlying the freedom crusade was the assumption that a representative democratic government would cooperate with the U.S. and not support terrorism or attempt to develop nuclear weapons. Aggressive unilateralism was seen as producing responsible democratic governments, the key to eliminating terrorism and assuring our command. It was a form of fantasy rationalization unrelated to sound foreign policy. The U.S. has supported authoritarian governments for years, especially in the Middle East. It helped tyrants suppress freedom movements that had the slightest touch of socialism, as freedom efforts frequently did. Idealism was applied only when it suited our interests. Neo-conservatives saw an aggressive push for democracy exactly the same way.

High minded ideals obscure the stark reality that the intent of unilateralism was to knock off anyone we chose as part of controlling the planet. Feeling free to invade other nations was probably not unexpected from those devoted to tax cuts for themselves and eliminating public services. They set themselves forth as the moral standard for the world without consideration of the immorality of their own actions. Worse than the hypocrisy is that unilateralism is a dangerous policy. It explains why we have lost the respect of the rest of the world and find ourselves in a hopeless position in Iraq and Afghanistan.

If neo-conservatives were clever at developing concepts, they were lost when putting them into practice. The details of conquering the Middle East, much less the world, were never addressed. They seem to have expected that an overwhelming display of military power in Iraq would bring the rest of the region into line. The authoritarian rulers in the Middle East, including the royal family in Saudi Arabia, would fall and the people would opt for freedom in a cooperative democratic form of government. The success of Israel against what appeared to be overwhelming odds indicated that Arabs respected force and resistance would be ineffective. If anyone, Iran for instance, resisted, they would be crushed. Iran's development of nuclear weapons was important to neo-conservatives not out of their use against Israel, an unlikely prospect, but because a nuclear Iran could not be controlled.

The scheme for world domination was always crazy. It depended on the Napoleonic idea that invaded countries would welcome our arrival, as he trusted they would welcome the revolution, so that the amount of direct military force could be limited. If it could be done, world domination would require an armed force of perhaps 5 million men and an annual military budget of over $1 trillion, including futuristic weapons whose development would lead to bankruptcy.

The neo-conservative method for overcoming these obstacles was to proceed with the present force and gradually transform to an entirely new military drawing heavily on control of space. All earthbound equipment would be mobile and much of it unmanned (aircraft carriers, for instance, would be scrapped as too easy to sink), with manpower of 1.6 million doing mostly "constablatory" jobs while the offense was run in the manner of computer games. The apparently deranged fixation of the Bush team on an anti-missile system that did not work, and if it did was extremely limited, was a first step in developing Reagan's Star Wars dream: an earth girdling system of space platforms that could pick off enemy missiles, including massed ICBMs, and deliver decisive blows against trouble spots. The offense included no compunction about using atomic bombs. The world could be ruled by a small army prepared to use nuclear weapons with no fear of retaliation. I am not making this up, the concept was laid out by the Project for the New American Century just prior to Cheney's election.

Not included in the planning was cost. Neo-conservatives claimed they could get the ball rolling merely by raising defense spending by $15 to $20 billion a year from the 2000 level of just under $300 billion until spending reached a mere 3.5% to 3.8% of GDP. These modest estimates clearly reflect their usual disguise to get the ball rolling. The true monetary cost is probably best reflected in the close to $200 billion already spent on the pathetic ABM system currently being deployed. The futuristic plans not only seem beyond visionary, if attempted they would ruin the economy.

Shockingly, neo-conservative plans also called for such things as encouraging inter-service rivalry in hopes of greater innovation, an approach that would add to the cost, and removal of civilian control of the military. Essentially, they were calling for an end of America as we know it and adoption of a military state, a requirement for having any chance of taking over the world. The developers of this plot spoke daily on such outlets as Fox news and held significant positions in government, while disguising their revolting dreams in words of freedom and democracy. They should be tried as traitors.

In proposing to free the military from civilian control, neo-conservatives may have been working against their goal, for just as civilian leadership stepped up intervention, the military became more cautious. The generals learned the lessons of Vietnam and Lebanon and Somalia, before they were reinforced in Iraq. They knew Iraq was badly planned beyond the purely offensive phase. Rumsfeld disparaged the generals, partly because left to themselves they would never have undertaken the invasion. Civilians, most notably neo-conservatives, were the ones with big plans for employing the military in aggressive ways. Incongruously, as more and more members of Congress and the executive branch lack military experience, they became more anxious to use force.

The demented nature of unilateralism can be seen in the cost in terms of the economy, our soldiers, our moral sense, and loss of constitutional freedom required to bring it about. How did neo-conservatives expect to make it U.S. policy? Here they followed the right wing method with free market economics – gradually selling the public through emphasizing the bright side and avoiding consideration of the negatives. Similarly to the free market, master of the world thinking was subtly attractive. Exceptionalism led to thinking Americans could do anything and dreaming of a blissful world at the end of the rainbow.

The process began, as it had with the right wing movement, in near obscurity. During the Clinton years, neo-conservatives worked at making unilateralism respectable by painting it as fulfilling American destiny. Fox news, the Weekly Standard, The Wall Street Journal, and the pronouncements of prominent militarists worked on the minds of Americans. Clinton seems not to have recognized where they were going. He waved the magic military wand just enough to encourage unilateral sentiment. Perhaps the most disappointing thing about the move to unilateralism was the scarcity of voices speaking out against it. Not taken seriously enough, it worked on the consciousness of Americans sufficiently that when formally adopted by Bush there was little resistance.

Desperation may have aided the cause. The United States was formed as an expansionist nation and was on the winning side in the great wars. Success inevitably created a feeling of military invisibility. With our manufacturing base under assault and future prospects not what they were, Americans began to feel vulnerable, encouraging militarism as a means of protecting our leading position. Manufacturing might be moving to China, but we could still beat them at war.

The problems in unilateralism were never addressed even after it was adopted as official policy in 2002. Prior to Iraq the right had no interest in nation building and neo-conservatives had no practical view of how to establish a democracy. Neither recognized the collateral responsibilities in throwing out the bad guys. The right did not believe in hand outs in any form, including to newly established nations wrecked by its military assaults. Afghanistan was neglected after a few token gestures and the amount of rebuilding funds for Iraq was tiny considering the broken down condition of the country. The right's penny pinching non-humanitarian ways removed the one expectation backward countries had when the U.S. came calling.

One of unilateralism's operational impracticalities was a lack of interest among Americans in the military commitment necessary to carry it out. If fancy high tech weapons are impersonal and popular to fund, people are another matter. Iraq revealed that much more manpower, probably including a draft, was required to pursue aggressive unilateralism. We never had enough troops in Iraq for the simple reason they were not available without giving up our multiple overseas bases. To keep up its inadequate manpower level, the armed forces had to resort to expensive civilian subcontracting, enroll less qualified men, sell citizenship through accelerated naturalization, bribe recruits with large bonuses, and use the National Guard in unintended ways. Direct purchase of mercenaries through employment of private armies was begun. It was Rome, Napoleon, and Hitler all over again. Exercise of unilateralism required a draft, but that would have exposed the harshness of the policy in a way that Americans would not have supported. The nation got a warm glow from the spirit of nationalism inherent in unilateralism, but it was not willing to commit its young men to unnecessary warfare.

Although it is not the purpose here to discuss alternative courses, a few words on the subject. Unilateralism is based on the Hobbesian view that man is a sinner not to be trusted to work out equitable solutions. Its supporters see the world as a dangerous place that left to its own devices will destroy itself in war. The only hope is for the United States to act as overlord.

This doleful view is not the only alternative. The U.S. is the natural world leader, but not in an oppressive military form. Its significant position means that with strong leadership troubles can be solved in cooperation with others. The world is less complicated than it used to be due to two factors: 1) nuclear bombs make large scale warfare impractical and 2) the primary objective of nations is economic prosperity rather than territorial expansion. War is worn out as a method for conducting international relations. Only the U.S. and Israel still believe in it. The greatest threats to the United States lie right at home: right wing/neo-conservative reliance on military solutions to assure preeminence and our own mis-managed economy that threatens to unhinge economic prosperity.

The unilateral hypothesis falls depressingly in line with theory for the rise and fall of great nations. Historically, leading nations become militarily extended and then embarrass themselves losing wars unexpectedly. The economic drag of militarism stresses a maturing economy. The pattern typically includes insufficient financing for the economy because of inadequate taxation or the hope that draining foreign dominated economies will make up for the shortfall. Iraq's own oil reserves were supposed to pay for the invasion of their country and its subsequent use as a base for U.S. Middle East operations. More broadly, globalization was assumed to accrue to our benefit and to the extent it did not the dollar franchise as the world's reserve currency would induce other countries to provide us their goods.

The Soviet Union is a recent example of the decline and fall pattern. By overextending our economy with unnecessary military spending and supporting the domestic economy through deficits and the dollar advantage, we are now in a similarly vulnerable position. To keep the economy going, taxes have to be lowered and borrowing encouraged, putting off a day of reckoning. The federal deficit is fixable with reasonable taxation, less military spending, and willingness to endure the sharp resulting recession, but satisfying the immediate longings of Americans and getting elected virtually requires continuation of our current economic course. The Obama economic stimulus is merely an attempt to get back where we were, true reform is not politically viable.

Unilateralism is not an unusual response for a country in the leading position. Wars have traditionally expressed relative strength between nations, as power increases and decreases in relationship to their greater or lesser military success. In thinking that the Cold War would inevitably turn hot, warmongers were guided by historical precedent. Probably no nation in history has gained as big a lead militarily as the United States following the end of the Cold War. For the first time it seemed possible for one nation to rule the world. Temptation to use that power was great and with such a lead the risks seemed minimal. In supporting continuation of an armed force that had no useful purpose other than forceful supremacy, they were thinking in a traditional manner.

The stronger the military, the more likely it was to be used and war is always a gamble. Wars were typically fought between neighbors relatively familiar with one another. The more distant the opponent, the greater the difficulty in evaluating how to conduct the war. The lesson of Iraq is to be extremely wary engaging in warfare under any circumstances. The lesson being applied, the need for a larger army, is exactly wrong because it will lead to more rather than less similar ventures.

Militarists failed to take into account that the Cold War, which remained peaceful because of the nuclear bomb, changed the historical certainty of war. Nuclear weapons made serious warfare unlikely. Militarists also failed to notice that the United States changed the rules on who had the power. We did not rise to the top on the field of battle, we got there through economic power. Our strength did not depend on an all powerful army. A surprisingly limited infantry was raised for both World Wars and the U.S. did not distinguish itself in ground fighting. Our approach to war was massive fire power rather than man to man combat.

A combatless struggle for superiority has shaped up in economic terms. Although we are still on top, the thirst for individual wealth unleashed by free market capitalism undermined our economic strength. The first step in assuring continued economic leadership is not guns, but ending the favored position of those who have despoiled our formerly overwhelming industrial power and rebuilding the vitality of our economy.

The United States has always been lucky and it was again in that unilateralism revealed its ugly nature in the relatively unimportant venue of Iraq. Confident in military power, Bush made the case for war by concentrating on grounds for action and disregarded cautionary signs. Saddam was an evil dictator and his removal a desirable objective. He was also weak, much weaker than in 1990, so that eliminating him would be almost like swatting a fly. For unilateralists, therefore, who had no interest in terrorism and sought control of Middle East oil, Iraq was irresistible. A vivid display of American power might put the entire region at our feet. It seemed so easy.

How could they justify a campaign of overstatement and partial truths to sell an unnecessary and probably unwise invasion? Their thinking went as follows. In planning the war on terror, two broad approaches were possible. We could strike back at the perpetrators of 9/11 or try to solve the broad problem through a combination of military power and improving the economic status of Moslem countries (which the Bush people simplistically thought of as establishment of democracies). The simple course of directly going after terrorists would not end the threat as other groups might try something similar (though quick victory and the amazing small scale win in Afghanistan would have impressed possible future terrorist organizations). The more ambitious goal was naturally preferred. By first going after Osama bin Laden in Afghanistan, confusion arose about the choice, but the neo-conservatives in control of foreign policy always intended on Iraq. For them, Afghanistan was the diversion.

Neo-conservatives were so smitten with the opportunity to pursue world conquest that they missed the requirements for pulling it off. To succeed required the following.

1) International support. The plan was too big to accomplish alone. Bringing in help meant being up front on the plan, rather than the empty pass at legitimacy through the UN. The approach had to be more Marshall Plan than military invasion (it was widely recognized that the invasion would be easy). Fighting terrorism by bringing backward nations into the modern world was a legitimate aim, but such a comprehensive plan required allies. Russia, China, India and other non-allies had to be persuaded that our intentions were not imperialistic through some form of international oil trusteeship of which they would be part. Although proceeding alone would do serious damage to our international relationships, the neo-conservative/right wing style was not to deal with limiting alliances or promises of aid. Reluctance about a coalition reflected a desire for sole control of the oil resources (of course they talked constantly about a coalition, but it consisted only of minor partners and the doggy-bone Brits).

2) The most careful planning was required to deal with a fractured, difficult to manage country and region. The only way the Iraq part might have been pulled off was immediate improvement in the lives of its citizens, but the aid resistant right would never have considered such a thing. Not only did they fail to allocate resources to reconstruction, they avoided consideration of the sanctions wrecked status of Iraq's economy. A hard nosed analysis of the cost would have checked their enthusiasm. And this was just for the Iraq portion of a much larger plan.

3) If the big plan was to proceed on the basis of minimal assistance, it required a much larger military, including a draft, but a draft would have been difficult for the propaganda machine to sell. A tax increase would be needed to pay the immense cost. Instead, they conveniently overestimated our military prowess and concluded that the region's own oil would make the cost self-funding.

Since these requirements diverged sharply from doctrine, they could never have been met by a right wing government. The right had no interest whatsoever in taxes to pay for armed belligerence, quite the opposite. As a reflection of their impracticality, the apparent completion of just the first stage of the grand plan was used to push through another tax cut. As victors in war, they felt entitled to concentrate that cut on their wealthy constituency. If the White House had thought through the difficulties merely in Iraq, and the thinking had been done for them, they would have recognized that such a bold stroke could not be accomplished without sacrifice, but careful deliberation was not the right wing style and another tax cut always was.

23

Capitalistic Totalitarianism

ALTHOUGH THEY TALKED A LOT about democracy, the actions of the right wing suggested no genuine belief. Democracy embraces the notion of a common good, the principle of equality, a truly representative government. The right did all it could to terminate laws supporting equality and created an economy that encouraged inequality. They subverted representative government with money and propaganda. The idea of a common good was scorned. While never openly stated, they clearly distrusted the democratic process and felt the riff-raff must be led by the superior few. When the country was controlled by the original European settlers and their successors, democracy was fine, but now that blacks had the vote and so many non-Europeans had come, they were dubious about the old system. That lack of regard translated into practices that went against the fundamental values of the founders. History has proven again and again that men thinking this way make unimaginable mistakes. Their minds are closed to protect their feelings of grandeur.

These were not traditional American conservatives, they sought a return to a class based society. Rather than hereditary selection, right wing chiefs were chosen by business success. Government could be run by subservient politicians skilled at convincing voters that what they were doing was the only reasonable course.

No better front man has ever been found than Ronald Reagan. He knew little of governing and did not care about the common man, but was expert at convincing the public. He was the supreme political snake charmer, the right's ideal stand in. The ease of Dick Cheney's move from politician to high government position to business leader to higher government position, scooping up tens of millions of dollars along the way, is indicative of the interplay. Business is not democratic, proof for them that successful organizations cannot operate on a democratic basis. But government is not like business and, while intelligent in mercantile terms, people thinking this way rarely do well as governors.

The negatives in aristocracy came powerfully to light in George W. Bush. Authority that passes by inheritance to those whose ability is impaired by their privileged background leads to the system breaking down. Bush was a perfect example of why it is a mistake: a man in control with little ability, a stunningly casual attitude toward the performance of his job, and eccentric personal hang ups that made him ill-suited to leadership.

If the right had no genuine interest in democracy, where were they headed? The answer is clouded by their derailing and the focus on making money, but the activities of George W. Bush, and particularly of Dick Cheney, and the necessities of carrying out a program of unilateralism provide clues to where they were going. Imagine where we might be if Dick Cheney had been president and Iraq a passable success.

In order to reach a conclusion, we must recognize that the right did not follow its own doctrine, that it was pap to attract a political following. All of the basic tenets, anti-government, the free market, and religious fervor amounted to feel good platitudes aimed at providing freedom to make money. The exception was assertive militarily based foreign policy and that is a separate indicator of intent. The ideology was built around a feel good model of life and playing on common fears (blacks, communism, and terrorists) that attracted voters who otherwise had no identification with the right. In other words, the purpose was not the ideology itself, but using the ideology to control the public.

This is revealing, for those using ideology in this way have a common characteristic - totalitarian forms of government. Prior to 9/11 there were only hints, afterward this direction was easier to see. In an embellishment directed at enhancing the power of his office, Bush incessantly extolled the responsibility of being a wartime president, despite the nature of this war never being comparable to others. Bush was always a somewhat pathetic figure, it was Cheney who set the course.

An example was the effort, generally associated with Karl Rove, to politicize most departments of government, notably the Justice Department. This time politicizing did not mean the normal practice of staffing with party members, it meant right wingers devoted to changing the way government operated. The criterion for selection was never ability, it was loyalty, something Bush never failed to emphasize. No president prior to Bush/Cheney ever expressed the loyalty theme so clearly or carried it out with such determination. Colin

Powell was much criticized for not blindly following Cheney's lead in foreign policy. The administration sought to remake a federal government of loyalists with little concern for ability to manage. Loyalty was the way the Nazi and Soviet governments were set up. It is the explanation for Nazi, Soviet, and Bush governments being so badly run.

The most obvious look alike was the emphasis on militarism. Since a characteristic of totalitarian governments is a desire to conquer, a strong military is necessary. There was no sound reason for tripling the defense budget so late in the Cold War, or perpetuating the worldwide reach after its end, or doubling again in reaction to a terrorist incident. The justification turned out to be unilateralism, or controlling the world militarily. While unilateralism covered its tracks in the ideal of democratization, it was above all a scheme for domination of the planet. This being America, the public never suspected the military would be used in this manner, when lo and behold, unilateralism was formally proposed and put into motion. The excuse was an attack from a small bunch of tent dwellers, similarly to the meager excuses employed by Hitler to precipitate his wars.

Another characteristic of totalitarian militarism is sacrifice of the nation's finances. Federal budgets managed by the right were more or less taken over by "defense", a fact disguised by claiming self-funded entitlements were what was straining our finances. At the end, the fully encompassed military budget reached almost 45% of government spending.

One aspect of totalitarianism is missing, but not completely. It relies on terror to control the public, not external, but internal fear of government. Rather than operating a police state, the right wing promised prosperity, but still made terror a force, this time exterior terror. Just as Hitler and Lenin converted rioting into power, the terrorist strike was the happening that allowed the right to proceed in a totalitarian direction. If not acting as ruthlessly as their predecessors, they were moving toward an authoritarian form of government, including reinterpretation of some of America's most basic principles.

Parallels with fascism were a regular feature of the right's period in power. At one time I collected fascist-like statements from Newt Gingrich, the right's leader during most of the 1990s. Claims of absolute truth for the ideology, dismissal of alternatives, and use of propaganda to sell the public was reminiscent of fascism. Practical likenesses could be found in methods for gaining and retaining power, namely uncompromising political truculence, militarism, racism, hatred of anything mildly socialist, disregard of the truth, and reliance on propaganda.

Fascists usually consisted of a tightly knit conservative group employing anti-social devices to inspire others to feel part of a movement, an apt description of the right. Maintaining control required distractions to keep the public intoxicated and uninformed. Right wing success could not be more exactly described.

In The Anatomy of Fascism, Robert Paxton defines the subject as follows: "A form of political behavior marked by obsessive preoccupation with community decline [seen in the many right wing antis], humiliation or victimhood [liberalism, communism, and terrorism], and by compensating cults of unity, energy and purity [rigid ideological certainty accompanied by eliminating social support programs that dilute national genes], in which a mass-based party of committed nationalist militants, working in uneasy but effective collaboration with traditional elites [old fashioned moderate Republicans], abandons democratic liberties and pursues with redemptive violence and without ethical or legal restraints [an effort to take over the judiciary] goals of internal cleansing and external expansion". The most striking similarities are excessive nationalism, militarism, racist demagoguery, and use of propaganda.

Few at home, though many overseas, noted that the right wing approach - exciting the people through the psychology of revenge and threatening possible foes, heavy doses of propaganda about impending dangers and questionable successes, racism, and focusing attention on ogre villains - was a political strategy developed by the greatest of all fascists, Adolph Hitler. The Hitler similarity is also striking in the form of a rigid ideological government devoted to the interests of a small elite. The right did not want to enslave the world, but through military force to assure that our interests overrode all others. Enslavement imagery is why thinking Americans and most of the rest of the world were appalled by the prisoner abuses in Iraq, Afghanistan, and Guantanamo Bay. An example of the hold the right had achieved was that the public did not seem to care.

Like fascists, the right recognized the power of uncompromising positions, propaganda, and militarism. Hitler's success was based on the depressed state of morale in Germany following World War I; the right succeeded because of racism, discontent arising out of the declining position of the middle class, and American's lost feeling of safety due to the Soviet threat and later destruction of the World Trade Center.

Among Bush's odd characteristics was emulating Hitler - the preening, strutting manner, the insistence on absolute non-discussive loyalty, and self-important talk of being a great leader, overt boasting that would be embarrassing to a normal person. Bush's emphasis on being seen as a leader was interesting considering that the German word for leader is fuhrer, Hitler's preferred way of being addressed. Bush invented a similar title, the decider, though he made so many bad decisions that it became a joke. These efforts were directed toward transforming boasting into the image of a tough fighting leader in whom unquestioning trust should be placed. It was a strategy for maintaining power despite working against the interests of the people. Bush, with his posturing, emphasis on appearance, and lack of substance, was more reminiscent of Il Duce than the fearsome Hitler, but he happened to be ideally suited to selling the reactionary course to Americans.

Reactionary government works best with a powerful leader, a difficult position for the right to fill because its devotion to monetary goals brought forth leaders lacking interest in public affairs. In a democracy leaders should have feeling for the people and sympathy for the less fortunate, qualities the right wing creed rejected. Businessmen have a poor record in Washington because they are attuned to authority rather than the public good.

As a result, the right struggled with leadership. Reagan was a feel good showman rather than a leader. His contribution was a benevolent image and the military to exercise the impulse for conquest. Gingrich was too obviously authoritarian for that stage of the right's development and he lacked the fortitude to withstand setbacks. In desperation, they got mixed up with George W. Bush, a man they should have realized was completely misplaced. Bush was a snob who looked down on the common man, fine with the right, and he was skilled in hiding his identification with them, but he was also extremely lazy. Disinterested in exercising his brain, he allowed the rabidly right wing Dick Cheney to guide him. Cheney tried to fill the void, but the position of vice president was too limiting. Probably because he was the rare individual who actually believed right wing dogma, Cheney had no judgment. Between the two of them, they brought the movement to an end.

Although totalitarianism is identified with powerful leaders, it does not necessarily start that way. Most began as non-religious hierarchies and developed a cult of the individual only later. The hierarchy was typically formed around a small core and a following built by assembling a variety of sympathizers. The sympathizers, who are not part of the core, become front organizations, attracting more and more followers to the cause. This kind of fractional coalition was exactly the way the small core group of wealth built its following. The sympathizers never got much payoff, but continually stirred up in the emotion of the movement, they remained loyal. The model was most obvious in the evangelical church following, but it was also present in the military, establishment conservative groups, and the moderately wealthy attracted to tax cuts.

While the absence of a strong leader was a problem, the totalitarian direction was boosted by the way elections became increasingly about money. Since no one has more money than the core group of the right wing, elections built around money put them in position to corrupt the democratic process to their own ends. Election of a man so unqualified as Bush demonstrated the future possibilities. A weak man was created as president, why not a strong one? If Bush could win, an unscrupulous man could as well.

The opportunity is all the more enticing from presidential elections becoming so demeaning, trivial, and compromising of principle that few honest able people are willing to take them on. The money centered electoral process might have been warm ground for an unqualified right winger like George W. Bush with a political gangster to guide his moves, but for a man of honor it has become a gruesome ordeal. The road is especially hard for Democrats, who must endure the vile right wing media, so expert at dumping on whoever is leading the polls. The dilemma for Democrats became interesting in 2008. An experienced well chosen Democrat stood to win in a landslide. Because they were the only viable candidates ambitious enough to take on the horrors of the system, Democrats were faced with a choice between an unpopular woman and an inexperienced black man, introducing the possibility of losing the election. Fortunately, the Republican candidate ran a terrible campaign and Obama was surprisingly strong. We may have lucked into an able president.

Bringing about a reactionary revolution in such a successful country seemed unlikely, especially when their basic premises were faulty. Gaining power required roughhouse tactics, a high degree of dishonesty, and undermining traditional American values. The right went at the task by putting up a smoke screen of idealistic propaganda so that the public would not realize what they were up to. Secrecy became a mania, accompanied by high sounding statements to disguise true intentions. Truth was always the enemy. Lying to cover up intentions became standard practice.

9/11 gave them the opportunity to claim a new world order requiring changes in established American traditions. They tried to centralize government in ways suggestive of totalitarianism, grabbing authority on the excuse that under wartime conditions the president was above the law. Legal machinations were attempted that acted as trial balloons searching for authority beyond the law. They spied on Americans, a standard totalitarian police state activity, when the same end could have been accomplished legally, in order to establish precedents and test the limits. Cheney was always pushing for more. They were not as smart or as forceful as the dictators and the system held them back, but a smoother operation in a less democratic country with a stronger leader would have advanced the effort a lot further.

Other totalitarian signals were attempts to control the press, trample on civil liberties, uproot the Constitution by getting rid of checks and balances, avoid accountability for their errors, and hide behind a structure of secrecy. Claiming to be the champion of democracy was a hoax.

The absurdity of right wing policy combined with the triumph of its propaganda left the country in a dangerous state of suspension. They stood against all that made this country great - avoidance of militarism, emphasis on peace, a progressive society, open-minded ability to deal with change, and a controlled form of capitalism that balanced opportunity with social justice. To the extent that the right claimed to be more concerned with individual freedom, it was a type of anti-social freedom that encouraged the strong to take advantage of the less strong. The nation had lapsed into a condition of unreality that brought forth a stubborn arrogant refusal to face up to growing problems. An America living in fantasy, ruled by those so greedy that mention of the public good set them to rage, was an America on a downward slide. As Obama said, we were desperately in need of change. Hopefully he is up to the job.